SAILOR'S LUCK
At Sea & Ashore In Peace & War

Rear Admiral Geoffrey P.D. Hall, C.B., D.S.C., D.L.

Sailor's Luck

At Sea & Ashore In Peace & War

by

Rear Admiral Geoffrey Hall

The Memoir Club

© Geoffrey Hall 1999

First published in 1999 by
The Memoir Club
The Old School
New Road
Crook Town
Durham

British Library Cataloguing in
Publication Data.
A catalogue record for this book
is available from the
British Library.

ISBN: 1 84104 003 7

Typeset by George Wishart & Associates, Whitley Bay.
Printed by Bookcraft (Bath) Ltd.

To the abiding memory of
Virginia
a much loved daughter
18.3.46 – 17.4.98

Contents

Illustrations

Foreword

by Rear Admiral G.S. Ritchie CB, DSC

GEOFFREY HALL succeeded me as Hydrographer of the Navy in February 1971, becoming the 20th incumbent of that honourable post since its establishment in 1795 to provide seacharts for the Royal Navy. When these charts were placed on the open market in 1823 the requirement for them began to expand as merchant ships of many nations set about using them world-wide.

During Hall's term of office as Hydrographer he was in overall charge of thirteen white-hulled naval surveying ships collecting hydrographic data at sea, and of the work of 800 civil servants at the Hydrographic Department at Taunton busy compiling, printing and issuing charts to the Royal Navy and commercial agents throughout the world.

Hall was the last Hydrographer to have been surveying at sea before the onset of World War II. On his own admission he was awarded each of his promotions from Lieutenant-Commander upwards on his last chance in each zone, so that on retirement in September 1975 he was nearing his 60th birthday and was the oldest man in the Navy.

During his long years he had enjoyed a widely varied, and often exciting, life in general service, Combined Operations and the surveying service in peace and war, and this included one general service and five surveying ship commands, each of about two years in duration.

Thus the author has a fascinating tale to tell. He writes evocatively, particularly when recalling events at sea – whether it be surveying off South Georgia under the daily stress of ever-changing stormy weather conditions; carrying out beach reconnaissance from a folbot on the Arakan Coast, where he nearly lost his life; making geophysical investigations in the Indian Ocean; or ocean sounding in the North Atlantic. Many found the latter activity boring – not so Geoffrey as the reader will find out on page 193:

> 'For me, however, it was far from boring. Quite apart from the interest and fascination of the developing survey, and my daily stint at hand-contouring of the bathymetry in the Chartroom, the whole business was immensely satisfying. I was aware that *Hecla* would almost certainly be my last sea-going command, and I intended to make the most of it. Standing there on the

bridge, or sitting in the Captain's chair, with nothing in sight except the vast blue ocean, the ship surging ahead on a steady course, engines throbbing and machinery humming in the background, officers and men quietly and efficiently performing their duties on all sides, I often thought what a marvellous job I had.'

In 1942 he undertook a six weeks N* course in HMS *Dryad*, and subsequently enjoyed putting the skills he had into practice. He always derived pleasure from handling his ship in close quarter situations, and was ever ready to take his vessel into tight locations such as the narrow lagoon at Aldabra Island, the constricted harbour of Heimaey in the Westman Islands, or the snuggest cove in South Georgia.

Unusual for this type of book, the tale is told in a very personal vein, an approach which will commend *Sailor's Luck* to historians fifty years or more from now.

The story of how Geoffrey became engaged to Mary Carlisle, a Wren Officer he had never met, by means of a letter written from a Commando camp in Ceylon, and their first meeting six months later in an hotel in Dorchester is delightful.

Once married, Mary packed and followed whenever possible, accepting Geoffrey's white mistresses; she was rewarded by being invited to launch one of them, HMS *Herald*. Today *Herald* is the grand old lady of the surveying squadron and as beautiful as ever.

Hydrographers of the Navy have always had to fight within the Whitehall corridors of power to obtain or even retain the ships they require to meet their responsibilities as they see them. Geoffrey Hall fought harder than most of us. Whether he won or lost may be judged by the reader of the final pages of *Sailor's Luck*.

Introduction

THIS IS AN ABRIDGED and heavily edited extract from my personal memoirs, written down a few years after my retirement for the information of my descendants. Having enjoyed the diaries and memoirs of some of my forebears, and been fascinated by the ambience of their times, I felt I owed it to later generations to pass on to them how one ancestor lived in the 20th century – and, in particular, an account of his career in the Royal Navy which they might find of some interest.

I had an unusually long naval career of exactly 41 years (1934-1975). Unlike one or two 'high flyers' in my group who rose rather rapidly to higher rank (and early retirement), I served the full span of years in each rank, being promoted in every case at the last opportunity! Thus, on retirement and approaching the age of 60, I found myself the oldest serving officer in the Navy – even including 'Their Lordships' (whose Severe Displeasure I was about to incur).

Since I enjoyed naval life, I was fortunate; indeed I am aware that throughout my career luck played a significant part in determining its direction and duration. When many officers would give their eye-teeth for a Sea Command, the fact that six of these came my way suggests at least a measure of good luck, rather than simply the Fortunes of War (or Peace). There were three or four 'Life-or-Death' instances where pure luck (or my guardian angel?) decided the out-come – and other occasions when crucial appointments occurred just as I happened to be 'in the right place at the right time'. Apart from these episodes, however, to have cruised every ocean, touched on every continent and visited many exotic and little-known places world-wide – all in the day's work and at no personal expense – seemed to me the essence of good fortune.

Hence the title of this book. The sub-title outlines its story.

G.P.D.H.

Editor's Note

THE MORE ONE LIKES a book, the harder it is to cut it. The task I was set was to reduce *Sailor's Luck* by about seventy thousand words through a combination of omission, compression and abbreviation. These constraints have cost me much anxious pondering and many a sigh of regret. Thus I have had to omit most of the author's account of his early years and his family life, and also his experiences in retirement. What is left is the enthralling narrative of his career in the Royal Navy. Recognising his own gift for writing, I have tried to keep to a minimum any editorial interpolations. It has been a true labour of love. What the reader now has before him is the Admiral's own story told in his own words.

David Bourke

CHAPTER I

Naval Cadet, H.M.S. *Frobisher*, 1934–5

'HEARTIEST CONGRATULATIONS. You have passed 5th into the Executive Branch of the Royal Navy'. I looked at the telegram from my father. My cup was overflowing. I remembered my years at Haileybury, my growing determination to join the Royal Navy, my studies in the Army Class and the written entrance examination, which I had taken at College over a five-day period. Some of the papers had been straightforward enough but others I had found appalling, and I had not felt that I had done well. I remembered the Practical Mechanics, in which I had performed better than I expected, the Interview at Burlington Gardens, which had seemed to go surprisingly well, my Medical, which, much to my relief (for I had had my misgivings about it), I had already passed. Now all this had been crowned with success; I had been accepted as a cadet in the Royal Navy.

At the time I heard the news, I was on holiday with my mother in Iceland, and this, my first experience of its charms, had already engendered in me a lifelong love of that country; it had become, and was to remain, the 'land of my dreams'. Now, with this happy news from home, I could relax and enjoy it to the full before joining my first ship at Chatham in a fortnight's time.

On Thursday, 13th September, 1934, clad in my new tailor-made naval uniform, I joined a throng of other 'new entry' cadets and entrained for Chatham to join H.M.S. *Frobisher*, the Cadet Training Cruiser. We were at once put to work. The ship was like an oven and we spent the rest of the day sweating profusely as we stowed baggage, shifted stores, underwent medical inspections and were classed, categorised, lectured and organised. Finally, after a meal and a long-awaited cold shower, we were permitted to sling our hammocks and 'turn in', just about 'dead to the world'. The next day was even more strenuous. Not only were we joined by over a hundred ex-Dartmouth cadets, but we had to prepare the ship for sailing down-river to Sheerness, where we moored to a buoy and proceeded to embark enormous quantities of ammunition.

We were off on the first of three training cruises which, spread over a twelve-month period, would fit us to qualify as midshipmen for service in the Fleet. The ex-Public School (or 'special entry') cadets – who were

regarded as completely inexperienced in the ways of the sea – were known
as 'Preliminaries', and this cruise was intended to bring them to the same
level of naval knowledge as their ex-Dartmouth contemporaries (who had
had four years of naval training and indoctrination). The 'Pubs' (as we were
commonly referred to) were, however, generally assumed to be better
educated than the 'Darts' and, because we had decided on a naval career at a
more mature age, we were better motivated and certainly more enthusiastic.
By comparison the 'Darts' tended to be more blasé. After five days at sea we
reached Gibraltar on September 20th and remained there for the rest of the
month. Everything was new to us: life on a warship, life in the balmy
Mediterranean, the sights, sounds and smells of Gibraltar itself, the glorious
sunshine and the heavenly bathing – and though the routine aboard ship was
tough and relentless, we enjoyed it. When pay day came, and we received
one shilling per day, we could hardly believe it. To have all this and to be
paid for it as well! It seemed too good to be true! Life for the cadets may
have been tough and strenuous, but it was anything but monotonous.
Besides working as crew members from 6.30 each morning, we were under
continuous instruction – both theoretical and practical – till late in the
afternoon, and this was interspersed with daily Divisions and Prayers,
Physical Training, drills, boat-pulling and sailing, armed landing parties,
ceremonial parades and inspections, visual signalling exercises by night and
by day, and all manner of ship's duties, to which we were frequently roused
by bugle calls at any hour.

Frobisher was a heavy cruiser, built in the 1920s and armed with six 7.5"
guns, four 3" anti-aircraft guns, and six 21" submerged torpedo-tubes. She
was a very fine-looking ship, on which 'spit and polish' had been lavished
unstintingly. The upper-deck screens and bulkheads were heavily enamelled,
the wooden decks scrubbed white and spotless, ropes everywhere 'cheesed
down' in immaculate coils, and every conceivable fitting of highly polished
brass. She was a ship to delight the eye of any sailor – and we quickly came
to take an enormous pride in her. Indeed, much of our time when not
actually under instruction was spent washing, scrubbing, scraping, sweeping
and polishing different parts of her – both on deck and between decks. In
those inter-War years, H.M. ships were expected to be 'spick and span' at all
times and much energy went into keeping them so.

The normal practice at sea (weather permitting) was for the ship to stop
for about half an hour at Evening Quarters in order to carry out various
drills. As often as not, all boats would be manned and lowered to pull round
the ship or to recover lifebuoys thrown overboard a mile or more astern, or
to recover torpedoes. Those not involved with the boats might be sent out

to exercise 'Tow For'ard' or 'Tow Aft' or 'Collision Stations' or 'Out Paravanes'. Alternatively they might simply double round the ship or do P.T.

Sometimes, as we moved eastward through the Mediterranean, the pipe would be 'Hands to Bathe'. Then we would all strip off and dive over the side. In depths of 1,500 fathoms, with the sea calm and a brilliant blue, this was an unforgettable experience. To open one's eyes under water and stare down into the abyssal deep was to witness a watery world of incredible purple. Then as one surfaced, one realised, rather alarmingly, that the ship had slowly drawn away (she still had way on), and one had to strike out hard with the others to catch her up.

Boat-hoisting was quite a performance – in fact, when all boats were down, a major 'evolution'. *Frobisher* had at least eight pulling-boats – four cutters, two whalers, a gig and a galley – as well as several motor-boats and motor-pinnaces. At sea it was often the case that all the pulling-boats were down together, sometimes under sail, and manned by up to a hundred cadets. A flag signal from the yard-arm would recall them, either separately or in groups. 'Clear Lower Deck – Hoist Boats' would be piped, the Royal Marine Band would muster on X-Gun Deck, and one boat on each side would sweep up to its falls and start hooking on (in a seaway this could be hazardous). 'Haul taut singly!' would be bellowed aft at the fifty or more hands manning the falls along the decks, then perhaps, 'Walk back ship-side fall!' or, preferably, 'Marry the falls!', followed by the order, 'Hoist away!' – when the band would strike up some rousing tune (e.g. 'What shall we do with the drunken sailor?') as the hands stamped their way aft in time to the beat and the boat with its crew would rise towards the davit-heads. As it approached them, another bellow, 'Handsomely!', and the band would slow its beat.

Then, 'Avast hoisting', and the music would stop – followed by the order: 'Ease to the life-lines!' as the boat's crew jammed further movement of the falls, which were then turned up on the stag-horns. This procedure was repeated for each boat on each side, but the whole performance might be completed inside ten minutes.

All that autumn we moved steadily through the Mediterranean on a 'clockwise' cruise, calling at exotic ports of which we had previously only dreamed: Naples (from which we visited Vesuvius and the ruins of Pompeii), Gravosa and Ragusa on the Dalmatian coast of Yugoslavia (where we fell in with H.M.S. *Queen Elizabeth*, the flagship of the Mediterranean Fleet), the Aegean Sea and the Greek Islands, Gallipoli and the Dardanelles, Constantinople (as it then was), where we paraded through the streets with band playing to lay wreaths on the Turkish War Memorial, and where we visited the Blue Mosque, the Mosque of St. Sophia, the Imperial Palace, the Seraglio – with its eunuchs – and the Treasury, where over a hundred million pounds-worth of incredible treasure was displayed. We spent the last week of October at Mudros and the first week of November at Haifa (from which we visited all the holy sites at Bethlehem, Nazareth and Jerusalem and bathed in the Dead Sea). Then we moved west to Candia in Crete, where we viewed the recently excavated ruins of Knossos. In mid-November we were at Malta, home of our huge Mediterranean Fleet. Moored in the Grand Harbour and Sliema Creek, and comprising six Capital Ships and a vast array of cruisers and destroyers, this made a tremendous impression of British naval power. After a week at Algiers, we moved to spend the last week of November at Gibraltar and returned to Chatham on 6th December. We spent the following week sitting examinations (during which my mother paid a visit to the ship) and got home for Christmas leave on 14th. What a tremendous experience our initiation into the Navy had been! Those three months had effectively dispelled any lingering doubts any of us might have had over our choice of profession.

Our next cruise was to the West Indies. We sailed from Chatham on 11th January, bound for Trinidad, and were ten days out when we hit the headlines in the national press. A 10,000-ton British oil-tanker was on fire in mid-Atlantic and was screaming for help. She lay 450 miles to the westward, without power or steerage, and with most of her engine-room crew either dead or seriously injured. A north-westerly gale was in progress and the tanker S.S. *Valverda* was wallowing in heavy seas. Six other ships were within 500 miles of her, three of them considerably closer than we were. But we had the speed, up to 29 knots. At 0730 on Monday morning, 21st January, as *Frobisher* rolled her way south-westward at the leisurely pace of 12 knots, we were electrified by the pipe: 'Ship will go to the rescue of an oil-tanker on fire'.

Altering course to starboard and working up to full speed, the ship was soon crashing her way through huge seas and shuddering from end to end from the impact of the waves and the vibration of her engines. Awnings were furled, boats turned in, all loose gear lashed down, and storm lifelines rigged along the upper deck. But as our speed increased, so the damage grew: two of our starboard boats were stove in, several reeled hawsers were torn from their deck-fittings and washed overboard, and most of the guardrails and stanchions on the starboard side were smashed or bent double. The motion was indescribable: everything for'ard of the bridge was either totally submerged or pointing to the sky, huge waves swept repeatedly over the fo'c'sle and 'B' Gun Deck, towering clouds of salt sea-spray obliterated

Frobisher *preparing to tow a stricken tanker, Mid-Atlantic, 1935.*

the foretop – and often the masts and funnels – and black smoke poured out from both funnels, obscuring the sea on the port quarter, while at every thudding pitch, the stern rose into the air and our four propellers raced uncontrollably. Nine thousand tons of heavy cruiser driven at full power into the teeth of a North Atlantic gale is an awesome sight – and we'd never experienced anything like it. So violent and unpredictable was the motion that it was impossible to move anywhere without clutching on to some fixture. Yet we spent that evening clad in oilskins and bringing down the heavy hawsers, manilas, grasses, towing pendants, slips and shackles on to the quarter-deck, ready for 'Tow Aft' – and getting drenched to the skin in the process.

I was Midshipman of the Morning Watch and at dawn on the Tuesday we received a faint message from *Valverda* saying that she could see our searchlights shining on the clouds; we were in contact. When we came upon her, there was a small French ship lying near – but doing nothing. She had been only 80 miles away when the S.O.S. went out and on seeing us, she pushed off. We had beaten all the other ships in the race to get there first and now it was up to us. Weather conditions were appalling, but the fire in the tanker was out. The whole after part of the ship was burnt out and blackened, the boats had been destroyed, the engines were out of action, the ship was powerless, one engineer was dead and several others were in a critical condition. During the day we eventually succeeded in passing a line across by Schermuly gun, and by evening we had our 6½" towing wire shackled to the tanker's chain cable, ten shackles of which had been veered out through her hawse-pipe. We started to move forward. The wire came up bar-taut, humming – and we held our breath. The tanker yawed right over to starboard, her rudder jammed hard over. The hum of the wire rose several octaves – and then everything went slack. It had surely parted. But it hadn't! It was *Valverda's* chain cable that had parted – in her hawse-pipe! It was unbelievable. Chain cables just don't part – they just don't. But this one had. We were left with 100 fathoms of 6½" towing wire and 10 shackles of chain-cable hanging from the after fairleads – weighing some 15 tons. That was more than our electric capstan on the quarter-deck could cope with. We had no alternative but to slip the lot.

For the next three days we wallowed – both literally and metaphorically. We wallowed in the troughs of the Atlantic rollers and we wallowed in rumour, speculation, indecision and frustration. H.M.S. *Guardian*, a net-layer equipped with special towing gear, arrived on the Wednesday and took the tanker in tow, but made no headway whatever. *Valverda* yawed wildly (as she had done with us), and during the night the tow parted. *Guardian* gave up and transferred her special 5½" towing wire to us. Gradually the storm abated and on the Friday, having put a skeleton crew of experts aboard the tanker and brought off her injured men, we got her in tow again. This time we had brought our own chain cable aft from the fo'c'sle and veered half a shackle (about six fathoms) of it through our after fairleads as a 'spring'. The other end of the tow was shackled to the tanker's cable, which, now that we had restored power to her windlass, was gradually veered out to ease the terrific strain on the wire as we forged slowly ahead. The same old trouble recurred: she couldn't steer and went off at right-angles to the line of advance, forcing us to stop repeatedly and go astern so as to avoid parting the wire. We made no headway. On the Saturday, with the tanker still miraculously 'in tow', our engineers succeeded in repairing her steering gear, and from then on things began to settle down. Gradually we worked up to about five knots.

For the next six days we struggled slowly towards the nearest land, Bermuda, 900 miles to the northwestward, with twenty thousand tons of deadweight wallowing astern of us (the tanker was fully laden). It was a long and testing interlude of hopeful anxiety. However, on the last day of January we arrived at Bermuda and lay off the coral reefs waiting for the dawn. The task before us was to manoeuvre the giant tow through the long narrow channel cut through the reefs into the sheltered waters of the lagoon. This meant a complete change of tactics, as well as of towing gear, for we now had to keep the tow close up under our stern so as to keep her from yawing into those deadly submerged reefs. The job took us all the next day and all the next night. Two more hawsers were parted in the process, but by keeping our searchlights on the tanker as we painfully weaved our way through the sinuous two-mile channel, we somehow managed it, and, as the last wire parted under the colossal strain, *Valverda* let go her anchor in calm and safety.

So ended the famous '*Valverda* incident' – a saga indeed. We found that we had made history. Not only had we featured prominently in the newspapers at home (with photographs flown home from H.M.S. *Guardian*), but we had broken records. We had been continuously at sea for longer (22 days) than any H.M. ship since the Great War, and we had accomplished the second longest non-stop tow on record (900 miles). By any standards it was a magnificent feat, but for us cadets it was an object lesson in determination, professional skill and practical seamanship that none of us would ever forget.

Of course the gilt on the gingerbread was the salvage money – announced many months later in an Admiralty Fleet Order. I think we all got rather more than we expected.

After our toils and anxieties, the coral islands of Bermuda seemed like Paradise. We spent two days there, resting, refuelling and repairing the damage. Then we set off (into the teeth of another gale) for the West Indies. Four days later we reached Barbados, where we found half the Home Fleet anchored off Bridgetown. Later we moved on to St. Lucia and from there to Montserrat. But it was the Virgin Islands that we really fell for, and here we spent our last week in the West Indies. The ship's routine and our courses of instruction were relaxed, and much of our time at St. Thomas and Tortola was spent in soaking up the sun, swimming, sailing and picnicking on the beaches. The islands seemed wild and virtually uninhabited, and we treasured the memory of them on the long voyage home. In April, while the ship re-fitted at Chatham, we got some well-earned Easter leave. When we returned in May, we found *Frobisher* had been equipped with a sea-plane and a crane to hoist it in and out. In the same month we took part in the celebrations for the Silver Jubilee of the King and Queen at Rosyth, where we dressed ship over-all, We were now Senior Cadets preparing for promotion to Midshipmen, and were largely preoccupied with working up to our Passing-Out exams. in two months' time.

Before we left *Frobisher*, however, we had one final summer cruise, beginning with a visit to Copenhagen (where we found ourselves bowled

over by the beauty of the flaxen-haired girls) and thence to Oslo and
Trondhjem (where we found the Norwegian girls, if possible, even prettier)
before returning to Scapa Flow for summer exercises, in which virtually the
whole of the Home Fleet was engaged. Here we were kept properly on our
toes. A constant stream of signals emanated from the Flagship and had to be
repeated down the lines, signals sometimes affecting us, sometimes not. It
was our third taste of the highly disciplined life of the Fleet, where no
mistake or slovenliness went unnoticed, calling forth a signalled reprimand
from one eagle-eyed Admiral or another.

It was quite a relief to resume our independent programme. We left the
Orkneys, rounded Cape Wrath and sailed down the west coast of Scotland
to Loch Linnhe, where we anchored off Ballachulish. Here the cadets
obtained valuable experience in handling boats under power and sail in the
very strong tidal streams flowing in and out of Loch Leven.

By mid-July we were anchored off Torquay and from there moved out
into the Channel to rendezvous with the 9th Cruiser Squadron of the
Reserve Fleet for the Spithead Review. The other ships of our Squadron,
Effingham, *Hawkins* and *Vindictive*, were all manned by Reservists and we
now joined up with them for elementary manoeuvres. We then took under
our wing the similarly manned 10th Cruiser Squadron (*Cardiff*, *Calypso*,
Caledon and *Curacoa*). Steaming eastward in Line Ahead, the eight cruisers
were joined by eight minesweeping sloops of the Reserve Fleet. The whole
formation, led by Vice-Admiral Commanding Reserve Fleet (in *Effingham*),
then steamed up through the Solent, keeping careful station, and took up
their allotted berths for the Review. It was an impressive evolution and
earned us a 'Manoeuvre Well Executed' signal from the Admiral.

The Silver Jubilee Review of the Fleet at Spithead took place on 17th
July, 1935. King George V was in the Royal Yacht, *Victoria and Albert*, and
the occasion was moving, spectacular and deeply memorable. The whole
might of the Royal Navy (excluding the China, West Indies and Cape
Cruiser Squadrons) was engaged, together with the big Ocean Liners
representing the Mercantile Marine, many foreign warships and hundreds of
yachts. They were ranged in parallel columns as far as the eye could see –
with every vessel dressed overall and with their crews manning the side.
Preceded by the Trinity House yacht *Patricia*, the beautiful and graceful
Royal Yacht steamed down the line with her two bell-topped funnels
gleaming, the Lord High Admiral's flag at the fore, the Royal Standard at the
main, the Union Jack (flag of an Admiral of the Fleet) at the mizzen. As she
did so, every ship in turn gave His Majesty three heartfelt and rousing
cheers. Flag-signals then broke out from every yard-arm, ordering the Fleet

9th and 10th Cruiser Squadrons followed by Reserve Flotilla of Minesweeping Sloops forming up for Royal Fleet Review, Spithead, 1935. Frobisher *is 4th in line.*

to weigh and proceed – and the whole vast array of battleships, cruisers, destroyers and sloops steamed out to sea in the wake of *Victoria and Albert*, led by Admiral of the Fleet, His Majesty, King George V. With the Fleet clear of the land, the Royal Yacht then turned about and passed down the lines at full speed, flying the signal, 'Splice the Main Brace'. H.M.S. *Frobisher* then broke off and headed for the French naval base at Brest, where we spent the last week of our final cruise. Here we got down in earnest to our Passing-Out examinations, both written and practical. These, so far as I can remember, comprised Seamanship, Navigation, Pilotage, Communications, Engineering, Gunnery, Torpedoes, Officer of the Watch and Divisional Duties. Rather to my surprise, I did quite well, and also won the Prize Essay. It was significant that every one of the top ten places was held by a 'Pub' (So much for the Dartmouth Entry!). Vacancies for Midshipmen in the Fleet – both at home and abroad – were promulgated before we broke up at Chatham in August. Six of us, who had habitually 'slung' in the airy After Control Room, opted for the six vacancies in H.M.S. *Dragon*, preparing for her last commission on the America and West Indies Station, and were duly appointed.

CHAPTER II

Midshipman, H.M.S. *Dragon*, 1935-7

AFTER A WONDERFUL LEAVE between appointments I joined my new ship, H.M.S. *Dragon*, towards the end of August. Hitherto, as Cadets, we had been more or less 'on probation' in the Navy. True, we had been Officer Cadets, but that position had carried no authority, no permanence. A Cadet was not considered an officer. As fully-fledged Midshipmen, however, we were classed as 'subordinate officers' and were part of the working complement of the ship – with a whole range of ship's duties – and were paid five shillings a day. The six of us who had occupied the After Control position in the Training Cruiser (and made it our exclusive preserve) formed *Dragon's* whole complement of Midshipmen. Three of us were Canadians (Mids. Caldwell, Russel and Boak), belonging to the Royal Canadian Navy, one (Mid. Mackay) was a New Zealander, while the other two (Mid. Highton and I) were English. We shared the Gunroom with one Sub-Lieutenant (who was President of the Mess), one Sub-Lieutenant (E), one Paymaster-Midshipman and one Paymaster Cadet – ten of us in all.

H.M.S. *Dragon* was a Light Cruiser of 4,800 tons, built at the end of the Great War. She was armed with six 6" guns, three 4" High-Angle guns, two 'Pom-poms' and four 3-pdr. saluting-guns. She also carried twelve deck-mounted 21" torpedo-tubes. Six boilers powered two sets of turbines, each of which drove one propeller shaft, developing 40,000 h.p. at full power – and giving a speed of 29 knots. Her full complement was about 600, including some 30 officers all told. She was commissioning (for what we thought was to be the last time) to rejoin the America and West Indies Squadron. We were due to sail on the Monday morning (26th August).

At the time we joined, the end of August, 1935, the international situation was deteriorating, with Mussolini becoming increasingly bellicose and intransigent over Abyssinia and Britain and France squaring up to him and demanding action from the League of Nations. Our Fleet in the Mediterranean was being steadily reinforced and most of the other cruisers of the Squadron were withdrawn from the Station, leaving *Dragon* to 'show the flag' in South America. Official visits by H.M. ships to foreign ports involved a high degree of ceremony and protocol, the detail of which was laid down meticulously in King's Regulations and Admiralty Instructions

(K.R. & A.I.), the Navy's bible. Knowledge of these details was part of a Naval Officer's stock-in-trade, and Midshipmen were expected to have it at their finger-tips. Flag-showing cruises and courtesy visits were intended to improve or consolidate friendly relations between Britain and her trading partners overseas – and, as was well known, 'trade followed the flag'. Although at this time our stock stood very high in all the South American countries, many of them were very 'touchy' in matters of national pride. It was therefore essential to the success of our mission that national susceptibilities should never be offended or appear to be slighted.

On entering the approaches to a foreign port for the first time, *Dragon* would hoist the national flag of the country concerned at the yard-arm and, with the ship's company smartly 'fallen in for entering harbour', and with the Royal Marine Band assembled, a 21-gun national salute would be fired. This would be returned with an equal number of guns, either by a warship of the host country or by a shore fort, or sometimes by a troop of field-guns lined up on the shore. If a foreign Admiral were present, his Flag would then be saluted with the appropriate number of guns (perhaps 17), depending on his rank, and that would be returned with the correct number of guns for a Post-Captain. As soon as we had berthed (or anchored), a Lieutenant or Sub-Lieutenant would be sent off by boat as Officer of the Guard, wearing his sword, with ensign and pendant flying (often under sail or being 'pulled'), to call on the foreign warship both as a matter of courtesy and to fix up details of any further calls, e.g. between the ships' respective Captains. At the same time, British representatives at the port (Consul, Vice-Consul or a senior Embassy official) would board the ship to conduct the Captain on a round of formal calls on the various foreign dignitaries in the area (perhaps the State Governor, the Naval C-in-C, the Port Admiral, the Mayor and the Harbour Master – and possibly the British Ambassador).

Later in the day each of the Captain's calls would be returned. As the foreign dignitary approached the ship, a bugle or pipe would sound the 'Still', and as he mounted the gangway, the bugler would sound the 'Alert', all those on the quarter-deck solemnly saluting, while if the caller were a naval officer, he would be 'piped over the side'. A Royal Marine Guard with fixed bayonets might be drawn up for his inspection, and while this was in progress, the Band would strike up the appropriate tune to which his particular office or rank entitled him, 'Rule Britannia', 'Iolanthe' or 'The Garb of Old Gaul'. This sort of thing might be repeated half a dozen times or more during the course of the day, and in tropical conditions it called for a certain stamina on the part of all those assembled to receive the caller: the Guard, the Band, the Commander, the Officer of the Day, the two

Midshipmen of the Watch, the Quartermaster, the Bugler, the Boatswain's Mate, the Gangway Sentry etc., all in full white uniform with swords, dirks and medals to the fore. If, as was often the case, the calls were made by boat with the ship at anchor, the Gangway Staff, supervised by the Midshipmen, was kept extremely busy, conducting the movement of the boats, ordering them to lie off (or at a boat-rope), and calling them alongside when required.

After a day or two the 'ceremonial' tended to fade out – but meanwhile the invitations had been flooding in: four officers for tennis, six officers for riding, eight officers for a cocktail party and dance, two officers for a week-end up-country, a cricket XI and a Rugger XV to play the locals, a sailing-race against the local Yacht Club, eight officers to play polo, all officers to be honorary members of the Country Club . . . and so on. It was made very clear to us Midshipmen that it was our duty to take up such invitations whether we liked them or not – and always to return the hospitality.

On one occasion we were visiting Buenos Aires at a time shortly after the death of Admiral of the Fleet Lord Jellicoe. On the Sunday, therefore, we had a ceremonial Church Parade to attend a Memorial Service being held for him in St. John's Pro-Cathedral. It entailed the whole Ship's Company marching through the streets of Buenos Aires with the Royal Marine Band playing.

Buenos Aires was a thriving city with a population, at that time, of over two million. Traffic was heavy even on a Sunday morning, and the streets were filled with cars and lorries. It was quite a long march from the naval dockyard to the Cathedral and my job was to go on ahead of the parade to warn the traffic police so that there would be no hold-ups. There were no traffic lights in those days, but at each street intersection a policeman wielding a white baton stood in a raised kiosk controlling the flow of traffic. My Spanish was none too good, but with some simple gesticulations and the words,'El crucéro inglès, Dragonne', I tried to convey my message – to no avail. The policemen, though puzzled, ignored me, cars and lorries continued to speed across the intersection, and all the while the sound of the band and hundreds of marching feet grew louder and louder behind me. Something had to be done or there would be chaos. So, throwing caution to the winds, I drew my dirk and holding it at arm's length, marched into the centre of the road, faced the on-coming traffic, and mustering all the authority that I could, held up my left hand (with the dirk outstretched in my right) and brought the traffic to a standstill. I'm not sure who was the more astonished, the policeman or the motorists – or me! But it worked and the parade marched on. At each of the following intersections I repeated the procedure, the traffic police simply gaping at me, and the parade reached the Cathedral exactly on cue. In the circumstances, of course, it was the obvious thing to do – but it certainly impressed the officers, and after it was all over, I was summoned to the Wardroom and plied with drinks.

It will be apparent how fortunate we were, at the tender age of nineteen or so, to have visited so many countries and ports. Over a period of 21 months we made no less than 35 visits, ranging from Rio Plato in the south to Newfoundland in the north and embracing the whole of the Caribbean and the West Indies. We visited two ports in Newfoundland, four in Canada, three in the U.S.A., two in Mexico, one in Argentina, one in British Honduras, one in Uruguay, seven in Brazil and eleven in various islands of the West Indies, as well as visiting Bermuda nine times.

It might be thought, from the foregoing, that naval life consisted of little apart from 'fun and games'. Nothing could be further from the truth. Sport, recreation and social activity were vital counter-weights to long days and nights of hard work, humdrum business and strenuous exercises. We were well aware that international relations were steadily deteriorating and that war was probably not far round the corner. Thus few opportunities were lost, on passage between ports or on ocean voyages, to practise our surface and air gunnery, multiple torpedo attacks, landing or boarding parties, emergency stations or damage-control exercises. Apart from that, the Midshipmen had very little spare time. They were watch-keeping at sea, and in harbour they were either 'day-on' or boat-running, while in normal working hours, whether at sea or in harbour, morning and afternoon, they were generally 'under instruction'. Occasionally, if there was a great deal of activity in the ship, or if we were required for other duties, 'Instruction' would be waived. But this was exceptional. In the ordinary course, our instruction would start in the Gunroom at 0900. At 1015 there would be 'Stand Easy' till 1030, followed by instruction in a different subject till 1130. In the afternoon there would be two periods, from 1315 till 'Stand Easy' at 1415 and from 1430 till 1530. The subjects in which we were instructed included Seamanship, Gunnery, Torpedo, Electrics, Engineering, Navigation, Pilotage, Wireless-telegraphy, Visual Signalling, Ship Construction, Mechanics, Mathematics, Meteorology and Modern Languages. The 'technical' subjects were normally taught by the ship's specialist officers, Warrant Officers or senior specialist ratings, while purely 'academic' subjects were the province of the Instructor Officer.

The purpose of our Instruction, apart from improving our professional knowledge, was to fit us for our Midshipmen's examination at the end of our two years, and for subsequent promotion. I may say that a Midshipman's all-round knowledge at that stage was pretty comprehensive, and probably superior to that of any other officer or rating, for the simple reason that officers, as they progressed in rank and experience, tended increasingly to concentrate on their own 'specialisations' and to put the groundwork behind them – while the Petty Officers and Chief Petty Officers, while highly expert in their own particular fields, lacked the breadth of training which Midshipmen of the Executive Branch received.

By the beginning of 1936 *Dragon's* Midshipmen had all received job changes, and I found myself appointed Navigating Officer's Assistant (or 'Tanky'), a job I had rather hankered after. This involved me in all sorts of theoretical and practical work connected with astronomy, nautical charts and time. To ease the Navigator's relentless task at sea, I would set up the Star Globe (showing the bearing and altitude of all the visible stars and planets) prior to the taking of the morning and evening star-sights, record the exact time and altitude of each 'shot', back up the sights with sights of my own, check the Navigator's calculations, work out the time of Meridian Passage for noon sun-sights and the times of sunrise and sunset at the ship's expected positions, wind, check and rate the ship's three chronometers against one another, check and rate the deck-watches against the chronometers or radio time-signals, and keep the large outfit of charts corrected up to date from Admiralty Notices to Mariners. It was a demanding job but extremely interesting, and, moreover, it excused me from night watch-keeping!

While the ship was at sea, opportunity was seldom lost to carry out some form of gunnery or torpedo practice. Full calibre shoots normally required a Battle Practice Target (B.P.T), which would be towed by a tug, but 'Throw-off' shoots, whether full calibre or sub-calibre, could be carried out using the ship's boats, one of which would be sent away with a 'marking party' with a Midshipman in charge. H.A. shoots were often carried out against smoke-bursts or flares – or, if another ship were in company, against a kite flown by that ship, or sometimes against 'met' balloons. 'Repel Aircraft' – to exercise our close-range anti-aircraft weapons – could also be carried out using improvised targets, though a sleeve target towed by a seaplane was preferable. Practice torpedo attacks, using the ship's boats as targets, would often be carried out at Evening Quarters, and recovery of the 'spent' torpedoes became a standard task for the Midshipmen in the boats. For exercise purposes the torpedoes were fitted with 'practice warheads', which were buoyant, the main body of the torpedo having slight negative buoyancy. Thus, at the end of its run, a torpedo would be floating vertically, the tip of its orange-coloured practice-head just visible among the wave-crests. The Midshipman in charge of the sea-boat (a five-oared whaler)

Dragon working up to full power, West Atlantic, 1936.

would direct the boat close up to the bobbing practice-head (being careful not to get too close, or the boat could be stove in), while the Torpedo Party in the bows would lean out, snatch a spring-hook on to the head-ring, slide a steel wire noose down the torpedo, and haul it up by the tail. With the torpedo securely lashed head-and-tail close alongside the boat, it would be rowed back to the ship and hoisted in. Torpedoes are extremely expensive weapons, and to lose one (which seldom happened) was to provoke an immediate Court of Inquiry.

Perhaps the most dramatic and interesting of these war-practices was to exercise 'Night Encounter', a relatively frequent occurrence as it was the Captain's favourite exercise. It would take place, normally, during the First Watch — well after dark. About 2100 the cutter, equipped for sailing and carrying an Aldis-lamp and hurricane lantern, and with a crew of 16 and a Midshipman in charge, would be lowered to within about six feet of the wave-tops. The officer on deck would then order 'Out pins', and would watch for the approach of a high wave-crest before ordering 'Slip'. With luck, the heavy boat would fall smack on top of the wave. With the ship slowly forging ahead, towing the cutter by its boat-rope, the boat would sheer out under helm, slip the boat-rope and hoist sails. The Midshipman's orders from the Captain would be to steer a certain compass-course for an hour – and show no lights. The ship, meanwhile, would gather speed and soon be lost to sight, perhaps her masthead steaming-lights being occasionally visible on the horizon as the cutter breasted a big wave. It was really rather an eerie experience to be cast away in mid-ocean on a dark night, with nothing but one's own slender resources to rely on – apart from a supreme confidence that the ship would somehow be able to find one again. The ocean seemed so huge and menacing when viewed from sea-level, and if the wind freshened, the cutter surged ahead and heeled more and more to leeward and started shipping seas inboard. Then the question was: should one luff up and shorten sail, or press on and risk it? As the hour approached and there was darkness on all sides, had the ship lost us? We would get ready to light the hurricane lantern to illuminate our mainsail – when suddenly a star shell would burst in the sky, far away on our beam, followed by another and another, slowly falling on their little parachutes and lighting up the whole wide ocean, silhouetting the cutter to the eyes of those on the ship's bridge and calling forth two blinding white rays as the great searchlights opened on us. The exercise would then be a success. We would be considered 'sunk'. But it was not always so. Sometimes, due to erratic steering, a drastic change in wind-direction or a faulty boat's compass, the ship would fail to find us. Our Aldis light would then be shone – and it would be the Middle Watch before we were recovered.

The last days of October, 1936 were spent in the West Indies but were later dominated by the grounding on coral reefs of a large Spanish liner (S.S. *Cristobal Colon*) off the north end of some outlying islands of Bermuda. Together with the dockyard tugs, *Dragon* did her utmost to tow the ship off. For four days we tried in every way we could, but the liner was impaled amidships on a transverse ridge, her double-bottom badly holed, her hull making water, and beginning to break up under the pounding of the sea. We were conscious throughout of undertones of the Spanish Civil War, then in its fourth month. The ship flew the Republican ensign and was on her way to Latin America with a cargo of coal to exchange for munitions of war. Her officers were incompetent and the crew rebellious. Her ownership was in doubt and salvage costs unlikely to be met. After enormous expenditure in effort and material, it was decided by the Governor to abandon the ship. Our Royal Marines stood by in case of mutiny, and the crew were removed in the ship's boats to a disused barracks ashore, together with their personal belongings. Slowly the lights dimmed, as water crept up to the ship's generators and, with a wisp of steam curling from her funnel, *Cristobal Colon* gradually died – forlorn and abandoned.

By January 1937 we were once more in the West Indies, and after an energetic but highly enjoyable time in Jamaica, we steamed westwards to one of its dependencies, the Cayman Islands. Here we spent a week, heavily involved in the Annual Regatta for the local schooners – beautifully built ships of up to 130 tons – mainly employed on the turtle trade with Honduras and Nicaragua. Some of us were fortunate enough to participate in the races, and I shall never forget the unique experience, and the excitement, of sailing in the brand-new schooner, *A.M. Adams* of 120 tons (the Caymanian favourite) against the highly unpopular reigning champion, *Goldfield*. They were the only two ships in the 100-ton Class 'A'. The race was to be over a 35-mile triangular course and the wind was a fresh north-easterly. It was a superb exhibition of old-fashioned seamanship, motivated by supreme ambition and intense personal animosity between the two ships' Captains. After narrowly averting a collision with *Goldfield* (which had suddenly luffed and crossed our bows, drawing forth a volley of abuse from our skipper), a formal 3-course hot luncheon was served on the roof of the after cabin. This was preceded by the Captain solemnly reciting a long and involved Grace while the race continued. A second sitting followed, at which Grace was said by the Mate. Meanwhile the two ships, having rounded the first mark with *Goldfield* slightly in the lead, were now racing neck and neck on the beat to windward. We rounded the second mark just ahead of our rival, and led her all the way down the 7-mile reach to the finish, crossing the line a mere 15 seconds ahead of her. Great were the shouts of joy and triumph as *Goldfield* was beaten, but they were short-lived. A signal to the Regatta Committee pronounced *Goldfield* the winner – on *time* ! Everyone was astonished, including the two ships' Captains, neither of whom was aware that they had been racing against time.

From the Cayman Islands we set course to the south-westward for a speck on the chart labelled 'Swan Islands', 150 miles away. Our mission was 'hush-hush', but the purpose of it gradually unfolded. As dawn broke, we peered ahead with binoculars, seeking vainly for the islands, till suddenly the masthead lookout cried 'Land-ho on the port beam!' We'd damned near missed them! Rounding up to approach from the south-westward, we anchored in the only possible place, at the S.W. end of Big Swan. It was a 'fairytale' desert island that we beheld, with a fine white sandy beach fringed with a profusion of coconut palms growing right down to the water's edge. To the right of the beach was a stone jetty with a flagstaff, from which – lo and behold! – flew the Stars and Stripes. Our mission was to lay claim to, and annex, the islands on behalf of the British Crown, their handful of inhabitants being exclusively Caymanians. While the Headman (and virtual owner of the islands) came off to see the Captain, I took the motor-boat in with some officers, and was fortunate to get ashore myself. The scene was idyllic, quieter and more peaceful than anything I'd experienced, and I was overwhelmed by its beauty and tranquillity. The only sounds, apart from the rustle of the wind in the palm trees, were the cackle of a few hens and the neighing of a nearby horse. I met one or two of the inhabitants, who had no idea what power, if any, claimed the islands, and who told me that the only reason they flew the American flag was that it was the only flag they had! (This was soon rectified: with our gift of a large Union Jack flying from their flagstaff, our captain was able to report 'Mission Accomplished'.)

By now, in 1937, the situation in Europe was causing mounting concern – in particular the blatant intervention of Germany and Italy in the Spanish Civil War. In the light of this, Britain had initiated a massive rearmament programme including the compression into two years of a ship-building programme that had been intended to extend over ten. As a result of this, two new modern cruisers, *Apollo* and *Ajax*, arrived on the Station and *Dragon* became obsolete. It had been decided that she should return to the U.K. and pay off into Reserve.

First, however, the Coronation of the new King, George VI, was to take place on May 12th, and all the ceremonies and celebrations marking the event had to be organised and prepared. The Squadron was to disperse from Bermuda to other parts of the Station to take up their duties as Guardships for the local ceremonies. *Dragon* was to go to Antigua before returning home, while *York* was to remain as Guardship at Hamilton, just across the Sound. Two days before the ships were to disperse, a Mr. Mackay, the owner of a magnificent yacht, invited *Dragon* to allow three of her young midshipmen to sail home in her with him.

This was one of those 'opportunities of a lifetime' which was simply not to be missed. Our Captain reacted with enthusiasm: 'It'll teach those young snotties a thing or two about seamanship – do 'em a power of good,' is apparently what he said. But permission had to be sought from the C-in-C, and even confirmed by the Admiralty. Meanwhile lots were drawn among our 'Executive' midshipmen for the three preferred places, and as it turned out they fell on Michael Highton, Pat Russel and me. (This was true justice, as the others had already enjoyed some long leave in Canada, whereas we three had had none for nearly two years).

Approval came through from the C-in-C the day before the ships dispersed – and after some hurried packing up and farewells to friends and shipmates, we three were transferred to the flagship for our last week in Bermuda. We were quite sad to wave goodbye to good old *Dragon* and to the others, as they steamed out of the Sound (*Dragon* flying her long paying-off pennant from the masthead), but we were soon absorbed in *York's* multifarious preparations for the Coronation ceremonies. As regards ship's duties, I found myself Mid. of the Day to start with, and Mid. of the Motor Boat shortly afterwards. On the 10th May, *York* proceeded across to Hamilton, where she moored close in front of the prestigious Royal Bermuda Yacht Club.

The following evening a big Dance was held on board, attended by all the local élite and a great many Americans. The whole town was in festive mood, with flags and bunting, coats-of-arms and decorated arches everywhere, all the yachts and ships dressed overall by day and ablaze with lights at night, and crowds of people singing and merry-making in the streets.

On Coronation Day the main event was a magnificent Parade, 21-gun salute, and March Past by the Navy and Army before H.E. the Governor, with massed bands of the Royal Marines and the Sherwood Foresters – and attended by huge crowds all 'dressed up to the nines'. It was a most impressive performance, which lasted all morning and was hugely appreciated by the thousands of spectators, among whom were hundreds of Americans who had come to Bermuda for the big occasion. It was followed, in the afternoon, by a big Garden Party at Government House, attended by everyone of note (including, of course, ourselves!)

This was our last day in Bermuda, and it was rounded off in unforgettable style by the Coronation Ball at the famous 'Bermudiana' Hotel, where 500 tables had been reserved for private parties. Mr Mackay, in whose schooner, the *Elk*, we were due to set out for England the next day, invited the three of us to join his party, starting with drinks on board the yacht. There followed a truly unforgettable evening of drinking, dining, and dancing in the superb surroundings of that magnificent hotel, with four or five dance bands playing in different rooms and another one out on the lawn. So ended Coronation Day in Bermuda, a fitting end to the many happy and eventful days we had spent there.

On Thursday the 13th of May we set sail for England in the 180-ton schooner, *Elk*, in which her owner, Mr. Mackay, had been cruising in the West Indies. His wife and two daughters had quailed at the Atlantic crossing and opted instead for a safer and more comfortable passage in S.S. *Orbita*, so we three midshipmen were allotted their quite sumptuous quarters. The yacht was 131 ft. in length with a 24 ft. beam, and carried, with all sails set, 7,500 sq. ft. of canvas. She also had powerful auxiliary engines. Her crew consisted of Master, Mate, Boatswain, Chief Engineer, Cook, Chief Steward, Steward, Assistant Engineer and six Able Seamen – 14 in all, plus the owner and us three passengers.

The very last thing we wanted, of course, was to be regarded as passengers (and that was far from our Captain's intention). It was quickly agreed, therefore, that we should be auxiliary members of the crew, and also that we should back up the Master's astro-navigation. For the first seven days of the voyage we were close-hauled and beating to windward while endeavouring to sail a Great Circle course. *Elk* was carrying jib, fore-stays'l, fores'l and mains'l and, with the help of the auxiliary motor, was making good about seven knots. We would have preferred to do without the engine. Not only did it interfere with the yacht's natural motion and with the way the sails drew, but it also caused an appreciable amount of vibration. However, the owner was keen to get home as quickly as he could. After a week the weather changed. The wind dropped and the sky cleared, and with just a vestige of S.W.'ly breeze, we hoisted the balloon jib in lieu of the jib and stays'l. The following day we encountered a heavy beam swell from the N.W. and, to take advantage of the slight westerly breeze, we took in the balloon jib and hoisted the large squares'l on the foremast (which was equipped with a wide yard for the purpose). Annoyingly, however, we were still using the wretched engine.

Meanwhile we three were 'pulling our weight' – literally! – pulling and hauling with the seamen when sails were changed, taking 'tricks' at the wheel (and *Elk* certainly handled beautifully), and doubling up on the Master's star-sights and sun-sights. We never did find out what method he used to calculate his position lines (it certainly wasn't the Marc-St. Hilaire method, at which we were adept), and we began to trust our own fixes more than his. But these were lazy days for us, and when not sleeping, drinking or eating, we spent much of our time reading and sun-bathing.

However, on the ninth day of our voyage the weather broke and we awoke to a grey, tumbling ocean surging up in white, foam-capped waves under a leaden, rain filled sky with a strong south-westerly wind. The time had come to revert to our original rig and to dispense with the motor. We were now running with the wind on our port quarter with all sails drawing well, and bowling along merrily. This was really sailing, and, with a heavy following sea lifting our transom high in the air, skilled helmsmanship was needed to prevent the schooner from broaching to.

The weather steadily deteriorated and by nightfall we were driving before a full gale, lee scuppers under and decks awash, making an incredible twelve knots. It was a most exhilarating sensation, sails bellying forward, rigging bar-taut, masts and booms bending, seas cascading over the decks and hatches, and the gale howling through the rigging. It couldn't last. Lashings were beginning to be carried away, and at dawn all hands were called on

The yacht, Elk *sailing home from Bermuda, 1937.*

deck to shorten sail. We took in the mains'l, all 2,300 ft. of it. It was a hell of a job and it took us over an hour to get it in, some of us being nearly washed overboard in the process. Later on we set the squares'l again, and the following day took it in again and set the main tris'l. This was the pattern of life for several days as the wind shifted from one quarter to another. We had little peace, and were frequently soaked to the skin by breaking seas or sudden rainsqualls.

After a fortnight's sailing the wind shifted again and blew steadily from the south, so we re-set the mains'l, hoisted the main-tops'l, and with the fores'l, forestays'l and jib already set, we were carrying more sail than ever before. As we reached along at a good eleven to twelve knots, we must have looked a magnificent sight. After 15 days we sighted our first landfall, the Bishop's Rock Lighthouse, and next day (26th May) we reached Hythe, near Southampton. We were home!

What a memorable voyage that was, and what a unique experience! We would recall it for the rest of our lives. We got in on a Friday and travelled up to London by train. How marvellously fresh and green the English countryside looked after all those months abroad! We had forgotten how beautiful our own country looked, being sated with the exotic attractions across the Atlantic.

Dragon had meanwhile got in to Chatham from Antigua and we telephoned her and obtained a week's leave. It was a great home-coming. I'd never been away so long before and I was greatly impressed by my parents' new home at Tumby Chase. We got ourselves down to Chatham and as *Dragon* was in process of paying off and there was no news of our next appointments, we were granted indefinite leave pending recall on re-appointment. This arrangement completed, I returned to Tumby.

CHAPTER III

Midshipman, H.M.S. *Southampton*, 1937

A WEEK AFTER OUR ARRIVAL in England I received a telegram ordering me to join H.M.S. *Southampton* at Portland – 'forthwith'. Though I could well have done with a bit more leave, this was indeed terrific news. *Southampton* was our very latest cruiser, the first of the new 10,000-ton heavy cruisers of the 'Southampton' class, and the Flagship of the 2nd Cruiser Squadron. I got down there the same evening and was delighted to find that my old friend Michael Highton was joining the ship with me. Arriving on board, we were confronted by the First Lieutenant, who peremptorily inquired why we had not sought permission to join p.m.! (The convention is that on taking up a new appointment, one should do so before 9 a.m.). We had evidently attached too much urgency to the word 'forthwith', and would have done better to have put ourselves up in Weymouth for the night.

The first thing I discovered was that I was Senior Midshipman, so I had to start taking over the duties of that office. Compared with *Dragon*, the ship was so large and modern that it needed time and effort just to get used to it. The Gunroom, which was designed for eight, was rather over-crowded. We now had a complement of two Sub-Lieutenants, two Paymaster-Midshipmen and eight Executive Midshipmen. However, we gradually 'shook down' and had a useful run up through the North Sea in company with our sister ship, *Newcastle*, before mooring two days later in the Firth of Forth.

For the rest of June and the first half of July it was exercises, exercises, exercises – surface and anti-aircraft gunnery practices, and drills of every kind – all designed to bring the new squadron up to a reasonable pitch of war-readiness. Some of these practices were carried out in the North Sea and some in the S.W. approaches to the English Channel, where large-scale Trade Defence and Coastal Defence exercises were mounted by the Home Fleet in conjunction with the R.A.F. and other services. In interludes between successive phases of intense activity, *Southampton*, together with many other units of the Fleet, usually anchored in Weymouth Bay or Torbay.

There was a lot for us to work up. We had the very latest weapon-

Southampton, *flagship of 2nd Cruiser Squadron, 1937.*

Victoria & Albert *awaiting the King and Queen for passage to Northern Ireland (with heavy naval escort), Loch Ryan, 1937.*

systems, with highly sophisticated control arrangements: 12 6"-guns in 4 turrets as main armament, 8 4"-guns in 4 mountings as anti-aircraft armament, and, for close defence, 2 0.5" multi-machine guns and 2 2-pdr. pom-poms with 4 barrels on each. We also carried 6 torpedoes in 2 triple-mountings and 3 'Walrus' amphibian seaplanes, which could be launched either side by an athwartships catapult. During our first full-calibre shoot at a Battle Practice target, we found our main 6" guns surprisingly accurate and capable of a high rate of fire. We also found our aircraft of enormous value in a reconnaissance role – particularly during the Trade Defence exercise.

On 28th July, in perfect weather, the King and Queen crossed from Scotland to Northern Ireland in the Royal Yacht, escorted there and back by a force of cruisers and destroyers led by *Southampton* – an impressive and memorable occasion.

Soon after these events, I was granted 16 days' summer leave – the first decent whack I'd had in two years – and spent most of it at my parents' home, Tumby Chase. On returning to Chatham, I was sent to undergo two weeks' 'destroyer-time' on two different ships, H.M.S. *Wishart* and H.M.S. *Wanderer*. *Wishart* was an Improved 'W'-Class destroyer, day-running in the Thames Estuary with seamen's training classes, and doubling as Emergency Destroyer for the Nore Command. She was based in the stream, just below Chatham, and usually picked up her training classes at Sheerness. Apart from a Lieutenant-Commander in command, she had no executive commissioned officers, and was under-manned in all departments. This meant that we midshipmen were given far more responsibility than we had enjoyed hitherto, becoming Officer of the Watch at sea, Officer of the Day in harbour, and Duty Commanding Officer at week-ends. In addition we took charge of all boat-lowering and hoisting operations during sea training. After a week we transferred to H.M.S. *Wanderer*, another 'W'-Class destroyer, which was working week-and-week about with *Wishart*. We completed our second week's destroyer-time in her.

A few days after we had re-joined *Southampton*, she sailed north for a concentrated period of exercises with other ships of the Home Fleet in the Cromarty Firth, operating out of Invergordon. *Southampton* had now been fitted with two radio-controlled pilotless seaplanes for use in anti-aircraft 'throw-off' shoots. They were known as 'Queen Bees'. We also had a bevy of R.A.F. and civilian 'experts' on board to control them. The day came when we were to launch 'Queen Bee' No.1 for the edification and exercise of the Fleet's A.A. gunners. Off it went, zooming into the sky and performing all kinds of spectacular manoeuvres, which gradually became more and more alarming. From the worried frowns on the faces of the 'experts' and their frantic knob-twiddling, we very soon deduced that all was not well. Eventually, as the plane began a series of inverted 'loops' and adopted an upside-down posture in flight, the experts announced that she was 'out of control' – whereupon 'Queen Bee' No.1 went into a tight spin and dived into the sea! We retrieved what was left of the wreckage and a few hours later we launched 'Queen Bee' No.2. This one did everything she was required to do: high-level runs, passing-runs, low-level runs and dive-bombing attacks. On each of these manoeuvres she was met by a thunderous hail of fire from the Fleet. The decibel count was certainly impressive; less so was the accuracy of the gunfire. As it died away, the 'Queen Bee' flew off. It continued to do so till it was not only out of range, but out of radio contact too. Its automatic emergency gear then took over and it crash-landed in the sea, buckling up both its floats as it did so. (Verdict on the day by the C-in-C: 'Thoroughly unsatisfactory. An inquiry will be held.')

Towards the end of September it was decided to send the ship's drifter down to Chatham. (Every major warship had its own steam drifter, manned by herself, lovingly cared for, and used as her tender). Ours was named *Lunar Bow*. Our Sub-Lieutenant (C.D. Madden) was put in command, and I and Roger Keyes (son of Admiral of the Fleet Sir Roger Keyes) were the two Midshipmen appointed as his officers. We sailed from Invergordon on the Monday evening, and on the Wednesday we put in to Hartlepool for coal and fresh water. Carrying on to the southward, we encountered a lot of fog and, during my Middle Watch, some hair-raising moments when we got in among a huge fishing fleet, the myriad lights of which were quite bewildering. Whenever we passed a light-ship we closed it, passed over newspapers and magazines and took off any mails, and in daylight hours we sometimes did a little bartering with passing trawlers for fresh fish. We entered Great Yarmouth on the Thursday evening on a full flood tide – and narrowly escaped being thrown against the breakwater. Here we spent a glorious night among the fleshpots. Next day we had trouble with our navigation – caused, I discovered, by the Navigating Officer misapplying the effects of Variation and Deviation to our compass course! However, as much by good luck as by good management, we got into Sheerness that night and were safely moored up in Chatham by noon on the Saturday (October 2nd) in time for week-end leave.

We were now to become directly involved in the Spanish Civil War. Because General Franco's Insurgents were being more or less openly backed by Hitler's Germany and Mussolini's Italy, whereas the Spanish Government enjoyed the sympathy of Britain and France, there was an increasing risk that these four Powers would be drawn into open conflict, thereby precipitating another European War. Already there had been an alarming number of 'incidents' (accidental or contrived) involving attacks on the warships of these countries, and this had driven the four Powers to conclude a Non-Intervention Pact. One of the provisions of this was the setting up of an International Naval Patrol (known as the Nyon Patrol). It involved the warships of Italy and Germany patrolling the coasts of Government-held territory, while those of Britain and France patrolled those of Franco-held territory.

Practically the whole of Northern Spain (except a small part of Asturias) was by this time held by the Insurgents, and this sector was allotted to Britain to patrol. When we rejoined *Southampton* at Sheerness on 8th October, we found that her 'B' and 'X' turrets had been painted over in huge red, white and blue stripes to indicate her nationality in unmistakable terms to marauding aircraft of either side. It also served to remind us, as we sailed next day for the Patrol Area, that we were now (for the first time in our lives) on Active Service. We took over command of the Patrol from the Rear Admiral commanding 2nd Battle Squadron in H.M.S. *Resolution*, and headed for our forward base at St. Jean de Luz. Here we made final preparations for Rear Admiral Calvert (CS2) to co-ordinate the patrol work of the four destroyers placed under his command: *Fearless, Foxhound, Electra* and *Escort*.

On 15th October we went into War Routine, with all armament closed up with live ammunition, extra-large ensigns at peak and fore, colours flood-lit, and sailed for the Patrol Area. Gijon and Aviles in Asturia were under heavy bombardment, at least six British merchant-ships were trying to evade the Insurgent naval blockade to get into the ports with relief supplies, and Franco's naval forces – notably the cruiser *Almirante Cervera* and the minelayers *Vulcano* and *Jupiter*, were ready to pounce on them as soon as they crossed the 3-mile limit of territorial waters. We were faced with a very tricky situation, which hung on the strict observance and interpretation of International Law.

As *Almirante Cervera* was in charge of the Insurgent naval forces in the area, we deemed it prudent to establish a polite working relationship with her – and cordial messages were exchanged with her at intervals, often at close quarters. The first incident we had to contend with was the arrest of a French merchant-ship by a Spanish armed trawler on the very edge of the 3-mile limit. We reported this to the French naval authorities at Brest, who immediately despatched two of their latest destroyers (*Le Fantasie* and *L'Audacieux*, as well as a third, *Le Terrible*). We kept them informed of the situation as they steamed at high speed through the Bay of Biscay during the night, and next morning they secured the release of the merchantman (which the Spanish maintained had simply been held 'for examination').

A few days later, while Gijon was being pounded to rubble by land and air, a potentially dangerous situation arose. A British merchant-ship, S.S. *Stangrove*, was arrested by an Insurgent armed trawler off Punta Coin. She had an International Observer on board and made frantic S.O.S. signals protesting that she had been five miles outside territorial waters when captured. She was carrying about 600 refugees, whom she had embarked at Gijon during the night, though these included a good many fleeing Government troops. *Southampton* closed the *Stangrove* and her captor at high speed to interrogate her, while *Almirante Cervera* circled round us. Both the ship's Master and the International Observer (who had been on the bridge with him at the time of capture) confirmed her position as 12 miles E.N.E. of Cape Torres (which would put her about five miles outside territorial waters), whereas the armed trawler swore she was only 2½ miles off Punta Coin. *Almirante Cervera* had not been present at the time of capture, but arrived on the scene with all haste and declared that when she had got there, both ships were within two miles of the shore. Our Admiral did not consider that this was good enough and he was faced with the dilemma of accepting one man's word against another's. If he gave in to the Spanish cruiser, he would be consigning hundreds of Asturian refugees to an appalling fate, whereas if he resisted the capture, he could well provoke a trial of strength between British and Spanish warships, and, at best, a serious international incident.

Ordering the destroyer *Foxhound* to join us at full speed, the Admiral signalled the *Almirante Cervera* that he felt obliged to escort *Stangrove* to safety and ordered the British merchantman to follow *Southampton* to seaward. Not unnaturally, the Spaniard protested volubly: 'I strongly protest at your intervention in favour of ship captured inside territorial waters, having on board certain combatants . . . who cannot be protected by invocation of humanitarian principles. I will inform my Government and will wireless it for general knowledge.'

Meanwhile both the cruiser and the armed trawler increased speed and started manoeuvring round us in threatening fashion. At this juncture we were electrified by the bugle-call 'Action Stations' (the first time many of us had ever heard it – hitherto it had always been preceded by the call 'For Exercise . . .')

The result was a real 'eye-opener'. A tremendous cheer resounded through the ship as the sailors, many of them crowded on the upper deck watching the proceedings, scurried off to their various stations, all too aware that this might be the 'real thing'. In a matter of seconds all quarters had reported 'Closed up and cleared away'. I had never seen so much radiant good humour and enthusiasm in so many men at the same time. All guns were loaded with live ammunition, and turrets, torpedo tubes and guns trained and elevated through full arcs to show our adversary that we were ready for anything. The sense of crisis was hardly bearable. Gradually the Spaniards fell astern as we drew *Stangrove* steadily towards Bordeaux and imperceptibly the tension ebbed away. After midnight we reverted to Night Defence Stations, left *Stangrove* to proceed independently, and returned at high speed to the Gijon area. The town had fallen. Thousands of refugees were streaming out of the port in hundreds of small boats, drifters and trawlers, trying to reach the small cluster of British merchant-ships lying just outside the 3-mile limit. *Foxhound* and *Fearless* were standing by, and the sea was littered with abandoned vessels whose occupants had already reached the safety of our half-dozen off-lying merchantmen. Meanwhile the Spanish warships were weaving in and out between the desperate little craft, rounding them up, firing upon them when they resisted, capturing them and herding them off in batches. The minelayer *Jupiter* was charging around as though she had completely lost her head, asking us to remove our ships from the scene, and admitting that the situation was 'out of control'.

Thousands of refugees, many of them armed Asturian soldiers, had succeeded in rowing, paddling or swimming off to the British ships, which, when full up, headed off towards Bordeaux, though not without considerable harassment en route from the *Almirante Cervera*. (She, meanwhile, true to her word, had broadcast to the world her version of the *Stangrove* incident, with a stinging denunciation of *Southampton's* breach of neutrality!) As the tragic day drew to its close, with thousands rescued but many thousands more killed, drowned or captured, we withdrew from the scene and returned to St. Jean de Luz. It had been an enthralling week.

A storm blew up over the week-end, and we had little respite, finding it better to go to sea again and ride the storm than lie rolling heavily at anchor. Soon we were at work again, having encountered a small steamer packed with some 50 wretched refugees, stinking to high heaven, whom we hauled aboard (tending to their manifold needs) before sinking their ship by gunfire. Next day we sighted another craft, an open boat, riding the huge seas many miles from land, and containing another 30 refugees, nearly all soldiers, but including a girl of about 17 and an older woman. The boat was laden with rifles, machine-guns and pistols, most of them loaded, which we threw into the sea. They had been adrift without food or water for a full week, were in an advanced state of despair and exhaustion, and had intended to shoot

300 defeated Republicans adrift in the Bay of Biscay without food or water for a week, 1937. They were rescued by Southampton.

themselves that night if help had not come to them. We went straight back to St. Jean de Luz to land this lot and next day put up one of our aircraft to search for more refugees, calling in *Electra* and *Escort* to assist.

Early on 26th October we sighted a small steamer of about 200 tons flying the Republican flag and crammed to the gunwhales with about 300 Asturian soldiers, as well as a handful of women and children. Hauling this lot on board was a hazardous task but we managed it without mishap, although there was a number of wounded, sick and injured among them. Hundreds of small-arms were removed from them and unceremoniously consigned to the deep – after which we placed a depth-charge with a time-fuse in the steamer's bunker and blew her to smithereens (a highly spectacular event). Further systematic searching throughout the day revealed nothing more, so we steamed off to La Pallice to land our thankful passengers.

By the end of the month our 'Spain Patrol' was virtually over, and after a further visit to La Pallice we re-joined the Home Fleet at Portland. There followed a fortnight of intensive drills, exercises and inspections before we returned to Chatham, and there Michael Highton and I successfully passed our Promotion Exams and pushed off on Long Leave for the rest of the year. So ended our two years and three months as Midshipmen. It had been quite an experience!

CHAPTER IV

Subs' Courses at Portsmouth; Sub-Lieutenant, H.M.S. *Franklin*, 1938, and H.M.S. Scarborough, 1939

O N NEW YEAR'S DAY 1938 I was promoted to Acting Sub-Lieutenant and appointed to H.M.S. *Excellent*, the Gunnery School at Whale Island, Portsmouth. After a month's Foreign Service Leave with my parents at Tumby Chase, I motored down there in my little red sports car and, on arrival, drove straight ahead across the Parade Ground. Halfway across, I became aware of shrill whistle-blasts from several directions, followed by the unnerving sight of an irate Gunner's Mate rushing towards me with his hand aloft. I stopped. 'Watcher thinkya doin' – sir?' he asked. 'Joining', I replied. 'Not that way, you don't – sir,' he answered, 'Dontcha know cars is not allowed on the Parade Ground?' 'Sorry,' I said, 'No, I didn't know'. Well, the upshot of that was that I was placed on a charge and ordered to double three times round the Island – my first taste of the notorious 'Whaley Discipline'!

We had embarked on the first round of our 'Subs' Courses'. These embraced all the main professional subjects in which we were required to qualify before we could be promoted to Lieutenant. They comprised a wide range, including Gunnery, Torpedo and Electrics, Mining and Minesweeping, Navigation and Pilotage, and Communications. Passes in these subjects, as the outcome of rigorous concluding examinations, were graded as 1sts, 2nds and 3rds. The grade achieved in a given subject determined whether the candidate would be allowed, or required, to specialise in that subject. Thus to become a specialist Gunnery Officer (not a prospect that attracted me), it would be essential to obtain a '1st' in Gunnery on completion of one's Sub's course in that subject, after which, in two or three years' time, one would be called back to Whale Island for the Long 'G' Course.

For our Subs' Course we were split into Groups of 15-20 young officers, a mixture of Dartmouth and ex-Special Entry, and we stayed in these Groups for all the courses. We were in 'U' Group. In general, we were appointed to, and accommodated in, the 'School' (or H.Q.) of the particular specialisation responsible for our course of instruction. Thus for the first few months we were in H.M.S. *Excellent*, for the next period in H.M.S. *Vernon* (Torpedo and Electrics), and for the final months in H.M.S. *Dryad* (Navigation and Pilotage) – all these shore establishments at Portsmouth being known as 'stone frigates'.

At Whale Island our 'cabins' were in wooden huts, rather reminiscent of temporary barrack-blocks, but well-equipped, furnished, with all 'mod. cons.', and pleasantly warm. In comparison with the sea-going accommodation (Gunroom and slung hammocks) that we had been used to for three and a half years, it was really luxurious, particularly as during the day we lived in the quite 'splendiferous' Officers' Mess. There was a very special atmosphere about *Excellent* (Motto: 'Si vis pacem, para bellum') – with a tangible 'Esprit de Corps'. The Gunnery fraternity certainly regarded themselves, not without reason, as the Navy's élite. After all, they felt themselves to be the 'cutting edge' of Britain's 'sure shield', the teeth to the British Lion.

The Gunnery Course was extremely interesting and also very strenuous. Quite apart from the technical complexities of the many different weapon systems and control systems and their munitions, and the theoretical and practical aspects of their use in different circumstances, we had to familiarise ourselves with the whole theory of ballistics and its applications. We also had to work the weapons themselves by participating in the repetitive gun-drills associated with each. We also spent lengthy periods on ceremonial parade-ground drill, including taking full charge of the parades, arms drills and movements of men on the march – and woe betide us if any slip-up on parade could fairly be laid at our own door! Then there were the repeated practices for the 'Brickwood Trophy', involving competing teams of gun- and gun-carriage crews racing to man-handle their heavy artillery across imaginary chasms, a truly frantic, hair-raising, and utterly exhausting business, though tempered with a wonderful spirit of good humoured camaraderie.

We moved about the Island, from one activity to the next, as a Group, on the march and usually 'at the double'. I remember one alarming occasion, as we came to the Officers' Mess for dinner, when our Group was suddenly confronted by a full-grown African lion. ''U' Group About Turn – Double March!' yelled the Sub in charge, and we reversed course and sped like lightning from the scene. ('Whaley' prided itself on its zoo, in which there were several lions. This one had escaped but was soon recaptured with the aid of a huge net).

Gunnery Officers were not a popular breed – though they were admired. Their special qualities of ruthlessness, assertiveness, self-assurance and leadership were not to everyone's taste, invaluable though they were to the profession and to the Senior Service itself. It was frequently said that the main reason why anyone chose to be a Gunnery Officer was that he would never have to serve with another one! Certainly it was not a specialisation that appealed to me, fascinating though its technicalities were. My heart was not really in it, and for that reason I feared I might well fail the final examination. I therefore put in an inordinate amount of study, and because marks were awarded for the quality, accuracy and neatness of one's illustrated notes, I produced a rather splendid, fully-typed volume of them. Far from failing the exam., when the time came to pass out, I found, to my horror, that I had achieved a '1st'. I was in line to specialise in Gunnery! (I managed somehow, however, to talk my way out of that!)

Though the discipline at Whale Island was notoriously severe, the conditions were civilised and the work generally interesting, so that all in all, we rather enjoyed our three months there. In April or May we moved to *Vernon* for our Torpedo and Electrics course, though except for meals, we were not accommodated there. In *Vernon* quite a different atmosphere prevailed; it was far more relaxed than in *Excellent*. As far as I can remember, I got a '2nd' in the exams. at the end of this course.

We were next re-appointed to H.M.S. *Dryad*, the Navigation School, for further courses, including Navigation and Pilotage. Though particularly interested in Navigation, I was even more taken with the idea of specialising in Hydrography, which apparently required no pre-qualification other than a '2nd' in Navigation plus a successful interview with the Hydrographer of the Navy. The life-style of the Surveying Service appealed to my sense of adventure and exploration in far-flung quarters of the globe and away from the Fleet. However, during the courses at *Dryad* I kept a fairly open mind about these options. It would partly depend on how well I did in the 'N' Course and the subsequent exams. However, my mind was largely made up for me by a private invitation to visit one of our Survey Ships which was alongside in the Dockyard. Here I was enthralled to witness the actual process of drawing a Fair Chart.

As July drew to a close, I finally made up my mind to join the Surveying Service, subject to the approval of the Hydrographer of the Navy, who summoned me for an interview at the Admiralty. First I had a long talk with his Assistant (Captain E.F.B. Law), who put me very much at ease and outlined the sort of life I should expect, saying 'We're a very friendly little Service, you know; we all know each other's wives and that sort of thing'. After this I was ushered into 'The Presence', the Great Man himself (Vice-Admiral Sir John Edgell), whose name was something of a byword. The interview seemed to go well and I was accepted.

As it turned out, I was awarded a '2nd' in Navigation, so fate had confirmed my choice. However, I managed several '1sts' in the other courses and was awarded three months' seniority, meaning that I had only another nine months to do as a confirmed Sub-Lieutenant.

After a lovely spell of summer leave, I was appointed as a Surveying Assistant 4th-Class (H4) to H.M.S. *Franklin*, then lying at Chatham. *Franklin* was the first of a new class of Surveying Ship, just commissioned for service in Home Waters. She was painted white with a buff-coloured funnel. I was her junior officer, referred to and addressed by my messmates as 'Sub'. I was expected to learn my new profession 'on the job'.

We spent that autumn surveying in the southern North Sea, charting the sandbanks and channels off East Anglia and Kent, mapping the coast of Norfolk, measuring the tidal streams north of the Dover Strait and monitoring the changes in the sea-bed of the Thames Estuary. I learnt how to erect and level tide-gauges, to coastline with sextant and ten-foot pole, to measure currents with log-ship and compass, to boat-sound with sextants and station-pointers, and to observe accurate angles with theodolites. We based ourselves at Lowestoft, Great Yarmouth, Sheerness and Dover, and often anchored for the night off Margate, Ramsgate, Deal or Southend. *Franklin* was commanded by a Lieutenant-Commander Charles Sabine, who was a 'Charge' Surveyor. Our First Lieutenant was a Lieutenant-Commander 'Bill' Dickinson, a Surveying Assistant 1st Class (H1). The Navigator was Lieutenant Robin Bill, and the Senior Watch-keeper was Lieutenant 'Egg' Irving (later to become Hydrographer of the Navy). We also carried a Paymaster-Lieutenant-Commander, a Commissioned Engineer and a Boatswain. The Ship's Company numbered about 120.

We worked very long hours and got little shore-leave, but the work was extremely interesting both 'in the field' and in the Chartroom, where we worked up the results of our day's labours and portrayed them in graphic form. It was not long, however, before I realised that our Wardroom contained both 'sheep' and 'goats', and that the latter were – not to put too fine a point on it – partial to more than a drop or two. This was later to cause problems.

One night we were anchored somewhere well off the Belgian coast, occupying an important Tidal Stream Station and observing and measuring the direction and rate of the stream every half hour over a continuous period of 25 hours. I had the Morning Watch and before turning in that night, I had left instruction with the Quartermaster that I was to be called at 0345. In fact I woke up on my own, realised it was about 0400, and rushed up on deck, where I gave the Q.M. a piece of my mind for not calling me.

'Oh,' he replied, 'we've stopped observing, sir. The Officer said to pack up observations two or three hours ago.'

I could hardly believe it. We were more than halfway through the series and to have broken off at this stage would have been to waste the past 16 hours' work. I glanced at the Tidal Stream Logbooks (in which the half-hourly readings were recorded) and saw that from about 0230 the entries were either illegible or non-existent. My suspicions were aroused. One of our 'goats' had had the First Watch and another the Middle. Both had been drinking and chatting happily when I turned in. As I walked aft to the Quarterdeck, I noticed that the Wardroom lights were still on and a glance through the windows confirmed my suspicions: the two goats, each with a glass in his hand, were sprawled over their armchairs barely conscious and fully dressed.

I yelled to the Quartermaster to veer the log-ship, and with his help I took the 0400 readings – several minutes late. I then went to the Chartroom and started drawing the curves through the earlier readings as far as they went. Between my half-hourly observations, I spent the whole of that morning plotting the past readings together with my subsequent ones, drawing the curves through them, extrapolating the curves through the obviously unreliable or missing ones, reading off the 'proper' observations from these curves, erasing the 'phoney' or illegible entries in the logbooks and substituting for them what were probably the correct readings. It was a 'fudge' but a reasonable one.

I was still engaged on this work when, shortly after 0730, the Captain entered the Chartroom. 'Morning, Sub – how's it going?' he asked. 'Er... all right, I think, sir,' I replied as the Captain advanced and, leaving the newly-drawn curves in the Tidal Log for his inspection, I hastily flipped back the pages of the rough record-book to the previous observations of some days earlier – so that there met the Captain's eyes an unbroken list of readings. While my pulse raced and my heart thumped within me, the Captain cast a somewhat bleary and superficial eye over the records, grunted a few cheery words of encouragement and walked out again. Whew! Well, I'd certainly saved the bacon of our two senior officers (little did they realise it!), but what had I compromised in the process? The accuracy of the survey or just my own professional integrity? I have sometimes wondered if I did the right thing. I'd acted on impulse. The thought of what would befall my two superior officers if the truth emerged was enough – and I had to act as I did. My conscience has not troubled me unduly.

In December *Franklin* returned to Chatham Dockyard for her winter 'lie-up' – to refit, give leave and draw up the Fair Chart and other results and reports of her surveys.

The great thing about the Surveying Service's traditional annual winter 'lie-ups' was that one could count on at least a month's leave – relatively little leave being possible during the active surveying 'season'. I suddenly realised what a golden opportunity this offered for me to go off to Switzerland and try my hand at winter sports, and I started making plans to do so. The upshot was that I spent one of the most memorable fortnights of my life in Davos with a winter-sports party, meeting a glorious girl, Pat Hussey, with whom I got on 'like a house on fire'.

When I returned to *Franklin* in February, I heard that she was scheduled to spend the coming 'season' charting the coast of Labrador, in the wake of *Challenger's* work of five years earlier. This appealed to me greatly, and I was very downcast when informed that I was to be re-appointed in March to H.M.S. *Scarborough*, a newly converted sloop about to re-commission for surveys in the Far East. I immediately asked to see the Captain with a view to remaining in the ship, but though he was obviously pleased that I wished to do so, he replied that I had been hand-picked by the Assistant Hydrographer to commission *Scarborough*, which he himself was to command! Though perhaps a little flattered, I was still despondent about not going to Labrador. However, there was really nothing my Captain could do about it, and he thought it might be 'undiplomatic' to forward my request.

After a spell of leave between appointments, therefore, I joined *Scarborough* at Devonport early in April. All the executive officers had been hand-picked by the Assistant Hydrographer, Captain E.F.B. Law, who was to command her. This, he reckoned, would be his last sea-going command and he was determined that it should be a happy one. Our First Lieutenant was a splendid extrovert called Michael Beach-Thomas, our Navigator a Lt. Cdr. Billy Petch, our Boatswain a delightful man known as 'Bo' Leader, and there was a most congenial Lieutenant called Phil Hocking. It looked like being a first-rate commission. Pat Hussey came down to Plymouth over the Easter week-end and was introduced to my brother officers, after which we had a rather emotional farewell.

We sailed for a brief visit to Portland. There, unless my memory fails me, I met my brother Roger, who had recently recovered from a severe nervous breakdown and was serving with the Royal Tank Corps at Bovington nearby. The following evening he watched from Portland Bill as *Scarborough* finally sailed off for the Far East. As she did so, I shipped my second stripe. I was no longer 'The Sub'. As I took a long, lingering look at England fading into the haze on our starboard quarter, I felt a new sense of responsibility.

We were bound, ultimately, for the East Indies Station, to progress major surveys off Sarawak and British North Borneo, but there were several tasks to be undertaken on the way. We stopped briefly at Gibraltar and spent a week-end at Malta (where we were impressed by the loyalty of the Maltese and the contempt in which they held Mussolini), before continuing to Port Said and the Suez Canal.

At Port Said we got a new Sub-Lieutenant, one Bryan O'Neill, who had transferred to the Surveying Service from one of the Mediterranean Fleet's destroyer flotillas. I was no longer the junior (H) officer, and felt slightly superior (with my two stripes) when addressing him as 'Sub'. We were now breaking new ground, as far as I was concerned, having never before been to Egypt or beyond. I found the Canal, in particular, an eye-opener. It seemed almost incredible that a hundred miles of wide waterway could have been sliced straight through the sandy desert – by hand. As one looked along it from the ship's bridge, one could actually discern (from the convergence of the banks) the curvature of the earth.

I remember one night in the Red Sea when I had the Morning Watch, I sighted the lights of a ship approaching fine on the starboard bow. We exchanged identities and she turned out to be one of our Persian Gulf sloops homeward bound. I called the Captain and gave him the name of the sloop. As she passed us a cable's length to starboard, she signalled with her Aldis lamp: 'Are you manned by naval personnel?' The Captain, who by this time was on the bridge in his pyjamas and consulting the Navy List, swore. 'Tell her to heave to!' he yelled to the signalman. The signal was passed and acknowledged but the sloop steamed on. We called her again and said: 'Stop! Send boat for despatches.' By this time she was several miles away and no doubt her Captain (a Lieutenant-Commander) had been called to the bridge. She stopped, letting off clouds of steam. We relished the probable scene on her bridge. Her C.O., realising he was dealing with a Post-Captain commanding a 'Major War Vessel', and having bawled out his O.O.W., was in process of rousing the Watch and calling away his seaboat's crew – half an hour before dawn. By the time *Scarborough* had stopped, they had about an hour's pull ahead of them – each way. Quite what the 'despatches' were, I never knew – but they included a personal letter from our Captain to theirs. Henceforth, we felt, he'd have a healthy respect for H.M. Survey Ships!

Having called briefly at Aden to re-fuel, we set course across the Gulf of Aden to Berbera in British Somaliland. We had instructions to consult the local authorities before undertaking our first survey further along the coast. With the Italians in occupation of Abyssinia, British Somaliland was now hemmed in by them on every side, and such was the defeatism that permeated our Government at that time, it was assumed that if war came, they would push our forces into the sea. Our job was to carry out a coastal and hydrographic survey of a place called Karin, a possible site from which British forces, such as they were (the Somaliland Camel Corps!), could be evacuated. It was a depressing prospect.

That survey completed, we moved out into the Indian Ocean and reached Ceylon in June – with the S.W. monsoon. We put into Colombo for a while, having a job to do in the approaches to the port, and I found myself surveying the coastline southward towards Mount Lavinia. Resting in the shade of coconut palms at the head of the beach as I plotted some of my field-work, I was joined by an affable and well-spoken Sinhalese, who sat down beside me and showed an interest in my work. 'Do you think there's going to be a war?' he asked with a worried expression. 'No,' I replied without hesitation, 'No, I'm sure there won't be.' I often held that against myself in later years, but at the time I simply couldn't believe that it was beyond the powers of world statesmen to prevent such a catastrophe as had occurred between 1914 and 1918, and which had been recognised everywhere as 'the War to end all wars'. I still couldn't quite face the fact that the forces of innate Evil were at large.

We went round to the east side of Ceylon to set up our advanced base at Trincomalee, and then started to put in hand our first major survey, between Point Pedro and Mullaitivu on the north-east coast. This was to be one of those 'classic' hydrographic surveys based on an extensive floating triangulation. The form and techniques of such surveys had changed very little over the years.

The island stood between us and the steady force of the S.W. monsoon, so that inshore the sea was as calm as a millpond, but as one moved out to seaward, it became increasingly rough. The terminal points of the survey were about 50 miles apart, and we were to work out to some 15 miles offshore, so that we had around 750 square miles of sea to sound.

From a professional point of view it was an interesting survey, and for us junior surveyors a highly educative one. But so far as the coastal and submarine topography were concerned, it was somewhat featureless. Behind the long, steeply sloping beaches of white sand lay flat grassy islets studded with tall toddy palms.

Our Captain had a relaxed personality with a rather dry sense of humour, and was not noted for overwork. He was no martinet. Regarding his ship more or less as a private yacht, he was determined that we should all enjoy the two months ahead. This outlook was reflected through the ship without in any way affecting her efficiency or discipline, and the general ambience of cheerfulness and good humour was compounded, for us, by an exceptionally congenial Wardroom. Thus, although we worked hard, often well into the

Scarborough *surveying off north east Ceylon, 1939.*

night, it was never too onerous, and we frequently stopped altogether at week-ends. Now and again we would return to Trincomalee for fuel – and to relax.

Setting up the floating triangulation was an exacting task, which involved all available hands and called for a high standard of seamanship. We carried 30 beacons and up to 12 of these would usually be in use at any one time. We laid them about five miles apart to form a network of equilateral triangles, each one moored with two heavy anchors and carrying a 12x8ft. flag on a 30ft. bamboo pole. They could be seen up to a distance of 10 miles. As each beacon was laid, the ship would move carefully up to it, placing her stem close alongside it, while perhaps half a dozen of us, each with a sextant, would observe the angles between the other beacons and any visible shore marks simultaneously at the order 'Fix!' All those angles would be used in the Chartroom to calculate and plot the beacon's precise position. The inshore row of beacons would be fixed first, by observing the angles subtended by previously co-ordinated shore marks, and by theodolite 'rays' observed to them from the shore marks. For identification purposes, each mark would be given a short name, and traditionally the beacons were always named after girls in alphabetical order, e.g. 'Ada', 'Beth', 'Cath', 'Dot', 'Eve', etc.

The inshore waters, out to about four miles, were surveyed by the two surveying motor-boats (S.M.B.s), using continuous echo-soundings fixed frequently by two simultaneously observed sextant angles between three shore marks, samples of the sea-bed being obtained by hand-lead at intervals along the sounding-lines. This work was normally allocated to the Lieutenants and the 'Sub', and I spent most of my days doing just that. Meanwhile the ship would be working in similar fashion (though in much greater comfort) in the deeper waters offshore. At sunset each evening the ship would break off sounding and come to anchor close inshore, where the S.M.B.s would rejoin her for the night. From then on all surveyors would be busy in the Chartroom inking in the day's soundings.

As the wind blew steadily off the land by day and night, and the sandy sea-bed seemed smooth and featureless, the ship took to anchoring ever closer inshore, where she lay head-to-wind in calm water with the boats at her booms. On the very last day of the survey, as the ship weighed anchor at 0700 and the boats got away, and as the ship was turning to port, there was suddenly a tremendous crash and she shuddered from stem to stern. The Captain uttered a loud obscenity, the Navigator shouted 'Get a fix!' and jumped on the chart-table with a sextant, and the Boatswain on the fo'c'sle bellowed 'Close all watertight doors!' I was O.O.W. on the bridge, and had just written in the Deck Log: '0700. Weighed and proceeded', when my pencil went through the paper.

At first I thought we'd hit one of the boats, but soon realised we'd struck a rock (in fact, as was proved later, it was the only rock in the entire survey-area – and we'd found it the hard way!). So I wrote in the Log: '0702. Struck rock'. Afterwards, while we were anchored and assessing the damage (which involved the loss of our Asdic-dome and little more), I was sent for by the Captain and found him in his cabin examining the Deck Log. 'Did you write this?' he asked, indicating my second entry. 'Yes, sir,' I replied. 'Why?' he asked. 'Well, didn't we, sir?' I ventured. He said nothing but took up an india-rubber and erased the entry, substituting for it the words: '0702. Came in contact with submerged obstruction.' 'What makes you think it was a rock?' he asked, dismissing me.

We finished the survey a week ahead of schedule, and in mid-August set course across the Bay of Bengal to Penang and finally to Singapore. Here we had our first real taste of the fabulous 'Far East' and we lost no time in making the most of it, spending the first few days in exploring its delights.

However, the scent of impending war was in the air, and plans were in a state of flux. Two other Survey Ships joined *Scarborough* at the Naval Base, *Herald* from the East Indies and *Endeavour* from the Pacific. They arrived in a state of uncertainty and apprehension, but there was a great 'get-together' of their officers as the three ships lay alongside the same wall. Under the local War Plan, our Captain was designated 'Extended Defence Officer' for the Port of Singapore and O'Neill and I were to be his Assistants. All three ships were to pay off, we heard, but as August drew to a close, nothing happened. We were told to take local leave and await developments. Phil Hocking and I put ourselves up at the Sea View Hotel to enjoy the flesh-pots while we could. What luxury, what bliss, what freedom! Next morning we got a phone call: 'Return to the ship'. Germany had invaded Poland.

That week-end we listened avidly to every news bulletin, to the BBC's Overseas News broadcasts and to Singapore Radio. Britain and France had previously warned Hitler that if he attacked Poland, they would come to her assistance with every means in their power. Why, then, were we not already at war? Saturday went – and still we had heard nothing. It was exasperating. But on the Sunday (3rd September) the Prime Minister was to make an important broadcast, and we crowded round the Wardroom wireless to listen. We were at war with Germany!

CHAPTER V

Lieutenant, H.M.S. *Derby*, 1939

IT WAS IN SOMBRE MOOD that we listened to Neville Chamberlain's broadcast announcing that we were now in a state of war with Germany. In a way it was a relief. After five years of vacillation and procrastination we had at last taken the right decision. Now at last 'the chips were down', and we felt we could hold our heads higher. Life seemed to have taken on a new meaning, and we certainly felt a new sense of purpose in all that we did.

The rumours of the past few days turned out to be partly correct. The three Survey Ships were to pay off. Their officers and crews were to commission a flotilla of eight Fleet Minesweepers that had been lying in Reserve at Singapore since the end of the 1914-18 War. *Scarborough* was to be re-converted to an A/S Escort Vessel and her Captain was to assume the post of X.D.O. for the Port of Singapore. I felt sorry for Captain Law – sorry too that such a promising commission should have been so abruptly aborted. He had been an excellent C.O. and a popular one too, who had enjoyed the company of his officers.

Our Navigator, Lt. Cdr. 'Billy' Petch, was appointed to command H.M.S. *Derby*, one of the old Fleet Minesweepers to be brought out of reserve, and I was to be his First Lieutenant. It was a big step for me – with a sudden access of heavier responsibility than I had ever shouldered before. Bryan O'Neill, our 'Sub', was to be our only other officer, with responsibility for navigation and other duties. *Derby*'s crew – of between 40 and 50 all told – was to be drawn entirely from *Scarborough*'s complement, so at least we knew them reasonably well. It was quite a challenge for us all. The general organisation of the ship, her watch-bills, duty-rosters and standing orders etc., fell to me to work out and promulgate, as did most of the arrangements for our minesweeping role. Within about a week, however, *Derby* was ready for sea, as were most of the other ships of the newly constituted 'Second Minesweeping Flotilla'.

The general idea at that time was that 'the Enemy' would start with an all-out assault on our maritime trade – a strategy that had brought Germany very close to victory in the 1914-18 War. It was also thought that in Far Eastern waters, Japan (with whom we were not at war) would perform a surrogate role in this strategy by mining the focal points of our trade-routes.

The approaches to Singapore were, of course, one of the most important of these focal points, and the role of the newly constituted Minesweeping Flotilla was to keep open the swept channels leading to and from the Port and the Naval Base on the Johore Strait. At the same time that our 'Swept Channels' scheme was being brought into force, a major operation was mounted to lay our own submerged minefields in secret areas elsewhere, to block access by enemy submarines, which, it was assumed, would be the vessels they would use as mine-layers.

Although our Minesweeping Flotilla was manned by professional naval officers and ratings drawn directly from the three Survey Ships, and although they were all reasonably conversant with the theoretical techniques involved in single and double Oropesa minesweeping, few, if any, had had actual operational experience of it. There was therefore a great need for each of the eight ships to work up, individually, to a satisfactory standard, and a subsequent need for the Flotilla as a whole to work together, in formation. Some of the narrower channels could best be swept by a single ship running a double Oropesa sweep, whereas wider areas were more suited to formation sweeping by four ships (sometimes all eight of them), each running a single sweep. All these variations in operational procedure had to be exercised and practised before we could regard ourselves as efficient.

On the quayside at the Naval base lay a huge pile of coal. It had been there for twenty years and had been eroded by wind and weather to little more than coal-dust. It was the fuel stock for the minesweepers, which were all coal-burning. They were affectionately known as 'Smoky Joes', but never had they belched forth such clouds of ash-laden black smoke as they did while steaming on this stuff. The ships were capable of speeds of around 18 knots at full power, but such was the quality of the coal they were burning that any attempts of that sort rapidly became a First Lieutenant's nightmare. The funnels would become red-hot and all the paint on them would melt and flow down to the decks, while a continuous rain of unburnt coal-ash would descend on all exposed parts of the ship. As we seldom spent long enough in harbour to do a proper 'paint ship', the upper-works, screens and bulkheads used to get painted as opportunity offered, so that 'Wet Paint' on many of the external surfaces was the norm rather than the exception. Moreover, as with ships in any fleet or flotilla, these minesweepers would vie with one another to present the smartest appearance. The effect of such rivalry in our circumstances was that prominent parts of the upper deck structure were often treated with high-gloss paints and enamels. The result, of course, was that when the inevitable rain of ash descended, these 'tiddly' surfaces, far from presenting a brilliant shine, took on the appearance (and feel) of emery paper.

It was my responsibility to supervise and take charge of operations on the sweep-deck, rigging the kite, otters and float, reeving the special sweep-wires through their appropriate blocks, streaming the sweeps, veering them out to the required depth, and then monitoring the tension in the wires as the ship worked up to optimum speed – as well as keeping the Bridge informed as we went along.

Apart from the actual sweeping, there was also the need to mark the areas swept, and one or two ships would be assigned to this task, which involved the laying of dan-buoys at intervals along the edge of the swept areas. There were well-rehearsed 'drills' for all these jobs, but things could – and sometimes did – go wrong.

I recall one horrific incident when one of our consorts was dan-laying. The mooring wires were 'stopped up' in a series of loops along the after guard-rails, ready to be released as the strain came on while the dan-buoy was streamed. Somehow or other some of the loops were released prematurely, fell into the water and fouled the ship's starboard propeller, which was turning. This put a sudden irresistible strain on the rest of the mooring wire, much of which was lying in coils on the deck. By a tragic mischance, one of the seamen was standing with one leg inside one of these coils and before anyone realised what was happening, it pulled tight and amputated his leg below the knee. There was an immediate alarm. The ship was stopped and a signal was flashed to *Derby* for assistance, we being the nearest to the scene. We placed ourselves alongside our helpless consort and the wretched seaman, with a sick-bay attendant at his side, was transferred to our quarterdeck on a stretcher. Leaving the other ship immobile to cope with her badly fouled propeller, we opened up all power and belted up the Johore Strait to the Naval Base, where an ambulance had been alerted to meet us, while morphine and other first-aid treatment were administered to our deathly-pale patient. It was only after he had been safely transferred to hospital that the enormity of the accident really sank in on us, but the whole Flotilla had learned a very salutary lesson. Henceforward extreme vigilance was observed on all the sweep-decks.

Other tragedies were to follow. One of our Boom Defence Vessels blundered into one of our own minefields, and two officers were quick to board her in the hope of guiding her out of it. One of these was *Scarborough's* erstwhile First Lieutenant, Michael Beach-Thomas, a delightful man, whom we all held in great affection. Tragically, the B.D.V. struck a mine, capsized and sank with all hands.

Meanwhile our minesweeping operations continued unabated, though they had now become a matter of routine. The fact that no mines were swept, while certainly taking the edge off our initial zeal, at least gave us the satisfaction of proving the safety of the vital shipping lanes and did much to set the minds of the Port Authorities at rest. Gradually, as the weeks passed, a trickle of Naval Reservists arrived in Singapore – both officers and ratings – and some of these were assigned to the minesweepers to relieve R.N. personnel who were needed elsewhere. Bryan O'Neill was the first to go from *Derby*, having somehow 'wangled' his way back to destroyers, but during the month of November more and more of the original 'ex-Survey' crews were replaced. By mid-December the Flotilla had become largely manned by reservists, with R.N.V.R. officers actually in command of some of the ships. Eventually the day came when it was announced that all (H) officers were to be withdrawn, as their services were required in the war-zone.

If by the 'war-zone' was meant Home Waters, who were we to complain? Thoughts of 'England, home and beauty' had never been far from our minds since we had left Portland eight months before. But in fact the war-zone might be anywhere, for the War, to date, had been rather conspicuous by its absence. We were living through what came to be known as the 'Phoney War', with little hostile activity anywhere, except on the high seas. Indeed, in one of her letters to me about this time, my mother had remarked: 'The war continues peacefully'! All in all, I cannot pretend that we shed any tears over leaving the 2nd Minesweeping Flotilla.

We were to fly home by Imperial Airways in their recently introduced 'Empire' flying-boats. I suppose there were about a dozen of us (from the three Survey ships), the others having already been re-appointed. We had a choice as to which flight we should take – half our number to embark next day, and the others two days later – so we drew lots. I drew against Phil Hocking – and lost. We were at the Seaview Hotel again, and Phil reckoned that an extra two days in Singapore would suit him very nicely, so he opted for the second flight. (It was to prove a tragic decision for him).

Air travel (as distinct from just flying) was something quite new to us, and the prospect of a 10,000-mile journey across Asia and Europe was really exciting. Instead of the five-week sea voyage, we were expected to be home within ten days, so there was an even chance that we'd be back by Christmas! Quite what 'Their Lordships' had in mind for us that warranted such urgency was an open question – but it added an extra element of drama to the whole venture.

The 'Empire' flying-boat, with its spacious interior, its armchairs, tables and settees – and its bar – was the acme of comfort. As our four Rolls-Royce engines thundered into life and we roared down the Singapore Strait

in a great flurry of spume and spray (which completely obliterated the view
from the cabin windows), and as we lifted up and up over the lush tropical
islets and swung gracefully round to a northern heading, we put all thoughts
of Singapore and minesweeping behind us and settled down to enjoy the
fascinating journey ahead.

It was a truly epic flight, all the more memorable because in those days it
was the custom to fly relatively low (at about 3,000 feet), so that we had
amazing views of the terrain reeling away beneath us, first the vivid green
jungles of Malaya, then the marvellously blue waters of the Gulf of Siam,
before we glided down, in the late afternoon, to the Bay of Bangkok, where
we stayed overnight at a sumptuous hotel.

After a brief glimpse of the countryside, we rejoined our aircraft and were
off again, this time over the jungles of Siam and Burma, then on across
India, putting down gently for the night on a calm and silvery lake. Where
that lake was I have no idea, but it was evidently one of Imperial Airways'
regular fuelling stops. For our next landing we flew on to Karachi, where we
changed planes to a Handley-Page biplane. In this we continued our flight
across Baluchistan and Southern Persia, crossing the Strait of Hormuz,
where the landscape of the Musandam Peninsula looming up on the Arabian
side was truly breath-taking: great jagged peaks rising sheer from the sea,
dark brown, bare and rocky, with numerous fjords penetrating inland. This
was the northern promontory of Oman. The following morning, after
spending a night at the desert fort of Sharjah, we made a short hop over the
Trucial coast and up to Bahrain, pressing on from there to Basra and another
overnight stop in Baghdad. After miles of flying across these arid regions, we
were astonished to find the landscape beneath us suddenly and completely
transformed from desert into green hills covered with vast acres of orange-
groves and vineyards, trees, streams and lakes. We had crossed over into
Palestine. No wonder the biblical authors had called it 'a land flowing with
milk and honey'!

From here we flew to Cairo and stayed the night at the prestigious
Shepheard's Hotel before changing aircraft again. The new plane carried us
first to Sollum on the North African coast, and then on a long hop down
the length of the Mediterranean to Marseilles, where we spent the night
before flying on to Bordeaux. It had been a memorable flight indeed! For
most of the journey, as the landscape reeled past beneath us, all had been
novel and absorbingly interesting but as we drew nearer to England, we
found ourselves becoming somewhat bored with air travel and longing to be
home.

As we flew into Bordeaux from Marseilles, we encountered fog and learned that it was thick over northern France, the Channel and the south of England. Air traffic was at a standstill. We were fog-bound and had to make the best of it. It was still frustrating in the extreme. We were so nearly home, yet not near enough. Eventually a decision was taken. Our pilot had a girl-friend in London and was determined to get there that night – and after a wager with another British plane, both of them decided to make a dash for it.

We headed north, above the fog, and, on crossing the French coast, descended virtually to sea level. We could just see the wave-tops a few feet below us as we scudded across the Channel, and feeling pretty apprehensive, decided to take our minds off the problem by gathering round and forming a poker-school with a pack of cards. Halfway through the game, the aircraft pulled up into a steep climb and banked violently to port, hurling the cards on to the deck. I looked out of the window and caught a fleeting glimpse of white cliffs rearing up to starboard with a lighthouse at their foot. It was Beachy Head – and we'd missed it by a whisker! A few moments later our pilot walked into the passenger cabin pouring with perspiration and said: 'God – I could do with a drink!', a wish which was immediately gratified. We saw nothing more till the orange flood-lights of the Heathrow runway loomed into sight . . . and then we were down and safe. An enormous sense of relief overwhelmed us. It had been a marvellous journey, but that last flight would remain with us for ever.

We went straight to the Admiralty to report back for duty. I was to be appointed to H.M.S. *Challenger* and, after Christmas leave, was to join her in Scapa Flow early in the New Year. I hurried home. It was Friday, 22nd December and I got there late that night – to the delight and astonishment of my parents (who thought I was still in Singapore!). It was a wonderful home-coming for me – but it was to be blackened by the next day's news.

I had promised Phil Hocking that I would ring his fiancée as soon as I got home to tell her that Phil was on his way – and this I did. Next morning we heard that a passenger plane had ditched in the Mediterranean and that there were few survivors. I immediately rang the Airline in London. Was it our follow-up flight? Yes it was. Who were the survivors? One was Bill Ashton (one of our colleagues), who had been picked up by an Italian schooner – but there were few others. The rest, including Phil Hocking, had perished. I felt his loss keenly, and wished to God I had never rung his fiancée. The blow to her must have been unbearable – and I had compounded it. And what if I had won the toss at the Sea View Hotel? Fate or luck had decreed that in this tragedy I was not to be the victim.

CHAPTER VI

Lieutenant, H.M.S. *Challenger* 1940–42

ALTHOUGH WE WERE STILL in the period of the 'Phoney War', there had, in fact, been quite a lot of action at sea. An unmitigated disaster of this period was the torpedoeing of H.M.S. *Royal Oak* at her moorings in Scapa Flow by a German submarine commanded by the redoubtable Lieutenant-Commander Prien, who had somehow manoeuvred his vessel through one or other of the supposedly blocked entrance-channels to the Flow, and, undetected, had made his escape by the same means. This was a major blow to the Fleet in what was thought to be an impregnable base – the loss of a capital ship with some 800 of her crew.

It was this episode that was responsible for bringing me to Scapa Flow to join H.M.S. *Challenger*. Her Captain, Commander W.C. Jenks, had been assigned the task of carrying out a number of large-scale hydrographic surveys of areas in which it was intended to lay controlled minefields and associated detector-loops – to ensure that such a disaster could never be repeated. *Challenger*, in her grey war-paint and with one pom-pom gun for'ard and another right aft, and Lewis-guns on each bridge-wing, looked much more business-like than when I'd last seen her (in the floating dock at Bermuda, with her boilers ripped out), and the rows of carley floats along her superstructure were evidence of the war-risks she'd be facing. But for the moment, as far as I was concerned, the risks were almost entirely from the elements, which seemed extremely hostile. When boat-sounding, Orcadian waters in mid-winter are no joke!

I soon found out too that Commander Jenks was cast in a different mould from previous C.O.s under whom I had served. He was an excellent seaman, a competent surveyor and ambitious. He was also rather shy and anti-social, an introvert and also a martinet. To him, the survey was everything. Nothing could take precedence over that. However, he was an excellent teacher, demanding a high degree of professionalism as well as extraordinary standards of human endurance. He spared neither himself nor his officers – nor his crew. He was admired but not liked. In the circumstances, however, he was the right man for the job: he got things done. He also kept a careful eye on morale, recognising the limits beyond which ordinary mortals could not be pushed.

We spent two strenuous months in the Orkneys, where the elements seldom let up, followed by further surveys of a similar kind in the approaches to the Kyle of Lochalsh, Plymouth Sound (where, to my delight, Bryan O'Neill joined us), Milford Haven and the Shetlands (where the Admiralty had its eye on the great firth of Sullom Voe as a possible Fleet Base or strategic anchorage). After this we returned to Scapa Flow, where we received orders to sail for a destination as yet undisclosed. It was not until after we had sailed that we heard where we were bound for: Iceland. Remembering the marvellous summer I had spent there six years before, my spirits soared. I would be returning to the 'land of my dreams'.

The 'pink charts' were laid out on the Chart Room table. Our immediate task was to survey Hvalfjord – the head of the fjord on a scale of 1:12,500 (6 inches to the mile) and the rest of it on half that scale (1:25,000). As the only man in the ship with first-hand experience of those parts, my comments and advice were somewhat at a premium – and were even sought by our Captain! As we plunged into the Atlantic, I was in the 'seventh heaven'.

The area had been chosen by the Admiralty as a major Fleet Base, capable of replacing Scapa Flow if that became untenable. The choice proved an inspired one, not only because of its strategic position, but also – as our survey gradually revealed – because its hydrographic and topographic features were ideally suited to our purpose. It was an extensive stretch of

Challenger *at Milford Haven, 1940.*

almost land-locked water, of adequate depth, virtually devoid of reefs, and surrounded by protective mountains.

After arriving at Reykjavik and 'making our number' with the newly installed Naval Authority there, we lost no time in pressing on to Hvalfjord itself. The task before us was to sound the entire area and map the surrounding countryside with particular thoroughness. Since no maps or charts of it existed on anything like a '6-inch' scale, we would be working from scratch. In such circumstances Commander Jenks was in his element, as we were soon to learn.

We came to anchor just short of the upper reach of the fjord and more or less in the middle of our survey-ground. This berth was to be our centre of operations for the next six weeks as the boats and shore-parties pressed on with the survey of the 'Head of Hvalfjord'.

The normal routine was for boats and field parties to return to the ship, after completing the day's work, about 6.30 p.m. Early in the proceedings I had just spent a long and particularly arduous day establishing, marking and occupying a Main Triangulation Station. Having accomplished the task, apart from one or two minor sounding-marks, I returned to the ship with my small party about 7.30 p.m. At the top of the gangway I was met by the Captain and asked why I had returned. When I gave my reasons, he replied that with plenty of daylight left, I was to return to the Station until I had finished the observation work down to the last detail. By the time we finally got back to the ship, it was 10.30 p.m.!

On another occasion a gale was blowing so fiercely that the glasses of our sounding-sextants were constantly being rendered opaque by the salt spray enveloping us. We returned to the ship with our boats' crews wet, cold and miserable, to report that conditions precluded further sounding. Since there was plenty of work outstanding in the Chartroom, this action seemed eminently reasonable. The Captain, however, thought otherwise. 'Can't see through your sextants?' he queried, 'Well, take a spare handkerchief with you – and get on with it!'

Interesting though the boat-sounding operations were, what I most enjoyed was the topographical surveying. This required me to traverse up the streams and valleys with compass and rangefinder, sketching in the contours with the aid of an aneroid barometer. Scrambling through this wild and peaceful countryside amid the sounds and sights of nature was a truly profound experience. The vivid green of valleys studded with vast fields of golden buttercups, the cold, crystal-clear rivulets cascading down through great outcrops of reddish-black rocks, the masses of little wild flowers, coupled with the calling and twittering of birds of all kinds, including eagles and ravens as they circled round the mountains – all this seemed to carry me into a world of romantic fantasy a million miles away from the down-to-earth urgency of the ship's task and a far cry indeed from the war raging in Europe.

Very occasionally, as a boost to morale, Jenks would take the ship down to Reykjavik for the week-end. One evening at a dance there Bryan O'Neill and I met two particularly charming and attractive girls. Having such delightful damsels in tow gave an added spur to our work and provided much to look forward to on our next visit to Reykjavik – whenever that might be. We fixed firm dates to meet them next time we came in.

Meanwhile in July we moved down the fjord to take in hand the much more extensive survey further seaward – including a large area in Faxafloi covering the approaches to the fjord – all on a '3-inch' scale. In general this was fairly straightforward but included in the area was another controlled minefield survey on a much larger scale than usual and calling for special techniques. The task was entrusted to Bryan and me and took us several days of hard, painstaking work, culminating in a huge sheet of densely packed soundings to be plotted and inked in. A great deal of adjustments were required to harmonise the sets of soundings involved, and one night we were kept hard at work in the Chartroom until about 3 a.m. Knowing that we would have to resume field work at 7 a.m., we decided to call it a day and turn in.

Next morning we were sent for by the Captain. Not only that, but the First Lieutenant (Lt. Cdr. 'Moss' Monk – a kindly soul if ever there was one) was ordered to bring us to him as 'defaulters'. We were even told to 'Off Caps'. The Captain demanded to know why the inking-in had not been finished. We explained that after a long and arduous day of boat-sounding, followed by six or seven hours' work in the Chartroom, we simply couldn't keep awake any longer. The Captain stared at us and said: 'When I was your age, there was no such word as "can't".' With that he dismissed us. We held our peace but for days afterwards we seethed with indignation.

On our next visit to Reykjavik we hired a car for the day and took the girls out to Thingvellir. In the evening we dined and danced with them back at the Hotel Borg. While sipping wine together by candle-light, and listening dreamily to the dance-music, we were rudely interrupted by a messenger. Would I please step outside for a moment as the Port Captain wished to see me urgently? (Consternation on all our faces) In the hotel foyer the Captain handed me a sealed brown envelope and said: 'Operational priority – take this out to your Captain immediately – get hold of a boat!' I took the envelope and looked at my watch. The last boat off was at midnight

– in a quarter of an hour. I turned to go back to the dining room and, lowering his voice, the Port Captain, almost whispering, said: 'A German invasion force is approaching Iceland, and is expected to get here by noon tomorrow.' 'Jesus Christ!' I thought as I returned to our table – to find all eyes turned upon me (even at the neighbouring tables). Thinking how dramatic this all seemed (like something out of a Viennese opera), I apologised to the girls and hustled Bryan out of the room and down to the quay.

As soon as the boat came in, we shoved off (if some of the others missed it – too bad!) and reached the ship, which was anchored some way out in the roads, about 12.15 a.m. I went straight to the Captain's cabin and found him asleep. He was far from pleased to be woken, but drowsily swung himself on to the edge of the bunk as I explained the urgency of my mission. Tearing open the envelope and holding the pink cypher-message in front of him, he read it out to me. The preamble repeated what I had already been told and it then went on to order the action to be taken by the various units of the Occupation Force: 'HMS *Challenger* is to continue her surveys'. 'Bloody Hell!' grunted the Captain, 'damned if I will. They can think again on that one.' Then turning to me, 'All right, Hall – you'd better get some sleep.'

I turned in with my heart thumping in my chest, wondering what the hell *Challenger*, with her puny armament, could do to resist a full-blooded enemy invasion. Flashing through my mind were mental pictures of the ship going down with colours flying and all guns spitting defiance to the last. I don't think I got much sleep that night. But when I woke up in the morning, things were strangely quiet. 'That's a bit odd,' I thought as I stumbled up on deck, 'surely we should be preparing for action?' Then I met the First Lieutenant, who was grinning sardonically. 'Relax, man,' he said, 'panic averted. We've just had another signal. Last night's was "For exercise".' Our Captain, however, who had been up all night, was 'Not Amused'. Despite the anti-climax, it was a dramatic episode, and one which I'm unlikely to forget.

By this time autumn was upon us and as the survey of Hvalfjord progressed seaward, our visits to Reykjavik became more frequent. One week-end the ship was at anchor outside the harbour when an exceptionally fierce gale struck us, causing us to set anchor watch. A second anchor was let go, we came to immediate notice for steam, and veered several more shackles of cable. During the night we 'steamed to the cables', the second anchor, underfoot, helping to reduce a dangerous yaw, which could lead to dragging. The aircraft carrier *Eagle* was anchored not far away and as the storm grew in ferocity, we could discern her lights moving slowly down wind. We held our position through the night (there were no flies on Commander Jenks when it came to seamanship), but when dawn broke, there was *Eagle* broadside on to the rocks of the outer breakwater. When the storm subsided, she eventually got off (spurning our assistance) largely through parading her ship's company on the flight-deck and having them jump up and down to the beat of her Royal Marine band!

One week-end Bryan and I had accompanied the girls to a village dance out in the country. At the time some Icelanders resented the British occupation of their country and British sailors were by no means universally popular. Wearing uniform, we were inevitably conspicuous, and not all the glances that followed us to our table were particularly friendly. There must have been 40 or 50 young Icelanders present and though we merged as best we could in the general dancing, singing, smoking and drinking, we became conscious of a certain hostility. When several burly young men moved over to the next table and started a conversation in their native tongue, we realised that a confrontation was brewing – particularly when some of them started removing their jackets and rolling up their sleeves. The two girls urged us to leave, but we were at the far end of the hall and our way was barred. There seemed to be nothing for it but to defend ourselves – and our girl-friends – though the outcome looked anything but hopeful. Suddenly at that moment the door was flung open and in walked a sergeant of the Military Police and two corporals, red bands on the sleeves of their khaki battle-dress. They came straight across to us and escorted all four of us out of the building. Then they whisked us back to Reykjavik in their truck. How they got wind of our predicament I shall never know, but we understood that they had been tipped off either by our taxi-driver when he returned to the city, or by a phone call from someone inside the hall. Whoever it was, we certainly thanked our lucky stars that night for the British Military Police!

As the Hvalfjord surveys drew to a close and our thoughts turned towards home, we received orders to survey several other fjords, among them Seydisfjord. This is a relatively steep-sided and narrow fjord with its little port nestling between high mountains at its innermost extremity. One Saturday afternoon, when we had been encouraged to take some exercise ashore, Bryan and I decided to climb a 3,400 ft. mountain called Strandatindur. It rose steeply from the south side of the fjord and was partly snow-covered. It took us several hours to reach the summit and by the time we arrived there, the sun had set and a mist was gathering in the valleys below. We rested awhile to take in the marvellous view, but decided we'd better get down before it became too dark. The gulleys on the north side of the mountain, facing the fjord, were filled with snow, and I found that by digging my heels into it, I could descend quite quickly. 'This is the best way down,' I called to Bryan, who was some way above me. They were very nearly my last words! Hardly had I uttered them when my heel struck ice and I was hurtling downhill on my back, totally out of control.

The mountain was steep, bare of vegetation, and composed largely of loose rock and scree. I was gathering speed down the ice-filled gully, trying vainly to arrest my fall by clutching at snow and ice. By the time I emerged on to the rocky scree, my speed was terrific and growing ever faster. Still clutching madly at anything within reach, I dislodged masses of stones and boulders, which slithered and bounced and roared down beside me in a veritable avalanche. It seemed to go on for ever, and knowing how precipitous the middle parts of the mountain were, I was convinced that it was the end of me. I had just about given up hope when suddenly I stopped. The crashing and rattling of the avalanche continued all about me and my ears were filled with the roar of rocks and boulders. Then a boulder struck me on the head and I blacked out. When I came to, the noise had stopped. It was pitch dark and I was lying on a ledge bleeding freely. From way up in the sky above me I heard a distant call. It must have been Bryan. 'Are you all right?' he seemed to be yelling. When I tried to answer, all I could manage was a croak.

For a long time I lay there bruised, battered and bleeding and with a splitting headache. All was quiet but the moon had risen. I took stock of my surroundings and got painfully to my feet. Just in front of me was a precipice. In the moonlight I could see well enough to traverse slowly across to another slope and gradually hobble and stumble down it. Still far below me I could see the fjord and the lights of the ship at anchor. It seemed to take hours to get down to where the grass and bushes began and I was feeling awful. At last the slopes became more gentle and I slowly traversed towards the head of the fjord. All of a sudden I was aware of a figure approaching and a voice hailed me: 'Are you one of the search party?' I was still confused. 'No. What search party?' I replied. 'One of our officers has fallen down a mountain. They reckon he's a gonner, but we've been told to search for him.' By this time I could discern several other shadowy figures strung out on the slopes. Next a torch blazed in my face. With my matted hair, face and hands covered in blood and clothes in tatters, I must have looked quite a sight. 'Oh my God!' exclaimed the man behind the torch, 'Lootenant 'All? You still alive, then? — Give me quite a turn, you did!'

By the time they got me back to the ship and into the Sick Bay, it was well after midnight. It all caused quite a stir. We had to fit the story together. I was still a bit hazy about my side of it, though it was beginning to come back. I remembered Bryan's last shout (after failing to get any response to his question as to whether I was all right), and I relished it: 'I think I'll try some other way down' (!). Apparently he'd gone back to the ship about an hour later and reported the accident to the Captain, saying he didn't think I could have survived. According to the Captain his words were: 'I'm afraid Hall's had it.' We subsequently worked out that I must have fallen nearly 900 feet. I was lucky indeed to have fetched up on that ledge!

Several other fjords were surveyed, but by mid-November *Challenger* had completed all her surveys in Iceland and we sailed for Scapa Flow. Here we joined a south-bound convoy heading down the War Channel through the North Sea. One of my duties was the custody of confidential books, cyphers and classified signals, and one of those signals which I took to the Captain contained a directive to merchant ships in convoy. They were not to open fire on enemy aircraft unless they themselves were actually attacked. Did this apply to us? Though not a merchant ship, *Challenger* was in the convoy and not part of the escort. In these circumstances one assumed that we were required to obey the directive like any other ship in the convoy.

Next afternoon the convoy was attacked. A solitary Heinkel seaplane came in from the east, skirted the flank of the convoy, and was fired on by an outlying cruiser, though without much effect. It banked, dived, and came in low across our port quarter. I was in charge of the after pom-pom. Should I open fire? It was not attacking us. I hesitated. The Heinkel glided quietly past our stern – and suddenly dropped a torpedo. 'Open fire!' I yelled and a shattering stream of 2-pdr. shells poured out in an arc towards it. Too late! It opened up full throttle and zoomed away to the north. An enormous spout of white water reared up against the port bow of the merchant ship on our starboard quarter, followed by a deep thud. She had been squarely hit.

'That bloody signal!' I thought. 'But for that I'd have opened fire a few seconds earlier and we might have averted the strike!' It was the first time in my life that I'd ever been in action and I felt both excited and frightened. I remember actually feeling my knees knocking together as we waited for the Heinkel to return and attack us. But it did not. Meanwhile the merchant ship had lost way and was settling by the head. *Challenger* was ordered to assist her. We lowered a seaboat and sent Bryan O'Neill and the Engineer Officer over to her. Two of her crew had been killed but the damaged forepart had been sealed off. The engines and boilers were unscathed and the Master reckoned he could limp into Tynemouth stern first. We left the ship to her fate and re-joined the convoy.

Our next surveying assignment took us to Ireland, where we were directed to survey Lough Foyle. The decision of the Irish Free State to remain neutral had, in effect, denied us the use of Bere Haven in the south and Lough Swilly in the north of Ireland, both of which would have been invaluable as bases for our convoy escort forces. In default of these, we were forced to rely on Londonderry, the approach to which lay through the whole length of Lough Foyle with its shallow and dangerous waters, in which ships frequently went aground. As the Admiralty Chart of Lough Foyle was hopelessly out of date, our first task in that spring of 1941 was to carry out a complete re-survey of the Lough on a fairly large scale.

It was an interesting survey, partly because the high ground bordering the Lough on the north-western side lay in the Free State and was therefore barred to us. Under normal circumstances the whole survey would have been controlled from this side, as all the other shores were low-lying and flat. Thus a good deal of improvisation was called for.

CHAPTER VII

The *Anselm* Disaster and the Surveys in Gambia, 1941–2

TOWARDS THE END OF June 1941 we received our sailing orders. We were to assume charge of a convoy consisting of the troop ship *Anselm*, carrying about 2,000 soldiers, with two escorting corvettes of the 'Flower' Class. It was a pretty puny escort, particularly as *Challenger* had no asdic or A/S armament, but the best that could be afforded in the circumstances. Nevertheless, it was a heavy responsibility for Commander Jenks. He placed *Challenger* in the van of the convoy, about five cables ahead of the *Anselm*, and one corvette on each flank, about five cables on either side of her. The whole formation advanced on a standard A/S zigzag, all ships turning together at predetermined times. Thus we headed out around Ireland and set our course southward through the Atlantic towards the Azores.

Each day we received the 'Daily U-Boat Situation Report'. It was broadcast in cypher by the Admiralty and gave the latest informed assessment of the positions of enemy U-Boats (based, we assumed, on D/F bearings of their routine radio-transmissions). These positions were at once plotted on the Atlantic Ocean chart in our Chartroom and marked by little red flag-pins. When our little convoy was about a week out from home, it became clear that at least two of these flags were getting uncomfortably close to us, and every now and again one or other of our corvettes would break off on an investigation of an asdic 'contact', only to report later : 'Non-Sub'. Doubtless we were all getting a bit jittery.

It was a beautiful moonlit night in July, with a slight sea, and I had the Middle Watch. We were making about 10 knots and *Anselm* was plunging along lazily astern of us with the corvettes spread out on either wing and easily visible in the moonlight. We were zigzagging 20° either side of a mean course, holding each leg of the zigzag for 10 or 20 minutes, and all was peace and quiet. But at the back of our minds were those little red flags inexorably closing in. I had steaming hot mugs of thick sweet cocoa ready for my relief, Jack Paisley, when he came up at 0355 to take over the Watch. Having briefed him and got him to sign the Captain's Night Order Book, I took my departure with the words: 'And for Christ's sake don't get us torpedoed!' Fully clothed, I lay down on my bunk and in no time was out like a light. Hardly had I lost consciousness when all hell broke loose. Alarm rattlers throughout the ship were making a continuous and appalling din, and a long succession of short blasts on the ship's siren roused every man from his slumbers, while the stamping and rattling of hundreds of feet on the iron ladders to the upper deck emphasised the sense of emergency. I was back on the bridge in a flash and arrived there just after the Captain.

Jack Paisley's face was white as a sheet and the Captain looked drawn and grey. It was 0415 and out on the starboard quarter *Anselm* was down by the head, stopped and listing to port. She had been hit on the port bow. The corvettes were careering off at full speed and dropping depth-charges. We increased to full speed too and started circling round the crippled troop-ship, expecting another attack at any minute – perhaps on ourselves. *Anselm's* decks were crowded with troops and frantic efforts were being made to lower her boats. Her bows were sinking lower and lower in the water, great clouds of steam belching from her funnel, and her rudder and screws were beginning to show. 'Up all hammocks – on the fo'c'sle!' came the order, and in a few minutes the foredeck was buried by lashed-up hammocks. 'Out all fenders, starboard side for'ard. Prepare to go alongside!' came the next pipe. Commander Jenks lost no more time. He placed *Challenger* close under *Anselm's* port quarter, twenty feet below her upper deck, which was steadily rising. 'Jump for it!' he bellowed through his megaphone, and swarms of soldiers leapt down on to the hammocks, landing in heaps, spraining ankles and breaking legs, and being shepherded aft to make room for more. They came down in hundreds, many writhing in agony as they landed from 30 feet above. It had become too dangerous. *Anselm* was beginning to stand on end, her stern rising ever more swiftly. 'Cut the ropes! – Full speed astern!' shouted the Captain, and *Challenger* backed off to a safe distance. *Anselm's* stern reared up into the air and she stood vertical, her funnel awash, for several minutes. A tremendous crashing mingled with the shouts and screams as every piece of loose gear on her decks swept down into the sea, and every soldier without a foothold or handhold was carried down with it. It was a horrifying sight. A cluster of men still stood on her stern, 200 feet above the sea.

The ship stood vertical with half her length in the air. Sea water was pouring in through her funnel and we expected her boilers to explode. There came a succession of dull thunderclaps as her bulkheads collapsed one after the other and she started to dive. The soldiers still clustered high up on her stern, sensing that they would be sucked down with her, started throwing themselves into the sea. From that height, almost 200 feet, they had no chance. They hit the water with sickening force, throwing up huge splashes, and were killed instantly. With horrible swiftness the ship went down and disappeared completely, leaving a mass of flotsam and wreckage heaving and plunging in a vast pool of oily turbulence. We watched it all at close quarters, almost paralysed with horror. *Anselm* had gone. It was scarcely credible. Many men were swimming in the oily water, some clinging to floating planks and gratings, others crammed into the lifeboats or else swimming towards them, while yet others clung to them for dear life. We had to act quickly. Our sea-boat was lowered and the two corvettes closed in with their scrambling nets down. I had to do something and got the Captain's permission to take away the skiff with one man on the oars. Several heads were bobbing about within a cable's length of us and we hauled them aboard covered with oil and gasping for air. As we paddled about among the drowned corpses and the wreckage, I was so overcome by the enormity of what had happened, and so resentful and indignant at the brutality that the Germans had inflicted on these men, that I found myself saying aloud, over and over again, 'The bastards! . . . the bastards! . . . the bastards!'

As there seemed to be no more survivors anywhere near us, we pulled back to the ship with the few wretches whom we had rescued. God knows, it was little enough in all conscience, but at least I'd done something to help. *Challenger* rescued no fewer than 900 men, and the two corvettes another 600 between them. All the while we were expecting another attack, though the corvettes had found no trace of the U-Boat despite all their depth-charging. 1,500 had been rescued. That meant that at least 500 had perished, and we heard afterwards from some of the survivors that about 400 of these had been trapped in the for'ard mess-decks, unable to reach safety due to the destruction of the ladders when the torpedo exploded.

With our own crew, we now had over 1,000 men aboard our small ship and, not unnaturally, the survivors were loath to go below. The upper deck and superstructure were absolutely packed with them and *Challenger* had become unstable due to the topweight. The ship's motion had become alarming, and there was no alternative but to arm our own men and force most of the soldiers below decks. All cabins and other accommodation were given over to them and the Sick Bay and passageways were crammed with the injured and dying. We had a major problem on our hands. The Medical Officer and the Supply Officer, with their small staffs, worked like Trojans to alleviate suffering and to sustain bodies and souls, but it was First Aid and couldn't be more than temporary. Meanwhile others had heard of our plight and the Armed Merchant Cruiser *Cathay* arranged to rendezvous with us next morning. So for another 24 hours the three little ships pressed on southwards with their huge burdens of suffering humanity.

Next morning the great bulk of A.M.C. *Cathay* (an ex-P.& O. liner) hove into sight. Oh what a relief! All three of our ships berthed alongside her in turn. She readily took every one of our 1,500 survivors (including the dead). Then we formed up to carry out a combined A/S sweep together. *Cathay* was now in charge (she had a Captain, R.N. in command), and disposing the ships in line abreast, she ordered a speed of 14 knots for the sweep.

The utmost *Challenger* could do was 13 knots, flat out. There was nothing for it but to spread our sails. We had a large mainsail with boom and gaff, which we used to set from time to time. It could give us an extra half knot and could reduce rolling. We also carried a large foresail – which was seldom, if ever, used. In the International Code of Signals there was a group of flags which meant 'Request permission to make plain sail'. This seemed appropriate, so we hoisted it at the yard-arm. *Cathay* was obviously a bit puzzled by this, as she kept her answering-pendant at the dip for some time.

After a while she hoisted it close up – and then broke out another signal in International Code. *Cathay* was clearly having fun, for this one was translated 'Affirmative. Do you intend to "Up Screw"?' (Much merriment all round). So we set our sails and just managed to keep up.

We were now bound for the western extremity of the African Continent and specifically for the mouth of the Gambia River. Here a Convoy Assembly Point was to be established, vitally important to shipping to and from the Far East, which at this time was routed round the Cape. Existing charts and maps of the area were virtually useless and we would have to start from scratch, surveying not only the hydrography of the river, but the topography of the surrounding countryside as well. In the end we found ourselves surveying the river as far up as it was navigable, but when we began we were unaware of this extra task to come. In all, the work was to take us seven months.

On my first sight of the low-lying, steamy and unhealthy-looking coast, the phrase that rose to my mind was 'the white man's grave'. The work itself, however, though arduous, was engrossing and challenging as well as being punctuated by many lighter moments.

We started by measuring a mile-and-a-half long 'Base' (with a dog-leg in it), laid out along the beach west of Bathurst. It was alleged to be the longest base-measurement in hydrographic history and, since it had to be done with meticulous accuracy, it took us well over a week.

We then had to work out the scale, position and orientation of the survey. The exact geographical position of one end of the Base had first to be established, and this was done by observing the transit, through an altitude of exactly 45°, of a series of pre-selected stars and planets. The observations (and there were up to 50 of them made by several officers working independently one of another) were taken with a 45° prismatic astrolabe with a mercury 'horizon' and the exact time of each transit was established by means of a chronograph – with a known error on G.M.T. Protracted preparations and subsequent calculations were needed, but by the end of a week or so a mean geographical position, in terms of latitude and longitude (to fractions of a second of arc), had been established.

We could now define the scale and position of the survey, and our next task would be to establish its orientation. A theodolite was set up exactly over the Observation Point (one end of the Base) and a True Bearing was observed by zero-ing the instrument on a relatively distant 'Main Station' and accurately measuring the horizontal angle between it and the sun (or a planet). This procedure was repeated a number of times on both 'faces' of the theodolite and on different parts of its azimuth circle. As the true bearing of each heavenly body at the time of observation could be precisely calculated, and the horizontal angles between them and the distant survey mark had been measured, a mean True Bearing could be deduced.

Even while this was being done, a number of other officers were already out in the field, setting up huge tripodial survey-marks as 'Main Stations' and proceeding with the main triangulation. Once all this had been accomplished, the master Plotting Sheet could be brought out and all marks meticulously positioned and 'pricked through' on to it. Thus the framework of the survey was established.

About the end of July I was assigned the task of tackling the coastline and topography. For this I followed a road leading westward over the mangrove swamps to Cape St. Mary. It was 'macadamised' and the heat thrown up from it not only tried me sorely in a physical sense, but very often created a mirage effect strong enough to prevent the use of any optical instrument. By the time I reached Cape St. Mary, I was heartily sick of that road!

I was next required to map the hinterland further up country. The method used was known as a 'Pacing Traverse'. In fact it consisted of a whole series of 'closed traverses', each starting at a fixed point and eventually returning to that same point. In this work I was accompanied by one faithful Able Seaman, a cheerful companion who shared the heat and burden of the day, carrying my equipment without complaint. He became quietly impressed by what he regarded as my uncanny ability to find my way back, after several days – in one case about a week – of apparently aimless 'safari' through jungle and parkland to my starting point. After one particularly long and convoluted 'safari', when we had duly arrived back at the peg marking our point of departure, he said: 'You know, sir, I reckon there's no one who knows Africa like what you do!' That day I truly felt my cup was full!

The lower reaches of the Gambia River are fringed with extensive mangrove swamps intersected with a maze of serpentine 'creeks'. The mudbanks, which dry out at low tide and are flooded at high tide, are infested with large crocodiles. I now had to start exploring and mapping this rather sinister area. I had with me a 16-ft. motor skiff and a 10-ft. dory in tow, with a crew of four sailors. The work took me practically a month. Sounding along each line, using a hand-bearing compass and a 'Leitz' range-finder for measuring distances, and making a series of zigzag traverses, we advanced steadily upstream, charting the shape, course, width and depth of each creek as we went. We had to be careful never to get completely lost, which in such a maze would have been all too easy.

One day as we chugged our way forward along a steadily narrowing creek with very high mangroves on either side. I was idly trailing my hand in the cool water at the side of the skiff when I noticed a group of objects a short distance ahead. It was the eyes and nostrils of a submerged crocodile. Suddenly out came its head and it lunged at me with wide-open jaws. I withdrew my hand in the nick of time just as the serried rows of yellowish teeth snapped shut with a sickening crunch a mere foot from the side of the boat.

Working parallel with us, but further up-river, was another party using similar techniques. The officer in charge was our senior Lieutenant (he may even have shipped his half-stripe as a Lt. Cdr.) and I refer to him as 'Sharpey' for short, as that is what we called him. We were steadily progressing our respective surveys towards each other, and would eventually meet. One day while we were working up our results in the Chartroom, I noticed that our work had overlapped at one point, covering the same ground but showing minor discrepancies in our findings. In effect we had a classic mutual misclosure and the orthodox solution was to accept the mean of the two positions and re-adjust the traverses leading to them. But I had not yet got the measure of Sharpey. Whereas I could adjust my traverse while transferring it to the fair tracing, Sharpey had already traced his work and would have to re-draw it. 'My position is correct,' he said, 'Adjust yours to agree with it.' 'Certainly not,' I replied, 'What makes you think your position is more correct than mine?' 'I am more experienced than you,' he answered. 'That may be,' I countered, 'but we've both used the same techniques and our final traverses are roughly the same length, so there's nothing to choose between them.' 'Well I'm senior to you, so do as I say,' he replied. In the end the Captain had to arbitrate and I'm glad to say that he stood no nonsense from that other officer. (That was the first of many disputes I was to have with him in future years).

It must have been late November by the time we'd finished the main survey, and Commander Jenks then decided to extend it further up-river. A new triangulation was required to cover the broad lower reaches, which were fringed on both sides with high mangrove trees. It was decided that a chain of full-size tripodial survey-marks should be established in the water, along the edge of the mangroves, to mark the Main Stations. This was easier said than done, and the problems fell to us to solve.

Consider the circumstances and the conditions. The ledge fringing the mangrove trees on each side of the river was of deep slimy mud. Most of the time it was under water but at low tide a foot or two of it was exposed to the sun. The tidal range was about six or seven feet, so that at high tide there were four or five feet of water above the mudbanks. A full-size Main Survey mark could be 45 ft. high, being constructed of three 30 ft. 'barlings' (similar to telegraph poles) lashed together at their apex to form a strong tripod with a 30 ft. bamboo flag-pole protruding from the top. For extra rigidity, wooden planks would be fixed across the barlings halfway up on all three sides, and the spaces above would be filled with wood-and-canvas triangles. Wire guys would be led from the bamboo pole to heavy iron stakes driven well into the ground, and a 12-by-8 ft. flag would be laced to the top of the bamboo. The whole contraption would be painted white for maximum visibility. These marks were extremely heavy and usually required at least eight men to erect them.

Now what might be practical on dry land was not necessarily so on soft submerged mud. We decided that we would have to compromise, making do with marks of about two-thirds full size and using 20 ft. hop-poles instead of the barlings, and 12 ft. boathook staves instead of the bamboos. But we had to prevent the heels of the tripod from sinking into the mud and also from floating out of it at high water. This was achieved by fixing 3 ft. square boards just above each heel and shackling on to the heel a ½ cwt. iron sinker. To prevent the heels of the tripod from 'splaying', the three legs were linked by steel-wire rope at ground level, while the wire guys from the flag-pole were led well out to boats' anchors buried in the mud.

Four of these marks were to be erected on the first day, to provide an initial quadrilateral from which the triangulation could be carried further up river. One of these, on the south side, was assigned to me to erect and observe from. I had a party of six and the 27-ft. whaler. Laden down as it was with all this heavy gear (and a good deal more), we found it easier to sail than to pull. We reached the selected site at low water, anchored the boat and leapt out on to the mud, sinking into it to our knees. It took us all morning to set up the mark and secure it, by which time we were floundering about not only in eighteen inches of slimy mud, but in a further eighteen inches of steadily rising water. Several crocodiles, which had been snoozing a short way off when we arrived, had now been submerged, and were watching our progress with baleful eyes as they circled round within twenty yards of us.

Now came the difficult part. Sending my party off to have lunch in the boat, and with the help of my S.R., I began the task of positioning the theodolite. To observe accurate angles, the instrument has to be firmly mounted and levelled, with its baseplate absolutely horizontal and its axis plumbed vertically below the flagstaff. To provide a reasonably firm platform for the legs of the theodolite-tripod, we made a large triangle of weighted planks and sank it into the mud as centrally as possible below the apex of the mark. We then placed the feet of the tripod on the submerged planks and screwed on the theodolite, which by this time was about two feet clear of the water. Levelling a theodolite is an intricate process at the best of times, and in these highly unusual circumstances it was well nigh impossible. Once levelled, the slightest knock or pressure on the tripod is sufficient to upset it, and with this unstable ground-platform, and the waves lapping against the tripod, one could only do one's best. To provide something to grip and lean on while peering into the theodolite and moving carefully round it, we drove a large heavy spade into the mud vertically below it. I was able to hold on to this as I started to observe.

By this time the water was above my waist and one or two of the crocodiles seemed appreciably nearer. Getting four rounds of angles is a time-consuming process and requires intense concentration on the part of the observer. I was apprehensive about the crocodiles and realised that as things stood, I would not be able to devote my whole attention to the job in hand. I therefore ordered one of my sailors to scramble up the mark with a rifle and ammunition and perch on the crossbar just above and behind me. I gave him instructions to shoot any croc which approached us. Thus protected, I got on with the business of observing, though every movement of my feet in the mud as I shifted position required a re-check on the level of the theodolite. I got my last angle just as the waves were beginning to lap the baseplate. It was quite the 'hairiest' bit of observing I'd ever done and I was more than thankful when it was over!

By December, 1941 the United States had entered the War, the Japanese had treacherously attacked, and almost destroyed, the American fleet at Pearl

Harbour and Germany had declared war on the United States. The War had entered a totally new phase and Commander Jenks decided that the classical style of our survey was too slow. He had set his sights on a new record: to survey the Gambia River as far inland as it was navigable. By normal methods that would take years, so we'd do what was known as a Running Survey. I won't describe the technique in detail, but it meant three parallel lines of soundings – by the ship, with an S.M.B. each side of her – while fixing by Taut Wire Measuring Gear and 'shooting up' features on both banks from each fix as the formation advanced up-river. Our goal was a place called Kuntur, about 200 miles inland. We covered 20 miles a day and moored up to the river-bank each evening, where we established a tide-pole. I had become the ship's Tidal Officer, so it fell to me to plot the many tidal curves obtained from the different poles, and to deduce the appropriate reductions to apply to the previous day's soundings. These reductions had to be 'smoothed out' as we advanced, and as the tidal range steadily diminished.

We reached Kuntur and spent Christmas there – a rather subdued Christmas as I recall – and we observed a Geographical Position on which to tie in our long traverse. The misclosure turned out to be much smaller than Jenks had expected and he was like a dog with two tails, dispensing 'seasonal cheer' to all the officers in the 'cuddy'. In all the two years we'd served with him, we'd never seen him so completely relaxed. Not only had we successfully completed the major survey assigned to us, but we'd also – off our own bat – done this tremendous running survey into the very heart of the colony.

It must have been mid-January when we finally left the Gambia, and few of us were sorry to see the last of it. None of us had been consigned to 'The White Man's Grave' and none had succumbed to the bite of the deadly Black Mamba (the local snake we'd been repeatedly warned about, against which we always carried a razor-blade and antidote). During the seven months we had spent there, it is true, several of our number had been invalided home with other forms of sickness.

We joined a north-bound convoy from the Cape and wished we'd been routed independently. One evening, just after dark, the convoy was attacked. One of our Escorts, H.M.S. *Culver*, was sunk with all hands. I was on the bridge of our ship when it happened, and we were all shattered by the catastrophe. Those 'lend-lease' cutters were not designed as warships. Having very little watertight subdivision, they were widely regarded as 'floating coffins'.

We arrived in Home Waters in early February and put into the Foyle to embark fresh provisions. Then we went round to Sheerness to re-fit and lie-up, and were welcomed home by the Hydrographer of the Navy (Vice-Admiral Sir John Edgell), who formally congratulated us all on our efforts and, in my case, at last agreed to release me to General Service.

CHAPTER VIII

Lieutenant, H.M.S. *Fraserburgh* (M/S 15), 1942

Having — TO MY DELIGHT — been released for General Service, I was sent to H.M.S. *Dryad*, the Navigation School, for an N⋆ course which, under the exigencies of war, had been reduced to six weeks. It was designed to fit us as Navigating Officers of cruisers and destroyer and minesweeping flotillas, and I found it pretty straightforward.

At the end of the course I was appointed Navigating Officer of the 15th Minesweeping Flotilla based at Granton on the Forth. The Flotilla was manned almost entirely by Reservists and the Leader, H.M.S. *Fraserburgh*, in which I was to serve, was commanded by a 'dug-out' R.N. Commander named Claude Plumer. Thus I was the only Active Service R.N. officer in the entire Flotilla.

Our initial task was the routine sweeping of the North Sea War Channel, which ran from Duncansby Head to the Thames Estuary. On one occasion, while working in the North Sea, we were suddenly enveloped in thick fog. With many inevitable uncertainties in our D.R. (Dead Reckoning), we had no means of fixing our position. 'Well now, Pilot,' asked Commander Plumer, pushing his head over the chart table, 'Where are we?' 'Well, sir,' I replied, indicating a vague position on the chart, 'We might be anywhere within three miles of this D.R.' I suggested that it might be prudent to anchor and wait for the fog to clear. 'No,' decided the Old Man, 'Let's go back to Harwich, Pilot. You'll have to do the best you can.'

Our 60-mile course for Harwich was beset by sandbanks and other hazards, including a strong southwards-flowing flood-stream. This was in the days before radar (at least as far as we were concerned) and we were absolutely 'blind'. I took the rates and directions of the tidal streams from the relevant data on the chart and, to the extent that I could assess their effect over a six-hour period, laid off a 'safe' course to the outer bell-buoy off Harwich, using my slide rule to assess probable 'speed made good' along the way. I was far from confident as to the outcome, but I'd done the best I could.

Doing about ten knots on a south-westerly course, and giving the regulation long blast on our siren every two minutes, we forged ahead even though we could scarcely see our own jackstaff. As evening drew on I said to the Captain, 'We should be within five miles of the bell-buoy now, sir.' We strained our ears – and carried on. By this time I was growing apprehensive. At least the echo-sounder was giving the right depths – more or less. The minutes ticked by and we listened. Not a sound in the still air! Surely we should be able to hear the bell-buoy by now? Of course, it was a flat calm. Since the bell was wave-operated, perhaps that was why it wasn't ringing. Just as I was saying to myself, 'Oh Lord, we should be altering course by now,' a sudden shout came from the bow look-out: 'Object on the starboard bow!' There it was, ten yards away, its name as clear as daylight and with the bell just audible! 'Oh joy!' I thought. 'Bang on! Well done, Pilot!' said the Captain as we ordered 'Starboard 20' and swung round for Harwich. 'Whew, that was quite something – my first navigational achievement,' I thought to myself.

All that spring the flotilla was in process of forming up. We were formed into two Divisions with *Fraserburgh* leading the first and (if I remember rightly) *Eastbourne* the second, with an R.N.R. Commander as her C.O. In July the whole flotilla steamed round the North of Scotland through the Pentland Firth to join up with the Deep Sea Minelaying Squadron in Loch Alsh on the west coast. We were required to sweep up a large minefield in which the Minelaying Squadron had laid all the mines at the wrong depth. This was the first time that a deep minefield had been swept and there were no obvious means of position-fixing or marking the swept areas. A plan of action was drawn up, but then every conceivable difficulty arose, and though we did work out a method of operation of sorts, the errors and uncertainties entailed were far too great for comfort. To make matters worse, weather conditions in the North Atlantic were surprisingly bad for August, and in September became almost prohibitive. Fixing and plotting our painful progress, we pressed doggedly on, often through mountainous seas. Although we managed to sweep up a few of our mines and sink them by gunfire, both the weather and the mounting beacon casualties were against us. Finally by mid-September, with the onset of the equinoctial gales, the operation was called off.

On one occasion off the north coast of Scotland we were caught by a sudden easterly gale and decided to seek shelter. With the flotilla following in line ahead, we set course to pass close under the lee of Cape Wrath and round into the Minches. Hunting through the chart folios for a suitable night anchorage, I discovered a delightful old 19th-century chart of Loch Laxford, which seemed to fit the bill nicely. I found that by drawing in the swinging circles of each of our eight ships, the whole flotilla could anchor safely in line ahead, 1½ cables apart, just clearing the rocks on either side of the loch – provided they kept perfect station while doing so.

Fraserburgh *at anchor off Reykjavik, 1942.*

We entered with the setting sun behind us and a superb scene opened ahead. The loch was completely sheltered and was surrounded by wild, rock-strewn country, apparently devoid of any human habitation. All went according to plan: we anchored in formation by signal, all ships 'letting go' together when ordered.

Towards the end of September we were assigned a new minesweeping task, this time off the east coast of Iceland. We had to clear part of the route followed by the Arctic convoys taking war materials to Murmansk for our Russian allies. This route took them close eastward of Iceland through water sufficiently shallow for minelaying, and several ships had been lost as a result. Our task, therefore, was to keep this area mine-free. Once again I was intrigued that we were to re-visit this fascinating land, and that we were to be based at Seydisfjord (which *Challenger* had surveyed two years previously, and where I had made my epic descent of Strandatindur!) Not only was I reasonably familiar with the coastal topography – the peaks and headlands – but my surveying experience of accurate position-fixing by simultaneous horizontal sextant angles was going to stand me in good stead for this particular operation.

Seydisfjord proved an ideal base for the 15th Minesweeping Flotilla, being spacious, fully protected and conveniently situated for our daily operations.

As we set out each morning, the dawn landscape was enthralling, with the rising sun directly ahead turning the snow-covered mountains on either side into a fantasy of pink and gold while the clear air of early morning provided a stimulus for the day's work.

The area to be swept lay roughly parallel to, and about 15 miles off, the east coast, and I was able to keep an accurate plot of our progress. Before long we started encountering mines, which, to our surprise, exploded with dramatic effect beneath the surface as we swept them up. We soon realised that these were the latest type of German 'S' mines, moored to float a few fathoms below the surface and designed to explode as soon as their mooring wires were cut. I felt absolutely elated at the key role I was playing in helping to clear what was obviously a major enemy minefield.

It was fairly certain that some of the mines had been laid by U-Boats, while we knew that magnetic and acoustic mines in our own waters had been laid from the air. We were therefore intrigued to observe, at times, one or more German aircraft circling us at a fairly low altitude and just out of range of our guns. We concluded that the areas we had cleared during the day had been observed by these planes and that a U-Boat acting on information from them had been re-laying fresh strings of mines in the areas we had just cleared. We decided that though there seemed to be no end to this cat-and-mouse game, if we persevered, they would be the first to give up. In fact it became rather amusing, each side knowing what the other was up to, and we actually reached the point of exchanging banter – by Aldis lamp – with the German aircraft circling outside our range.

In mid-November we were ordered to steam round to the north to carry out a series of searching sweeps in the Denmark Strait, between Iceland and Greenland. Weather conditions here were so atrocious that often there was nothing for it but to order 'In sweeps' and run for shelter. On one such occasion, in thick, blinding snow driven by a north-easterly gale, I had had little chance to fix our position for several hours. 'Well, where do you think we are?' asked the Old Man. I could only suggest steering south-eastward until I could get a fix.

I estimated that the nearest shelter would be Isafjord – if we could get there! With the rest of the flotilla wallowing astern of us, we headed blindly towards that fearsome, iron-bound north-west coast of Iceland, peering intently through binoculars in the hope of seeing something before we hit it. Suddenly, right ahead, I saw looming through the murk, snow-covered horizontal terraces and, by the grace of God, a white light flashing. As we swung round to port parallel to the land, by counting and timing the flashes, I was able to identify it beyond doubt and get a running

15th Minesweeping Flotilla leaving Seydisfjord to continue work off-shore, 1942.

fix. Though by this time it was dark, I reckoned we could make Isafjord for the night and we pressed on into the teeth of the gale. Eventually we got a lee and the appalling motion of those stubby little ships subsided. We were inside the mouth of Isafjord. With the moon rising and visibility improving, I reckoned that our best shelter would be in one of the north-easterly arms called Hesteyrifjord. Drawing on our experience at Laxford, we made a perfect approach in formation and, shortly before midnight, anchored the flotilla in complete calm. As we rang off engines and prepared to turn in, a boat came alongside with a message for me from the Captain of *Lyme Regis*: 'Congratulations, Pilot – but which fjord are we in?'

For our next series of searching sweeps we were based at Hvalfjord, where we arrived in late December. It was immensely satisfying to me to realise the use to which *Challenger*'s 1940 survey had been put and to see the large number of warships now moored there.

We had quite a happy little Wardroom and I developed a close friendship with our Gunnery Control Officer ('Guns'). He was an R.N.V.R. Lieutenant called Stephen Pyke, in private life a solicitor. He was a congenial character, as was Sub-Lieutenant Griffin R.N.V.R. The latter was horribly prone to seasickness but, to my great admiration, would never allow himself to succumb to it and would always bring a bucket up to the bridge when he was Officer of the Watch.

A few days after Christmas the whole flotilla sailed home. Up to this point nearly all my navigation had been of a coastal nature and, except for our passage up from Scotland in the autumn, I had had little occasion to practise any astro-navigation. This, however, was to be a longer passage, which lent itself to routine sun-sights and star-sights, in which all the ships participated. As we approached Scotland, conditions deteriorated and I was anxious about our landfall. That night, however, I managed to get a good fix from the moon and one planet. Since there is no means of checking a fix based on only two position lines, it has, of course, to be treated with considerable reserve. Three P.L.s are regarded as the minimum on which one can rely. Notwithstanding this, I felt pretty confident of my sights, and anyway, that night nothing else was visible. So I laid off a course from that fix direct for Skerryvore. Sure enough, in the small hours we sighted it fine on the starboard bow. There could be no mistaking the flashing light, bright and clear and about twenty miles off. My spirits soared. I felt a great sense of achievement, not only on that score, but over the fact that I had succeeded in navigating the flotilla safely in all sorts of conditions throughout the year. My morale and self-confidence were sky-high.

We berthed at Greenock on the Clyde and took leave in two watches. I was to take second leave and most of the others had already pushed off when a pleasant-looking, dark-haired Lieutenant came aboard. 'Hall? Good morning, my name's Lyne – Geoffrey Lyne,' he said, 'I'm your relief.' 'I don't want to be relieved – what's all this about?' I asked, genuinely puzzled. 'Let's go for a walk and I'll explain,' he replied, and we drifted off together along the dockyard wall. He had an extraordinary story to tell.

CHAPTER IX

Combined Operations, 1943-4

I LISTENED WITH AMAZEMENT to the tale that Lyne told me. The previous autumn, a month or two before the Allies invaded Vichy-held Algeria, he and a military colleague had been taken by submarine to a pre-arranged spot just off the Algerian coast. From here, under cover of darkness, they had paddled ashore in a collapsible canoe, their purpose being to reconnoitre and gather intelligence concerning the composition and gradients of the beaches, the exits from them, and details of their fortification. After completing their night's work, they were to return to a previously planned rendezvous with the submarine, which had meanwhile remained submerged on the sea-bed.

During the night a gale blew up and on their return passage they were blown too far off course to make the rendezvous. By daybreak the submarine had had to withdraw and their canoe had been swamped, leaving them drifting helpless and in danger of drowning. Picked up by a fishing trawler, they were taken to Algiers, where they were promptly arrested. They tried to pass themselves off as ditched aircrew, but though they had managed to discard all documents and incriminating evidence, the Vichy-French authorities remained suspicious. Possessing, as they did, detailed knowledge of the invasion plans, they were, of course, greatly at risk from intensive interrogation and possibly even of torture. Eventually they were freed from their cells by the Allied invasion force in the brilliant operation code-named 'Torch', which was the first amphibious assault of the War and forerunner of the Second Front. How easily the capture of our two young officers might have doomed it to failure!

'Well,' concluded Lyne, 'that's why I'm relieving you and returning to General Service. In a way we're doing a swap, because you're required to take my place in Combined Ops.' When I protested that I didn't want to be relieved, he reminded me that some time before, when I had been itching to become more directly involved in the war, I had responded to a call for 'Volunteers for Hazardous Service'. Though I had subsequently forgotten this, my then C.O. had evidently forwarded my application and this was the result!

Hoist with my own petard, and though sorry to give up a job in which I had been happy and had had some success, the only course open to me was to obey orders and report to Combined Operations Headquarters in London. Here I was to ask for a Lieutenant-Commander N.C. Wilmott, D.S.O., R.N., who would brief me on what lay in store.

Nigel Wilmott was a remarkable man. He had been Fleet Navigating Officer under Admiral Sir Andrew Cunningham, The Commander-in-Chief, Mediterranean Fleet. At a time when tentative plans were under discussion for an assault on the Italian-held island of Rhodes, Wilmott had persuaded the C-in-C to allow him to swim ashore by night from a submarine and explore the gradients and composition of the beaches on which the attackers would have to land. The information he gained proved of crucial importance and the success of this venture led to a recognition of the obvious value of such reconnaissance operations. Drawing on his own experience, Wilmott obtained permission to train up other units to perform similar functions. This led to the creation of small, highly specialised, clandestine reconnaissance units known as COPPs. (The initials stood for Combined Operations Pilotage Parties, which reflected their secondary role. Their primary one was Beach Reconnaissance, but any reference to that in their abbreviated title would have compromised security).

Wilmott was appointed to set up and command a COPP Training Establishment at Sandy Point, Hayling Island, in Chichester Harbour. He had selected me to be trained as Senior Officer of one of the first COPPs to go through the course, telling me first to take three weeks' leave and then to report to his Base in the Yacht Club buildings at Sandy Point.

By the time we assembled at Hayling Island, Wilmott had got together a small staff of instructors, both naval and army officers, each of whom had had operational experience in the type of work we were to be trained for. He had also acquired an impressive array of special equipment, much of which he had developed himself: waterproof swim-suits, collapsible canoes (folbots) designed to go through the torpedo hatch of a submarine, infra-red homing devices, under-water writing tablets, pocket lead-lines, beach-measuring lines, waterproof watches, night-reading compasses, explosives, revolvers, stilettos and 'blood-chits'. The Yacht Club itself had been converted into a workmanlike school with classrooms, 2-berth cabins, store-rooms, galley, mess-rooms etc. Wilmott ran a pretty 'taut ship', with few formalities and just sufficient discipline for a highly motivated group of trainees.

Three new COPPs were to be formed, Nos. 5, 6 and 7, and I was to be Senior Officer (S/COPP) of No.7. Each COPP had a total strength of eight: the S/COPP or C.O., a naval officer as principal assistant (A/COPP), an army officer of the Royal Engineers (E/COPP), a naval officer for administration, store-keeping and maintenance (M/COPP), and a junior naval officer to help the M/COPP, (AM/COPP). Two naval ratings and one R.E. soldier were added for general duties, canoe-paddling etc.

My A/COPP was Lieutenant J.D.R. McLean R.N.V.R. who, I noticed, was wearing the Croix de Guerre. From our first meeting we seemed to take to one another easily and naturally and after a time he suggested that we should use our Christian names. For reasons of good order and discipline I felt that this would amount to over-familiarity, and then discovered that his Christian name, though pronounced 'Rory', was spelt 'Ruari'. 'Good Lord!' I exclaimed, and left it at that. Nevertheless, Ruari was destined to have a profound influence on my life thereafter.

Officers of COPP7:
Left to right: Norman Jennings, Ruari McLean, the author and Bill Lucas, 1943.

My E/COPP, Captain Bill Lucas, R.E., was an intense and dedicated young man with a slight stammer. An overt Christian, he was nevertheless fearless, resolute, filled with zeal in a righteous cause and endowed with a nice sense of humour.

Norman Jennings, my M/COPP, was very different. Rather older than the rest, he had been a Savile Row tailor in civilian life. He had a pleasant, easy-going personality, was conscientious and meticulous in his duties, and had no heroic ambitions whatever. His assistant (AM/COPP), Midshipman Peter Gimson, was a rotund, genial and rather cheeky youth, with bags of 'go'. All in all we made a promising team with a keen and willing spirit.

We were classed as Commandos and since much of our training was on Commando lines, and since we wore a modified form of the Commando uniform, we felt ourselves to be members of that prestigious Corps. We learnt the virtues of stealth and surprise, the skills of self-sufficiency and survival, the techniques of under-cover sabotage, and how to kill an enemy in silence – with our hands, with a piece of wire, or with a dagger.

Most of our training at Sandy Point, however, was in nocturnal canoe work, in the course of which, incidentally, we strengthened our arm muscles by much paddling. The canoes, made of canvas and wood, would normally be paddled by two men, the officer who was to swim ashore and an assistant paddler to take charge of the canoe during his absence. We would make prolonged trips both in harbour and out in the open sea, swimming to beaches, measuring their gradients and testing their varying compositions, and also practising the infra-red homing technique. We became fairly expert at drawing views of the land at night from the sea, as it would be seen by officers or coxswains of landing craft approaching the coast and needing guidance from landmarks to reach a particular beach.

In the course of our training we made two visits to Western Scotland, one for general 'toughening up', the other for training with a submarine. We practised the complete operation cycle we would have to use, bringing up the two canoes through the torpedo hatch, launching them with their occupants from the for'ard hydroplanes, submerging for several hours while they were away on their missions, re-surfacing with a low profile at the pre-arranged time, and homing the canoes back with an infra-red transmitter.

It was while we were in Scotland that Ruari McLean returned from a short spell of leave with the news that he had become engaged. He asked me to be his best man and after some initial hesitation I agreed, influenced in this, I must admit, by a photograph of the bride's sister, whom I considered far more attractive than the bride herself, and who was to be the chief bridesmaid.

In June I was informed that COPP 7 was to be used in the Mediterranean prior to the long-awaited 'Second Front', and plans were drawn up and arrangements made for our journey to North Africa. We were due to sail from Liverpool and, by coincidence, Mary Carlisle, the girl who was to be chief bridesmaid at the forthcoming wedding, was working there as a Wren. To Ruari's and my frustration, however, we were prevented, for security reasons, from seeing her and all I could do was to write to her about the wedding arrangements, leaving the letter to be posted ashore after our departure.

This was the time when the invasion of Sicily was imminent and we were actually sent to North Africa in the hope that we might play our part in this. However, on arrival in North Africa, we found that no one was expecting us or had any plans to use us. After reporting this to COPP Headquarters, I received a reply to my signal saying simply: 'Proceed to India'.

This was a surprise but at the same time an exciting challenge. I had to use my own initiative in planning what was a major transfer of personnel and equipment to a completely different theatre of war, and one in which no COPP party had operated before. However, with the help of the Staff Officer (Movements), we were able to 'hitch a lift' on the battleship H.M.S. *Barham* as far as Alexandria. The only event of significance on the voyage was a highly embarrassing episode in which one of my sailors accidentally shot one of *Barham*'s senior ratings. He had been practising loading and unloading his revolver when it went off, striking a Chief Petty Officer in the buttocks. *Barham*'s Commander was naturally furious – as were we – and there was a certain coolness until we had disembarked at Alexandria.

Our COPP party encamped on the outskirts of the city while Bill Lucas and myself went ahead to India by plane to arrange where we were to be based. After some initial difficulty, we made contact with Admiral Miles, the Senior Officer, 'Force C' in Old Delhi. 'He,' we were told, 'is responsible for fighting the Japanese.' Until we arrived, however, he had been confined to planning for our eventual invasion of Japanese-held territories. He had had no operational personnel at his disposal.

The idea of reconnoitring beaches in advance of an invasion had hitherto hardly occurred to Admiral Miles and his staff, but once they understood what we could do, they embraced us with enthusiasm, giving us all the encouragement and support that we could wish for. They invited me to select a suitable base from which to train and operate and allowed Bill Lucas and me to comb through the charts of India's east coast. Eventually we fixed upon a place called Coconada, about a hundred miles south-west of

Vizagapatam and some three hundred miles north of Madras. From the details on the chart we considered it promising and resolved to take a closer look at it. On arrival we found that the only two European residents were the Port Officer and the Bank Manager, but both proved eager to help. The port and harbour facilities were to our liking and we were offered the exclusive use of a large warehouse for our stores and equipment. The Bank Manager then offered to let to us a large and quite palatial two-storey bungalow set in its own spacious grounds and with outbuildings. This was to be our residence and headquarters.

By about the end of August our whole party, together with a mountain of equipment, had joined us, and from then on we entered upon a period of intensive night exercises along the coast, simulating as far as possible the conditions we would be likely to encounter in real operations.

In October we were given our first real assignment and Bill and I were summoned to Delhi for briefing. The plan was for an amphibious assault on the island of Akyab and we were required to reconnoitre the beaches, their gradients, exits and defences, and then prepare view-sketches of their off-shore aspects. Several miles out, and guarding the seaward approaches to Akyab, was a small islet (with a disused lighthouse) called Oyster Island and it was vital to establish whether or not it was held by the Japanese. This, then, was to be our first objective.

We chose a moonless period for the operation and, since conditions off the Burmese coast were unsuitable for submarines, we secured the use of an M.L. as our 'carrier' in conjunction with one of our own L.C.Ps. The M.L. joined us at Coconada and proceeded to Calcutta to liaise with Force 136, a secret and somewhat eccentric organization, which nevertheless did all they could to help us and provided us with valuable information as to conditions on the Burma coast and enemy dispositions in the Akyab area. They also supplied us with a crate of carrier pigeons and, on our departure, pressed into our hands a bottle of pills inscribed: 'Instantaneous Death Tablets: To be Taken with Discretion'!

Next evening, as the light was fading, we pushed on southward, with the L.C.P. in tow, to Oyster Island. My plan was to carry out a 'reconnaissance-in-force' with half a dozen of our party creeping forward across the islet in extended line abreast. I impressed on each man the importance of moving forward together and preserving the line. It was a starlit night and we could just see the man next to us. We were to open fire without hesitation on any person encountered during the advance. I was in the centre of the line and controlling the pace of our sweep, which was slow and deliberate. We stopped at frequent intervals to accustom our eyes to the darkness and to take in the low grassy features ahead, any one of which might be concealing a Japanese defensive patrol.

At one stop, about half-way across, I was sure I saw a movement about ten yards ahead and to my left. I froze and stared hard in that direction. There was certainly something there. It looked like a man's head. Was it staring at me or was that my imagination? All was silent – and motionless. 'It must be a Jap soldier,' I thought. I cocked my revolver. I had never killed anyone in my life and my heart was thumping in my chest as slowly and silently I took aim. 'Better safe than sorry,' I thought to myself as my finger curled round the trigger. Then suddenly the dark shape turned and slowly faced me. It was a white face without a cap. 'My God!' I hissed, 'You bloody idiot!' Such was my fury and the sudden relief of pent-up tension within me that I was actually shaking. I had recognised my red-haired Leading Seaman, who had been positioned on my left. He had gone well ahead of our line abreast and had been within a split second of being shot. In a loud whisper I gave him the fiercest tongue-lashing of his life. Had I shot him, I dread to think what the consequences would have been for myself and for the entire operation.

We continued the sweep and found nothing. Oyster Island was unoccupied. Returning to our canoes, we paddled back to the M.L. Our first night's work had been a positive success – but oh how nearly it had ended in ghastly catastrophe!

The following night we moved in upon the beaches of Akyab. We took the ship, completely darkened, to within about two miles of the shore and launched our two canoes. Ruari and I were in the first and our task was to do the beach-work. The second was manned by Bill Lucas and his R.E. paddler. He was to investigate the exits and defences. It was a calm night with only starlight to guide us, and as we came within a cable or so of the beach, Bill and I slithered into the water and started swimming steadily towards it, trailing clouds of blue-green shark repellent as we did so. Meanwhile Ruari and the sapper paddled their canoes out another cable or two and anchored them well outside visibility distance from the shore. There they settled down to wait for us.

We arrived on the beach without incident and checked our waterproof watches against one another before inching away on our separate reconnaissance tasks. Mine was to measure four gradient lines, spaced about 30 yards apart. I was equipped with two lines, a distance-line, with spike attached, to measure distances from land to sea and a lead-line to measure depths. I would drive the spike into the coarse sand of the beach and then crawl backwards into the surf unwinding the distance-line as I went. Then at a measured ten yards I would lower my lead-line and measure the depth of water, check the time from my illuminated wrist-watch, and write down my findings on the special white tablet strapped to my arm. Once through the surf, I would swim on my back, unreeling the line until I felt two knots marking the twenty-yard distance. Then I would take a further sounding with my lead-line, and so on. I would then swim back inshore, move the spike some 30 yards further along the beach, and repeat the whole process for my next gradient line.

Quite apart from the ever-present possibility of being discovered by Japs, throughout the whole time-consuming process I had to be constantly on the alert for sharks or possible landmines, and all the time I was being battered relentlessly by the surf. I had completed several lines and was taking a final sounding in deep water when I became aware that my lead-line had entangled itself both round my legs and round my distance-line, preventing me from swimming properly. As I kicked to keep my head above water, I became more and more entangled and found myself, despite all my efforts, gradually being dragged under. In desperation I switched on my water-proof torch and held it above my head, sweeping its blue light out to sea in the direction of the canoes. Finally I sank beneath the surface and lost consciousness. I was all but drowning.

The next thing I knew was that I was being hauled across the canvas fore-part of Ruari's canoe, coughing, retching and 'bellowing like a water-buffalo giving birth' (to use his description!), as I sought to expel gallons of salt water from my lungs. Ruari had seen my blue torch flash and paddled towards its last sighting. Finding no sign of me, he had noticed a bluish glow under water and had realised that it was my torch still attached to my belt and still shining beneath the surface. He had grabbed me by whatever he could lay hold of and hauled me out. It was a very close shave. Another minute and I would have 'had it'.

A further night's work was needed, so the following night we crept back to continue the operation, except that this time Ruari would be doing the swimming and gradient work while I did the paddling. Bill Lucas, as the only R.E. officer, would again have to work on the defences and exits. Apart from an R.A.F. air-raid on Akyab itself, all went as planned, though we were far from pleased to see enemy searchlights and flares, which seemed to light up the whole landscape and made us feel horribly exposed. Afterwards, with no sign of the M.L. at the R/V, we had to fall back on our own L.C.P. Heading north till daybreak, I then closed the land (risking enemy occupation) to make faster progress through sheltered channels along the coast. At full speed all day, we managed to reach base at Chittagong just before nightfall.

That autumn two more COPPs joined us at Coconada, so that by the end of the year we had become quite an establishment. About the end of December a long signal in cypher arrived which I asked Ruari to help me to de-cypher. It proved to be a eulogy on our recent operations and conduct and went on to congratulate Naval Party 735 'on the award of the Distinguished Service Cross to Lieutenant J.D.R. McLean, R.N.V.R. (delight and surprise on both our faces and more than a touch of envy on mine!) . . . and to . . . (we had to de-cypher each word separately) Lieutenant G.P.D. Hall, R.N. . . . (euphoria now on both sides) . . . for courage and determination during clandestine operations in the Far East.' We could hardly believe it! It was fantastic, incredible, marvellous. That evening we had quite a celebration as the whole establishment rejoiced with us.

One aspect of our training which had been largely ignored, and about which we felt increasingly concerned after the Akyab episode, was that of Jungle Warfare: the ability to move, fight and survive in the tropical rain forests of South East Asia. Had we been marooned or stranded on one of those Burmese beaches, our chances of getting back would have been minimal. We therefore embarked on an intensive programme of exercises in the thickest Indian jungles we could find. On the first of these exercises we very nearly lost ourselves completely, only finding our way back to base by discarding compass-work and following topographical features such as valleys, rivers and streams.

On the second exercise we travelled in our own convoy of trucks and lorries to a spot somewhere in central India. We were armed to the teeth with rifles, sten-guns and explosives (with a view to bagging big game), but we had hardly commenced when I suddenly fell ill with what proved to be a severe bout of jaundice. I can just remember handing over command to Bill Lucas before being bundled into the back of a truck and removed from the scene.

By this time (early 1944) Lord Louis Mountbatten had been appointed Supreme Allied Commander, South East Asia, and had established his H.Q. at New Delhi. From here he moved his headquarters to Ceylon and as part of the general move, I received orders to transfer the whole of our establishment there and to select a suitable base for it as soon as practicable. It was agreed with the Staff at Delhi that I should look for a base that would be suitable not only for our own COPP establishment, but for a considerably larger force of Army and Royal Marine Commandos.

I had now an urgent need to get to Ceylon and for this I would need a Priority Air Movement Order from the Transport Authority. Anything less would have meant hanging around for days on end. We decided to 'pull a fast one' on the Transport people. We rang them up and told them that a Priority Movement Order was required for Captain Lucas and Lieutenant Hall, Royal Navy – 'and this is Captain Lucas speaking'. Captains, R.N. were pretty thin on the ground in India, and the response was predictable. 'Yes, sir – of course, sir. We'll have the papers round to you this evening.' The 'ploy' had worked and, true to their word, the Movement Order reached us at our hotel soon afterwards. We had been accorded the highest priority in the book! Next morning when we arrived at the airfield, we found that a Brigadier, no less, and his A.D.C. were having to wait for a later plane while we boarded one that was just departing. We had supplanted them and they looked livid. I must admit to feeling both smug and rather guilty!

We had already decided, from a close study of Admiralty charts, where we should concentrate our reconnaissance, and after a visit to the Staff of the Commander-in-Chief, Eastern Fleet, we were granted all that we needed for our immediate purpose. We then departed for the Kayts Peninsula, the north-western tip of Ceylon, which we had already fixed upon as the most promising location.

The charts had shown a wide stretch of sheltered water, backed by an extensive area of flat, grassy, palm-studded land with an off-lying fort joined to it by a causeway. That is exactly what we found. Hammenhiel Fort had been built by the Portuguese in the 16th century, had later been taken over by the Dutch, and had subsequently been allowed to fall into a state of dilapidation. But it was a stronghold and it was empty. Apart from the low causeway, which could be guarded, it was accessible only by sea, and it seemed a perfect storehouse for all the high-security equipment, arms and explosives which an expanded Commando Training Base would require. Moreover the flat grassy acres fronting on to long white sandy beaches looked absolutely ideal for a large encampment – or for the construction of more permanent buildings. The off-lying islets and the expanses of sheltered water were just what we needed for training and exercises with canoes and swimmers. We had found what we wanted and had no need to look further.

We returned to Colombo to report and to start making arrangements for the Big Move. At this point, however, I was waylaid by the Flag Lieutenant. 'Ah, Hall,' he said, 'I missed you when you were down here before. The Admiral wants to see you and has told me to produce you dead or alive!' 'Good God!' I thought, 'What the hell have I done now?' 'It's about one of your Progress Reports, I think', continued 'Flags', 'You'd better wait here and I'll find out when he can see you.' I was told to return at 3 pm and spent a pretty apprehensive lunch hour.

At the appointed hour I was ushered in to Admiral Sommervell's presence. He held open a file containing a Progress Report I had written the previous January, addressed to the Commander-in-Chief, Eastern Fleet, from the Commanding Officer, Naval Party 735. In it I had deplored the lack of operational activity in recent months and the consequent over-training and stagnation of the COPP parties, leading to a decline in morale. I had rounded off the report in these words: 'In my opinion the situation is far from satisfactory. This opinion is shared by all my officers.'

Admiral Sommervell looked at me and said: 'That is not the sort of thing a junior officer ought to say to his Commander-in-Chief . . . However, I understand your sense of frustration – and I take note of your zeal . . . But think twice before you give vent to your feelings in official reports.' 'Yes, sir – I'm sorry, sir,' I replied, turning to leave. 'As a matter of fact,' continued the Admiral, 'I did exactly the same thing myself when I was a lieutenant – and got reprimanded for it. But it didn't do me any lasting harm.' He gave me a warm smile as I withdrew, greatly relieved.

I had first written to Mary Carlisle from the troop-ship in Liverpool, way back in June. She had replied warmly and light-heartedly and since then we had carried on a very pleasant correspondence.

By late March or April all our people had moved down from Coconada and set up the new camp at Hammenhiel. There we were joined by several more COPPS straight out from England, one of which was commanded by Denis Mackay. Each COPP was more or less autonomous and had its own little camp-precinct in the shade of the coconut and toddy palms and close to the beach. As the hot weather built up, we became increasingly informal in our dress, often being attired only in sandals and a native 'lungyi'. From time to time, however, formalities were imposed to prevent any slide from discipline.

We began a further stint of Jungle Warfare training, with an ambitious and protracted exercise in Eastern Ceylon along the banks of the Mahwheli Ganga River. I remember an occasion when three of us had bivouacked in the open air near the river bank, lying on a carpet of dead leaves. In the middle of the night I suddenly awoke from a dream in which a slow train was steadily bearing down on us ('chuff-chuff-chuff'). Raising myself on my elbow, I observed a great black shape lumbering towards me through the forest. I froze. It was a huge buffalo, head down and swinging from side to side as it shuffled its way towards the river. I lay immobile as the beast's right horn passed inches from me, and when dawn came, I measured the distance between me and its hoof tracks: just three feet!

On another occasion, while Bill Lucas and I were carrying out an evasion exercise on one of the long east-coast beaches at night, our canoe (which we'd hidden in the bushes) was discovered by some of the Tamil natives. They alerted the nearby village, and before long scores of natives, armed with sticks and accompanied by dogs, were sweeping along the foreshore, chanting, shouting and banging drums or tin cans – enough noise to awaken the dead. The din spread to other villages further along, and out came more bands of searchers, scouring the beach for tell-tale footprints. Bill and I lay up in a dense thicket some way behind the beach-head, fervently hoping to escape detection. In their present mood, there was no knowing what these marauding bands would do if they found us. Would they accept our 'bona fides', or jump to the conclusion that we were enemy agents in disguise? The exercise had become extremely realistic – in fact too realistic for comfort – and we were genuinely alarmed. Some of the searchers passed very close to us – fortunately without dogs – but gradually the hubbub faded into the distance and we breathed more easily. We lay up under those bushes all the following day and at nightfall, when all was quiet, we made our way stealthily back to where we'd hidden the canoe. It was still there, surrounded by hundreds of footprints. Maybe they thought it was booby-trapped. It hadn't been touched. We got it back into the sea and paddled away into the night. It had been a really useful exercise.

It was about mid-summer that the Small Operations Group (S.O.G.) arrived at Hammenhiel under the command of Brigadier Tollemache. From then on everything changed. Gone were the COPPs' autonomous lifestyles, their informal attire and their camaraderie-based discipline. No longer did each Naval Party have its Commanding Officer (with direct access to the C-in-C). Instead the C.O.s were re-styled 'Officer-in-Charge', and reported to the Brigadier. Though this was obviously sensible, it nevertheless caused considerable resentment and not a little friction. I personally felt somewhat humiliated – having myself selected the base and built it up into a going concern – at having to revert to a relatively junior status and start paying homage to a 'parvenu pongo', however exalted. Nevertheless we settled down eventually, and fairly amicably.

Meanwhile the base had been considerably expanded. We now had units of the Special Boats Section (S.B.S), a clandestine military organisation specialising in under-cover sabotage, as well as a contingent of Royal Marine Commandos. Many more army tents had been erected, and the Brigadier now decided that a semi-permanent Officers' Mess should be constructed, complete with bar facilities. This turned out to be quite an asset in enabling the officers of the various different units and services to get to know one another.

It was during this time, and while listening to a favourite piece of classical music played on my gramophone, that I threw caution to the winds and sitting in my tent by the light of a hurricane-lantern, wrote a letter that was to change my life. I proposed to Mary Carlisle. It was some time later (on 'D'-Day, I think), while we were on a jungle exercise in central Ceylon, that I received a telegram – brought to us by a courier – which said one word: 'Yes'. I was engaged! I was in the seventh heaven, albeit in the middle of the jungle, and I don't think I took too much further interest in that exercise.

With the opening of the long-awaited Second Front by the Allied invasion of Europe through Normandy, things began to start moving again in South East Asia. The planners in Kandy had conceived the idea of invading the Dutch East Indies (now Indonesia) with an amphibious assault on the northern tip of Sumatra. COPP7 was required to reconnoitre the landing beaches there. We were briefed in detail by the Staff, and ordered to join H.M. Submarine *Tudor* in Trincomalee. We took four canoes and the usual mountain of special equipment, and somehow managed to squeeze ourselves into the narrow confines of the already crowded submarine. *Tudor's* Captain was a Lieutenant-Commander 'Sam' Porter and her First Lieutenant was a delightful man called Gordon Tait (whose paths I was to cross in later life). *Tudor* had a dual mission on this three-week patrol. She was to attack enemy shipping, and she was to facilitate the operations of COPP7. The former task would require her to patrol submerged along the Malayan coast and sink any vessel encountered – on the assumption that she was trading on behalf of the Japanese. The latter task would require her to remain for several days and nights, during a moonless period, off northern Sumatra. It took us about five days to cross the Bay of Bengal, running submerged by day and on the surface by night. When we got to the patrol area, there was very little traffic to be seen, though we spotted the occasional Japanese aircraft.

On one occasion, however, we observed a large motorized junk heading north along the coast. Sam Porter decided to sink her by gunfire. We surfaced, manned the gun on the fore casing, and closed the range. We opened fire on the junk, pumping shell after shell into her until she was ablaze, and then submerged. I then watched through the periscope as the junk slowly capsized and her crew (or what remained of them) threw themselves into the sea.

Sam Porter took a last long look at the sinking junk, ordered 'Down periscope', then turned to me and said: 'I feel like a bloody murderer.' I saw his point and sympathized. Every now and again we were forced to go deep due to sighting enemy aircraft, and on one occasion we became the object of an A/S search by a Japanese warship. We went down and sat on the bottom, switching off all machinery and fans to maintain complete silence. We stayed there for hours, waiting to be depth-charged, and in fact we could hear depth-charges exploding, but they were not very close.

The day came when we were to start the COPP operation. We approached the northern tip of Sumatra in daylight, running submerged at periscope depth. This gave me the opportunity to make a quick view-sketch of the land features as they would appear to an approaching invasion force. As we crept in towards the coast at slow speed, our 'asdic' started detecting contacts ahead – small ones, apparently, and Sam Porter ordered it to switch over to the Short Transmission Unit (S.T.U) and sweep down both sides. More small contacts were then detected, both ahead and abeam. A minefield! Sam looked anxious and ordered 'Stop both'. Then he looked at me and said: 'Are you married?' 'No', I replied. 'Well I f***ing well am', retorted Sam, 'Full astern together!'

After that little setback we waited till nightfall and then approached again on the surface. Conditions remained almost perfect. There was enough light from the stars to pick out the dark rising land to port, and the outline of the off-lying islands to starboard. *Tudor* stopped engines and slid silently in to a mile or two from the Sumatran coast, while we man-handled the canoes up through the torpedo-hatch and on to the for'ard casing. We got away without (as sometimes happened) capsizing a canoe, and paddled our way stealthily in to the white sandy beaches. The sea was calm and there was not much surf to worry about. We anchored the two canoes a safe distance outside the surf, and Alec Colson (an R.E. Captain from COPP8, standing in for Bill Lucas who was ill) and I swam in to carry out our well-rehearsed tasks. All went according to plan, and about three hours later, tired and soaked to the skin but pleased with ourselves, we paddled out towards the pre-arranged R/V position. We had now been equipped with a new homing-device, colloquially known as a 'bongle'. I dipped it into the water beside the canoe and started turning the handle (it was rather like an egg-whisk). This set up an under-water noise which could easily be detected by the submarine's 'asdic' as she lay waiting for us on the sea bed. Her 'asdic' would give her an accurate bearing of the 'bongle' transmissions, and she would then move up to periscope-depth and home in towards the canoes, surfacing as soon as she saw them.

All went entirely according to plan (as far as I remember, there were no hitches whatever) and the following night we repeated the whole process on another sector of the beach. This time Ruari and I exchanged roles, while Alec again did a second stint behind the beach-head. Everything went so smoothly, and we acquired so much data, that these two nights' work, coupled with another day's periscope observations, actually completed the entire operation. We retired gratefully to our camp-beds in the submarine's passage-ways and slept the clock round. Though we hadn't sunk much in the way of enemy shipping, the COPP operation had been an unqualified success, and *Tudor* felt that her patrol had been eminently worthwhile. For our part in it, we were 'Mentioned-in-Despatches'.

Not long after the Sumatra operation, we had word from COPP 'HQ' at Hayling Island that our party, the first in the field in the Far East, was to be withdrawn by the end of the year. This was welcome news indeed. Mary had written to say that she was thinking of getting herself appointed to Ceylon, and I now had visions of us passing each other on the high seas, going in opposite directions. So I lost no time in giving her the news and asking her to stay where she was.

As COPP7 was to be disbanded on return to U.K., and we were all to revert to General Service, I wrote to the Naval Assistant to the 2nd. Sea Lord (N.A.2.S.L.) to raise the matter of my next appointment. After almost two years in Combined Ops., I felt distinctly rusty as a Navigating Officer, and I certainly didn't fancy another hydrographic appointment. In fact, I told N.A.2.S.L. that the only thing I really felt qualified for was a sea-going command! (I knew that several of my contemporaries were already commanding corvettes, frigates and destroyers, so I comforted myself with the thought that I was not really being as brazen and presumptuous as might appear). In due course N.A.2.S.L. replied to my letter, offering me command of a Fleet Minesweeper. This was not at all what I had in mind (having already served two stints in minesweepers), so I took my courage in both hands and wrote back to say so, adding that what I felt best suited for was a 'blue water' job. A corvette or frigate would do me nicely, I thought. I received no reply to that letter, which was hardly surprising, so there the matter rested for the time being.

CHAPTER X

My First Command,
H.M.S. *Bigbury Bay*, 1945-7

AFTER AN UNEVENTFUL voyage home (apart from a few U-Boat scares as we entered the Atlantic), we berthed in Liverpool and made arrangements to entrain for Havant. I rang up my fiancée, whom I had never met, and had a pleasant chat with her. She was now a Third Officer, WRNS, serving as a Staff Officer at Portland. We agreed to meet 'on neutral ground' at 'The Antelope' at Dorchester as soon as I had wound up my COPP duties at Hayling Island and had obtained some well-earned leave.

Arriving at the hotel about twenty minutes early, I was in the middle of a quick shave, and had just walked down to the reception desk in my shirt-sleeves to ask for a towel, when in walked Mary. We embraced and I apologized for my appearance. It was our first meeting and we had much to talk about. We got on rather well together and I was very happy. Mary had a few days' leave before returning to Portland, so the next week-end we met in London and travelled down to Louth. I had previously wired my parents to expect me – 'with my fiancée'. It had come as a complete surprise to them – they had had no idea that I was engaged, and asked for more information, which I at once gave them. Once at my family home at Legbourne, we got on famously. I knew that they would adore the girl and they did.

The next major event was Ruari McLean's wedding to Mary's sister Antonia, announced two years previously. I was best man and took the opportunity to make myself known to Mary's parents and formally to ask Dr. Carlisle for the hand of his daughter Mary, which, after quizzing me closely, he gracefully conceded.

Soon after these events, I went to see N.A.2.S.L. in Queen Anne's Mansions about my next appointment. I was in some trepidation, having heard nothing since the letter I had written him from Ceylon about two months previously. 'Aha! So you're the man who turned down command of a Fleet Minesweeper!' were the ominous words with which he greeted me. Then, to my astonishment, he said he understood I was thinking of getting married. 'So how would a building job suit you? We have one of the new

Bay-class A.A. frigates building up at Aberdeen – *Bigbury Bay*, not a very attractive name, I'm afraid, but we'll need the C.O. to stand by her from April onwards. Meanwhile you can fill in the next couple of months with a round of refresher courses, and you'd better 'make your number' on Commodore, Contract-built Ships in Newcastle, as you'll be borne on his books. How'll all that suit you?' Of course it suited me perfectly. I'd been hoping for command of a corvette – and a frigate, a brand new one at that, had hardly entered my dreams.

One of the courses I was doing was a gunnery course at Greenwich. While I was there, the V2 rockets from Peenemunde were falling intermittently around us as the gunnery course proceeded. Some fell quite close to us and we interrupted one session by going out to view the devastation caused by a 'near miss' on the Naval College.

Mary was still at Portland, and together we gradually worked out the arrangements for our own wedding. It was decided that it should take place on Easter Sunday, 1945 at Mary's home at Heswall. Bryan O'Neill was to be my best man and it was to be very much a naval wedding, with a naval Guard of Honour. The whole ceremony went off perfectly and that evening we set off on a brief honeymoon in the Lake District.

On our return I went to call on the Commodore, Contract-Built Ships at Newcastle to be briefed on my functions and duties in this unfamiliar appointment.

Soon after this I went up to Aberdeen, where I was to take up my appointment to H.M.S. *Bigbury Bay*, then being built in the docks. A few days later, Mary (still a serving Wren Officer) came up on leave from Portland and we found ourselves suitable 'digs' nearby. That first evening, we took a stroll round the docks to have a look at my new ship. We could hardly have missed her. Among the crowded fishing trawlers and drifters moored up to the walls, she towered above their masts like a veritable whale amongst the minnows. Even in her partially constructed and unpainted state, she was an impressive sight. As we gazed at her slightly awe-struck, Mary turned to me and said: 'Isn't she a bit big for you, darling?' (A remark I was never to forget!)

While the War in Europe was drawing to a swift conclusion, the Pacific War was still raging with great ferocity, as the Americans steadily closed in on the Japanese homeland, with mounting casualties on both sides. It was now largely an amphibious war, with Allied naval power permitting the land forces to occupy island after island in the face of intense opposition from enemy garrisons, and with the American and British Fleets subject to murderous attack by the Japanese 'kamikaze' aircraft.

Bigbury Bay – *the author's first command, 1945.*

The new 'Bay-Class' frigates (of which mine was one) had been designed specifically for the Pacific War, in which the British Pacific Fleet, under Admiral Fraser, was now participating alongside the American Fleet. The emphasis in these new frigates had been shifted from an anti-submarine role to an anti-aircraft role (with the 'kamikaze' threat particularly in mind). Though fully equipped with the usual A/S armament, they had a much more powerful array of close- and medium-range A.A. guns, and a more sophisticated Fire Control system, than the earlier 'Loch-Class' frigates.

While the construction and outfitting of *Bigbury Bay* slowly proceeded in Aberdeen during April, May and June 1945, I was joined by a gradual trickle of key officers and senior ratings, whose supervisory functions in their own developing departments of the ship became steadily more important. Meanwhile I was kept busy drawing up 'Captain's Standing Orders', 'Captain's Permanent and Temporary Memoranda' and other organizational directives, while at the same time deliberately delegating as much as possible to my new officers, to whom I assigned their special duties in the ship. A running organization slowly developed, as the ship herself approached completion. Meanwhile the War against Japan increased in ferocity and was edging slowly towards its climax. The overall aim was an amphibious invasion of Japan itself, and we secretly feared that we might be too late for it!

The day came for our first sea-trials. Handling the ship for the first time was a test for me – and also a test for most of the crew. It was blowing hard, and I made a hash of turning the ship round in the basin – without tugs – damaging the wharf in the process. We learnt a lot of lessons in this brief escapade: control and handling of the berthing-wires was far from efficient, but the lesson I took to heart was the need to take seamanlike precautions against my own over-confidence. I ought to have accepted tugs – at least to stand by. When we did get away, the ship handled beautifully and I was 'over the moon'. But during speed trials off-shore one propeller-shaft overheated and we had to close down that engine. I had sufficient confidence in myself, however, to steam the ship back into port on one engine despite the adverse weather, and having berthed her carefully and without assistance, I was able to put the earlier incident out of my mind, knowing that I had also restored the crew's confidence in their Captain.

We commissioned about the end of June – with all due ceremony. I had suffered agonies in preparing my address to the ship's company assembled en masse on the ship's quarterdeck, with the White Ensign now flying proudly behind them. I had a complement of about 160, including 10 officers, all of whom, except the Warrant Engineer Officer and myself, were reservists, and I felt that it was important to strike the right note at the outset. In the event my speech went down quite well and I was pleased with the way the whole ceremony had gone.

We were well into July by the time we finally left Aberdeen, with all tests and inspections satisfactorily completed and the ship, freshly painted, a going concern at last. We headed north through the treacherous Pentland Firth and round to the Minches. We were due to join the Commodore, Western Isles, for a fortnight's 'Work-up' at Tobermory, and I had arranged to arrive off the entrance to the loch at 0800 next morning. The Commodore, widely known as 'Monkey' Stephenson, was a retired Rear Admiral who had been called back for the specific purpose of putting newly commissioned small ships through their paces, sorting out their troubles, and working them up to an acceptable pitch of efficiency before letting them loose on the Fleet. His reputation was formidable.

We were called up by the Signal Station as soon as we hove in sight, and were ordered to berth at 'B' buoy inside the almost enclosed loch. There was a strong off-shore wind blowing as we prepared wires, cables and sea-boat for coming to a buoy, a manoeuvre we had not previously tried. As we entered the loch, we saw that it was crowded with other frigates and corvettes, all lying to their moorings head to wind, and leaving quite a narrow passage down to 'B' buoy, which was close to the far shore. There was practically no room to manoeuvre if we failed to pick up the buoy. We approached it at dead slow speed, towing the sea-boat with the 'buoy-jumper' from our starboard bow, and stopped a few yards from it. The worst happened. The 'buoy-jumper' failed to secure the picking-up strop through the buoy-ring, the ship's head started paying off to port in the strong head-wind, and there was nothing for it but to turn the ship on her engines, steam out of the loch, and start the whole manoeuvre again. We came in the second time, stopped dead alongside the buoy, but again they failed to pick it up. This time the ship's head started paying off to starboard, and the buoy disappeared under the ship!

Out we went once more, turned the ship in a wide circle, and crept back into the loch at dead slow speed, determined this time that nothing should go wrong. As I stared ahead, lining the ship up precisely on the approach course, I became aware of a small, scruffily dressed figure standing beside me on the bridge. 'Everything all right, Captain?' it asked – quite gently. I spared it a quick glance and realised, to my astonishment, that it was none other than the Commodore himself! He had apparently sneaked alongside in his pinnace as we entered the loch for the third time, and unobserved, had leapt over our guard-rail and walked straight up to the bridge. It was quite a habit of his, I was told later. Anyway, despite the fact that his presence at my elbow did nothing to improve my confidence or concentration, on this third occasion we were successful – thank God! – and when safely shackled on, and engines rung off, the little man, in his barely recognizable salt-stained uniform, took me aside and, in the nicest possible way, gave me some very helpful advice on ship-handling, which has stayed with me to this day.

'Monkey' Stephenson, the Commodore, Western Isles, was a curious mixture of steely ruthlessness and genial compassion. He could be a 'holy terror' one moment, and the soul of good humour and kindness the next. He and his highly competent staff went through every ship with a small-toothed comb, identifying weaknesses of organization, equipment, personnel, morale – and command. Several C.O.s, First Lieutenants and other key officers had been told to pack their bags and go – and, at times, the Commodore had incurred the wrath of Their Lordships when suddenly faced with his demand for immediate replacement of an officer when no such replacement was available. The Commodore had become almost a law unto himself, and few cared to contest his will. But, my goodness, he certainly licked those ships into shape – and sent them out to do battle! It is no exaggeration to say that no single person contributed more to the successful outcome of the Battle of the Atlantic than did Commodore 'Monkey' Stephenson.

It was a nerve-wracking, frenetic and strenuous fortnight for us at

Tobermory. Orders, counter-orders, directives, signal criticisms, 'blasts' and congratulations came thick and fast – at all hours of the day and night – and there was no rest for anyone from start to finish. Every conceivable 'alarm and excursion' was exercised – and repeated 'ad nauseam' till the Staff were satisfied with the efficacy of our response – and, as the ship's efficiency improved, so did our morale.

I remember one occasion when I was summoned to dine with the Commodore aboard the *Western Isles*. It happened to be an evening when I had arranged to take Mary out somewhere (we had found 'digs' for her in a cottage nearby), so I regretfully declined the invitation on those grounds. Apparently it was 'not done' to decline the Commodore's invitations – they were in the nature of a Royal Command – and I was immediately sent for. Full of apprehension that I was going to be reprimanded for having my wife in the port, I mounted his gangway and was 'piped aboard' with full ceremony, saluting smartly as I faced him. He took me by the arm and walked me along the deck saying: 'I had no idea your wife was in Tobermory. Why didn't you tell me? You must arrange to bring her to dine with me some time.' He then proceeded to give me a long lecture on a man's duties towards his wife!

It was a beautiful day in early August, and we were carrying out main armament gunnery practices among the off-shore islands near Staffa, steaming up and down the range in a flat calm, and having a good look at Fingal's Cave as we turned. We were in the middle of a rather crucial shoot, and I was conning the ship from the Compass Platform, when I was called up on the voice-pipe from the T.S. down below: 'Captain, sir, news has just come through that we've dropped a new kind of bomb on a place called Hiroshima, and it's killed 50,000 people, and Japan is on the point of surrender. Are we to continue the shoot?' A great cheer went up as the news spread, and I found it hardly credible. How on earth could one bomb kill 50,000 people? Anyway, I replied, 'Carry on with the shoot', and we did. *Bigbury Bay* was ordered round to Portsmouth to adjust complement and grant leave prior to sailing for the Far East. It was while we were at Portsmouth that the War finally ended – and VJ-Day (marking victory over Japan) was officially announced. Mary and I were staying at the 'Keppel's Head' hotel on the Hard, and I remember feeling an appalling sense of anti-climax. We had been single-mindedly fighting the War for the past six years, and now, suddenly, we'd lost all sense of purpose. Adjustment to 'peace' was going to be a difficult process, and I doubt if I was the only one who felt unable to put my whole heart into the Victory Celebrations.

I still had another year or so to do as a Lieutenant, but in September

Their Lordships decided that officers in command of Bay-class frigates should hold the rank, and receive the pay, of Lieutenant-Commanders. It was a reasonable decision, as the ships were large enough to warrant the higher rank, and it placed their Captains a step above their own officers, many of whom were Lieutenants. Officers promoted under this scheme were known technically as Quasi-Acting Lieutenant-Commanders, but we made light of that and simply shipped our half-stripes.

I received orders to sail for the Far East in company with another Bay-class frigate, H.M.S. *Whitesand Bay*, which, as senior officer, I was to take under my wing for the passage to Colombo. *Whitesand Bay* was commanded by a man called Brian Longbottom. He was a pleasant chap and we got on quite well together. Leaving Portsmouth was a rather sad business for all of us, partly because we had little idea how long we were to be away (perhaps a full two years), and partly because, in my case, I was leaving behind my newly-wed wife.

We sailed via Gibraltar, Malta and the Suez Canal. Having a sister ship in company made a lot of difference. Apart from continuous station-keeping in different formations, we were able to practise all sorts of competitive manoeuvres and evolutions, as well as plenty of visual signalling. We also frequently compared notes on internal administrative problems. Being the Senior Officer gave me very much the upper hand in all this, and on the whole I really enjoyed my first experience in command of a formation of H.M. ships at sea.

From Singapore we sailed on to Manila in the Philippines (or what was left of it after the Japanese occupation – which wasn't much). The Japs were still holding out on Corregidor when we passed it, apparently not having heard that the War was over.

At Manila I received orders to take two minesweepers under my wing and escort them to Hong Kong to join the British Pacific Fleet. Halfway across the South China Sea we ran into a typhoon and got separated. For several days we battled against enormous head seas, and due to low cloud and poor visibility, we were unable to get a fix of any sort. When within a hundred miles or so of Hong Kong, I asked the Wireless Station there to give me a D/F bearing, and eventually obtained one, though of low quality. Using that, we managed to make a landfall, and, considerably the worse for wear after weathering the typhoon, finally crept into the shelter of the main harbour. I had orders to place myself under the command of the Captain, Escort Forces, and immediately went over to call on him.

Captain Aubrey John St. Clair Ford was a delightful man and gave me a warm welcome. He and his staff could not have been more helpful, and they very soon made a thorough inspection of the ship and ironed out many of the problems that had developed during our long voyage. Among other things, they discovered that one of the main steel structural beams that ran through the engine-room deck-head had cracked due to the stresses generated by the typhoon. This was regarded as a very serious matter, and for some days the whole future of the ship was in doubt. However, Christmas was now upon us, the first peaceful Christmas for seven years, and action was deferred. It was a really joyous Christmas throughout the Fleet – and throughout the Colony – and it was really heartening to see the Royal Navy in strength amid the beautiful hills and islands of Hong Kong, once more a British possession. Moreover, despite the havoc and pillage wrought by the Japanese through their four-year occupation, the bustling colony still had many delights to offer the war-weary sailors of the B.P.F. – and we made the most of them.

Meanwhile *Bigbury Bay* was busily integrating herself into the Escort Forces organization, taking over local patrol duties and acting as 'Duty Destroyer', while playing her full part in the Fleet's activities in and around the colony. Early in the New Year, however, there was a great shaking of heads among the senior technical officers of the Fleet about what was to be done with us, and whether, in fact, the ship was worth repairing and refitting, or whether it would be better to pay her off and sell her for use as a ferry between Hong Kong and Macao. These rumblings caused us great distress and a noticeable lowering of morale. I felt strongly that the ship was basically sound, and I knew that I had an efficient and enthusiastic ship's company. I was not going to let all that we had done during the previous nine months come to nothing if I could help it.

I paraded the ship's company on the jetty alongside the ship (now freshly painted and looking her best) and told them what was in the wind and what I felt about it. I then asked them to indicate, by a show of hands, whether they supported me in resisting the termination of the commission. Almost all of them did so. I then sent a signal to the Commander-in-Chief (Admiral Sir Bruce Fraser) asking if I might call on him. I had already put a strong case in writing through 'the usual channels', and the C-in-C demurred. However, I was determined to see him, and I tried again. This time he agreed to see me and I went over to the flagship (H.M.S. *Duke of York*) dressed in 'full fig', with sword and medals. He received me quite affably and said: 'You're a very persistent young man, aren't you?' I then stated my case with some vehemence, and told the Admiral that the whole ship's company was aghast at the prospect of paying-off and that we had not come all this way out to join him in order to be broken up and dispersed before we had achieved anything. I finished by asking him to come over personally, with his staff, to inspect the ship and her company and judge for himself what a fine ship he had.

About a week later we received a full and thorough inspection by the Commander-in-Chief. We were fully prepared for it, the ship's company was smartly turned out, the officers cheerful and alert, and the ship herself 'spick and span'. It was a great success and Bruce Fraser was impressed. Afterwards he and his Staff Officers came down to the Wardroom for drinks, and he was quite charming. I remember discussing with him the significance of the atomic bomb and the world-wide concern that was being voiced about the 'morality' of its use – and even its existence. It was something I found difficult to understand. How could one distinguish the ethics of killing 50,000 people with one atomic bomb from the ethics of killing a similar number with high explosive bombs dropped from a thousand aircraft? 'Surely,' I said, 'it's just a bigger and better bang?' Sir Bruce thought for a moment and then replied, 'I rather think there's more to it than that.'

Anyway, my initiative in going 'straight to the top' paid off. We were reprieved. It was arranged that *Bigbury Bay* should be taken in hand by the Taikoo Dockyard, to remedy the poor workmanship of Hall Russel's ship-building work-force, particularly in regard to the many welding defects that had come to light, and which reflected so badly on the Admiralty Ship Overseer at Aberdeen.

The Taikoo Dockyard, situated on the north-east side of Hong Kong Island, was unique in possessing enormous slipways which could accommodate sizeable ships. Instead of placing them in a dry-dock (as was normal practice), it employed huge winches and cables to haul them up the slipways on wheeled cradles. It was a most uncanny experience to stand on the ship's bridge, slowly tilting upwards, and watch the ship being steadily hauled out of the water and on to dry land.

By the middle of February all repair work had been completed and a period of sea-trials and exercises followed, with the Captain, Escort Force, embarked, and with *Whitesand Bay* once more in company. Having satisfied all the authorities that *Bigbury Bay* was once again fully operational, I received orders to proceed to Taku in North China to embark a large number of Allied internees who were awaiting repatriation from formerly Japanese-occupied territory. In the Formosa Strait we encountered a Chinese merchant-ship, crammed with passengers, that had broken down and was drifting. As she was apparently bound for Formosa (Taiwan), we took her in tow, and in the middle of the night, entering the port of Keelung unnoticed and unobserved, left her there. I reported the incident to the Senior Officer, Force 'S' (who was flying his flag in H.M.S. *Swiftsure* at Shanghai), and received, rather to my surprise, a congratulatory signal from him.

Shanghai was quite an eye-opener for us. The Whangpoo River was crammed with American warships, completely outnumbering the handful of British warships which were also present. Whereas we had seen to it that the Americans took a back seat in Hong Kong (where all the central berths were reserved for our ships, while U.S. ships were moored well out of the way), the Americans were determined to assert their strength over ours in Shanghai, where their writ clearly ran. However, the two Navies maintained quite friendly relations, and there was plenty to be enjoyed ashore. I fell in with some very hospitable White Russians (there was a whole 'colony' of them in Shanghai), who taught me a thing or two about vodka and how it should be drunk.

Having been fully briefed by S.O. Force 'S' (under whose orders I was now operating), we sailed northward through the Yellow Sea, into the Gulf of Pohai. and across the bar off Taku, where we had to wait for the tide. Once over the bar, we headed for an American naval support ship which was lying at the wharf, and aboard which the 70 internees were assembled. As we drew alongside her, and the Americans were taking our lines, I overheard the following exchange between one of their young sailors and one of our 3-badge ABs:

American sailor (pointing at our man's chest): 'Say, what are all the hero-bars?'

British sailor (coiling up his heaving-line): 'I got those before you joined!'

American: 'You Limeys – you're all alike – full of hot air!'

Briton: 'That's all right – it takes an Englishman to be a Limey. Any bastard can be a Yank!'

(Incidentally, was it not at Taku that an eminent person first remarked that blood is thicker than water?)

Most of our ex-internee passengers were women and children, though about twenty of them were male civilians. They had obviously had a pretty thin time under the Japs during the previous four years, and were clearly delighted to find themselves at last under the White Ensign. All our officers gave up their cabins to the women and children, and the Wardroom became theirs for the voyage. I moved up to my sea-cabin under the bridge. During the night, halfway down the Yellow Sea, we ran into fog. We could get no fix of any sort, 'Loran A' was not operating, our radar was 'on the blink', and even our echo-sounder was giving trouble. Moreover, our charts of the Yellow Sea (which had never been properly surveyed, though apparently pretty featureless) were far from informative. So I was reluctant to press on with our plan to make a dawn landfall on the islands fringing the approaches to Shanghai.

During the Middle Watch I stopped the ship every half-hour and took a sounding with the hand lead-and-line, and only when satisfied that this was vaguely compatible with the charted depths, was I willing to move on. We were therefore well astern of schedule when the fog lifted and we were able to discern the outline of the islands ahead. However, we got into Shanghai eventually by steaming flat out up the Whangpoo River (which rather upset the Americans), and disembarked our 70-odd passengers to await repatriation.

One evening in March, when the ship was on Escort Duty in the Yellow Sea, I was having dinner in my cabin when my trusted Coxswain (Leading Seaman Hoskins), who was serving the meal, came in and said: 'Congratulations, sir!' as he deposited a signal on my table. I picked it up and read: 'Virginia Anne born March 18. Mother and daughter both well.' What marvellous news that was! I was both relieved and delighted. I had suddenly become a father – a sobering thought indeed. There was not a great deal I could do about it at that distance, of course (apart from writing euphoric letters to my loved ones), but when we got down to Sydney, I bought my little daughter a large stuffed Koala bear ('Billy Blue Gum'), which I sent home to her.

For the next month or so (March/April) we were employed escorting merchant ships against piracy and mines up and down the coast. On one occasion, while escorting a ship up to Tientsin, our young Sub-Lieutenant suddenly fell ill. He was a robust young man, hale and hearty, and very popular – the ship's Sports Officer. Our Medical Officer, unable to diagnose the trouble, ordered him to turn in. Next morning he was worse, and the M.O. said he should enter hospital and that it was urgent. I ordered the second boiler to be connected and raised steam for full speed, heading into the Gulf of Pohai. I sent a Plain Language signal to the Russian authorities at Port Arthur (the nearest port) asking for permission to land an emergency hospital case, and reported the situation to S.O. Force 'S', at the same time abandoning the merchant ship.

I got no reply from Port Arthur, but very soon received a signal from S.O. Force 'S' ordering me on no account to enter Port Arthur without further instructions from him. Meanwhile the M.O. asked me to come down and have a look at his patient, as he was extremely worried. I did so and, to my astonishment, realized that he was dead. I could hardly believe it – nor could anyone else – but there was no doubt at all. I slowed the ship down, reported what had happened, and proposed that the deceased, Sub-Lt. Williams, R.N.V.R., should be buried at sea. This was approved and we immediately started making preparations for the funeral ceremony. I dug out my Prayer Book for the funeral service. That same evening we cleared lower deck, lined up a Guard of Honour, placed the corpse in its weighted hammock, covered with a Union Jack on a hinged platform by the quarterdeck guard-rails, and performed the ceremony, committing our erstwhile shipmate to the deep. As the Salute was fired, very few of us were not in tears.

It was a traumatic experience, the first and only time in all the years I spent in command of H.M. ships, that I ever conducted a Burial at Sea. But that was the straightforward part. The aftermath was not. When something of that sort happens, affecting all of us quite deeply, commonsense tends to rule one's actions. My first thought was to break the news, as gently and sympathetically as I could, to the young man's parents. I spent a long time composing the letter. The First Lieutenant was concerned to muster and list the deceased's personal effects. The Medical Officer was concerned to fumigate the cabin and prevent an outbreak of an unknown disease. The Supply Officer was worried about the deceased's Permanent Loan list, and the recovery of valuable items. The Wardroom Mess Treasurer was concerned about outstanding Mess bills and wine bills. There was a host of minor – even trivial – administrative matters to put straight, and we put them straight.

One thing that did not cross our minds at the time was the need to refer to King's Regulations and Admiralty Instructions, or to the tomes of Admiralty Fleet Orders stacked away in the Ship's Office book-shelves. This was unfortunate, because, as we found out later, the actions and procedures decreed in the many chapters, articles, sections and sub-sections in these volumes, following a death at sea, have nothing whatever to do with commonsense. This omission earned me some very stuffy signals and letters from the Flagship.

We returned to Hong Kong and spent the month of May patrolling round the islands on anti-smuggling and anti-piracy duty, taking our turn at Emergency and Guard Duty, and participating in the many local Fleet and Escort Force activities ashore and afloat. As summer approached and the weather warmed up, the Fleet began to disperse to other parts. *Bigbury Bay* had been in commission a full year, and it was decided that she needed a break in a 'white' country. To our delight, we were ordered to sail for Australia, to spend several weeks of relaxation, recreation and recuperation at Sydney.

We sailed in June and threaded our way south-eastward through the Philippine and Indonesian Islands and into the Coral Sea. Here, a couple of years earlier, had been fought one of the most decisive naval battles of all time, between the American and Japanese fleets. It was a sea/air battle of tremendous importance, in which the Japanese were defeated and their sea-power virtually destroyed, marking a turning-point in the Pacific war. To reach Sydney by the shortest route, we had to penetrate the Great Barrier Reef and navigate through the myriad intricate channels between the reef itself and the whole length of the Queensland coast. Normally a pilot would be embarked for this part of the passage, a compulsory requirement for all but H.M. ships, which were exempt and free to choose for themselves. The Admiralty charts, which I had carefully studied beforehand, were extremely good, and the Sailing Directions clear, so I decided that we would do without a pilot, navigate the ship ourselves, and then claim the Pilotage Fee (which eventually amounted to over £100).

It was an unforgettable experience and a fascinating one. My Navigating Officer (Lieutenant Rowell, R.N.V.R) and I remained on the bridge continuously, day and night, throughout the passage. The charts were on a fairly large scale, so that we moved from one to the next quite quickly, and it was essential to keep the ship's position continuously plotted on them, since the channels between the reefs were often intricate. My technique was to take frequent gyro-compass bearings, singing out each bearing to Rowell as I took it, while he plotted the fix, and to repeat the process as soon as I'd seen the fix on the chart. Thus I was able to con the ship accurately along the recommended track through the reefs (which were marked here and there by beacons, buoys and transit-marks) and into the relatively open waters inside the Barrier Reef itself.

Thus we continued our way south along the Queensland coast to Townsville, which we put into to re-fuel, grant leave and to give ourselves a bit of a rest. I slept like a log for about 12 hours and did not go ashore.

We reached Sydney early in July and were given a big welcome. I think we gave 10 days' leave to each watch, and plenty of hospitality was extended to us by the Australians, both privately and and by various organizations. Before granting leave, I cleared Lower Deck and addressed the ship's company on the Quarter Deck, giving them the scheduled sailing-date and outlining our further programme. Because there had always been a high rate of absenteeism (and even desertion) from H.M. ships in Australia, I was at pains to stress the penalties involved, and the fact that I would be in no mood to accept excuses from anyone who over-stayed his leave or missed the ship on sailing.

I decided to take leave myself towards the end of the period, and to go up to the Snowy Mountains for a winter sports holiday. I went to the Hotel Kosciusko, most of the way by train. I found some good skiing and plenty of congenial company, so I was soon enjoying myself.

I met two very nice New Zealanders, Bill and Jan Williams (cousins, apparently, of my old friend, Denis Mackay), who persuaded me that an even better time was to be had at 'The Chalet', some considerable distance higher up the mountain. A day or two later several of us set off to climb the track leading to the Chalet, complete with our skis and luggage, in an enclosed sled drawn by a caterpillar tractor. About halfway up the track we got caught in a blizzard which completely obscured the track and built up huge snowdrifts, in which the tractor became buried and stuck. We had to leave it there and complete the journey on skis.

Skiing from the Chalet was certainly better than from the Hotel, but the accommodation and fare were relatively austere and the social life rather less promising. In the sunny periods between heavy snowfalls and blizzards, however, we did get some excellent downhill runs, though I must say I found the stunted blue gums a very poor substitute for Alpine pine-trees.

I had arranged to get back to Sydney the evening before we were due to sail, but I had not bargained for the blizzard which struck us towards the end of our stay, and which raged for three days. All communication was cut off. We couldn't get to the hotel, and the bus couldn't run from the hotel to the railhead. Time was running out. We decided to make a dash for it – on skis. We had to leave our luggage behind, packed locked and labelled.

In view of what I had told my ship's company about overstaying their leave, it was a matter of real urgency for me to get back to the ship next morning, as I had arranged to sail from Sydney at 0900. My companions were not so pressed, but they entered into the spirit of the thing and provided welcome encouragement. The railway station was fifteen miles away and we had to catch the evening train. Carrying what we could in rucksacks on our backs, we skiied the whole distance through the snow, and though it was mostly downhill (and sometimes quite fast), it was an exhausting journey. I rang the ship from the railway station and told the First Lieutenant to have the ship's jeep at the Sydney terminal at 0830 next morning to meet my train. Fortunately it was on time, and we sped through the streets to the dockside, where the ship was singling up her wires in readiness to cast off. I climbed over the guard-rails at 0850, dashed up to my cabin, changed into uniform, and reached the bridge with two minutes in hand. The jeep had been hoisted inboard and we sailed exactly on schedule. (Whew!)

We took the northern route round Australia, up the Queensland coast and through the tricky Torres Strait, then westward through the Indonesian archipelago to Singapore, arriving at the Naval Base in mid-August. We were due for a three-months refit. It was decided that we should de-store the ship and move the whole ship's company into shore accommodation, a sensible move but one which took time and led to a great deal of disruption. In the process we found that one of our Confidential Books was missing, which concerned me not a little. I happened to mention it to the Captain of a destroyer flotilla with whom I was playing squash one evening, and he jocularly advised me to report that the C.B. had been accidentally lost overboard. When I did report the loss (as I had to), a Board of Inquiry was ordered — and who should be appointed as its President but the Captain (D) himself! He was a delightful man, and I remember his embarrassment when the Board was convened. I can't remember the outcome, but it was assumed that the C.B. had inadvertently been included with others to be destroyed, and I think my C.B. officer was reprimanded.

We emerged from the refit at the end of November, and carried out various sea-trials among the islands in the Singapore Strait. While doing so, I was delighted to catch sight of the R.F.A. Stores Ship from Australia as she headed into port, for on board her was the locked suitcase (containing, amongst other things, my best uniform) which I had left behind at the Kosciusko Chalet in the Snowy Mountains four months before. I was determined not to sail without it, and although it was apparently at the bottom of one of the ship's holds, I sent a boat over with an officer to wait alongside her berth with instructions not to return without the suitcase. This seemed to work, for after a few hours the boat reappeared with my coxswain proudly holding the long-awaited suitcase on high. Thereupon, without more ado, we set sail for Hong Kong, having a rough passage through the South China Sea, but reaching our destination safely early in December.

About a week after we arrived, *Bigbury Bay* was ordered up to Japan to join up with the U.S. Navy and operate under American command. We reached Tokyo in mid-December. The city was still in a shambles, but re-building was going ahead fast. In fact, despite the destruction, it was a hive of activity — and there was plenty of night-time entertainment. My chief interest was the Imperial Palace, which had not been touched, and I drove out there one day to take in the scene and to reflect on the extraordinary events over which the Emperor had presided, and which had had such cataclysmic effects on friend and foe alike.

At this time we were still operating under British command, as part of a task force comprising a cruiser, two sloops and two frigates. Sometimes we would work together and sometimes separately, exercising, patrolling and carrying out guard duties. One day, while *Bigbury Bay* was patrolling off the east coast of Honshu, a Japanese destroyer called us up with a signal lamp and flashed a message which read: 'Igotosasebo'. We asked for a repetition and got the same thing several times. Realizing that this meant little to us, she tried again and flashed: 'May I go to Sasebo?' There was no reason that I knew why she should ask my permission, so I replied: 'Yes, as far as I am concerned'. This clearly stumped the Jap, for she then flashed: 'As far as where, please?' By this time my signalman was almost in stitches, and I thought I'd better conclude the exchange by simply replying: 'Permission granted'.

In late January we were ordered south to Sasebo (in Kyushu) to join an American Task Group operating from Fukuoka. We got a big welcome from the Americans there and it was a novel and interesting experience to find ourselves integrated into a flotilla of their Escort Vessels. Their function was to maintain a continuous anti-smuggling patrol in the Straits of Tsushima, opposite Korea (the scene of the great Japanese naval victory over the Russian Fleet in 1904).

U.S.S. *Mansfield*, a Destroyer-Escort, was our flag-ship for these operations and we used to lie alongside her. Very friendly relations developed between the two ships, and the Americans introduced us to aspects of Japanese social life ashore, including the Tea Ceremony with Geisha girls.

In mid-February I received orders to proceed to Kure to embark 13 Japanese servicemen accused of war crimes (including a Vice-Admiral and a Lieutenant-Colonel) together with their Australian Army guard, and to take them down to Hong Kong to stand trial for their alleged atrocities. I reinforced the Australian guard with an equal number of my own men, and divided the prisoners into two groups (one army and one naval) to occupy the two messes opening on to the ship's quarterdeck. I appointed the Vice-Admiral (Imamura) as 'Leading Hand' of the naval mess and Lieutenant-Colonel (Fukumoto) in charge of the army one.

I had dossiers on all these prisoners, outlining the various charges that were to be brought against them. Vice-Admiral Imamura had been the Japanese Naval Commander-in-Chief at Singapore when the officers of the Japanese cruiser *Tone* had run amok after a Wardroom party at sea and murdered 60 prisoners of war on the quarterdeck. He had also presided over an incident in which Japanese naval ratings had beheaded a number of British naval telegraphists, the alleged culprits in both these atrocities being among my prisoners. Lieutenant-Colonel Fukumoto was accused of responsibility for the massacre of about 500 Chinese civilians at Singapore.

Although these men had not been tried (and must therefore be deemed 'innocent until proved guilty'), we had no doubt in our minds that they had committed the most appalling crimes (the description of the beheading scene on the cruiser's quarterdeck was enough to freeze the blood), yet I could not help feeling sorry for them, particularly the senior officers accused of 'responsibility'. So much so, in fact, that one evening while on passage south, I invited Vice-Admiral Imamura to dine with me. He spoke excellent English and we had a pleasant evening of small talk and reminiscences. He could not have been more courteous. I heard later that the whole lot of them were found guilty and that most of them were hanged.

No sooner had I disembarked the prisoners at Hong Kong, than word reached me that my relief had been appointed. After a few days of local manoeuvres and amphibious exercises, I brought *Bigbury Bay* into harbour for the last time, and a Lieutenant-Commander Hutchinson came aboard to take over from me. It was early in March that my first command came to an end, after two interesting and highly fulfilling years. I had been extremely fortunate to have had such a command at so early an age, and I had thoroughly enjoyed the experience. Most of all, I think, I had revelled in handling the ship, a process from which I derived immense personal satisfaction, particularly as my skill and self-confidence grew.

With the War over and the Navy rapidly contracting to its peacetime level, I knew that my next appointment (if I remained in General Service) would be mundane in comparison – perhaps as First Lieutenant in some Training Establishment – so I had applied to return to the Surveying Service, asking that, if possible, I might be appointed as Navigating Officer of a home-based Surveying Ship. To my relief, and somewhat to my surprise, the Hydrographer agreed to take me back – and even seemed to welcome my return.

I came home in the troopship S.S. *Ranchi*, leaving Hong Kong in mid-March. I had been appointed O.C. Naval Draft, which was a bit of a bore, as I had been hoping for a thoroughly relaxed month at sea. However, there was a young Lieutenant (H) by the name of Hammick, and a competent Chief Petty Officer in the draft, and I was able to delegate most of the routine work to them, while at the same time asserting my rights and privileges as O.C. Naval Draft (which included an upper-deck cabin to myself!). We came home by the usual route, via Singapore, Colombo, Aden and Suez, and reached Southampton on April 14th.

CHAPTER XI

Lieutenant Commander, H.M.S. *Seagull*, 1947-9

W HEN *RANCHI* CAME ALONGSIDE, my wife was waiting for me on the jetty. An order went through the ship that due to the impossibility of opening up the baggage holds so late in the day, no one would disembark until the morrow. I had other ideas, however. Having an upper-deck cabin to myself, I had taken the precaution of having all my gear with me in the cabin – and there was a lot of it. I saw no reason whatever to remain on board overnight – particularly with Mary standing there on the jetty. It was the work of a moment for four of my sailors to hump the stuff ashore and, wishing me the best of British luck, they waved me on my way.

We went to Legbourne for the start of my leave, and there I saw my daughter Virginia, 13 months old, for the first time. It was early May and I was anxious to take Mary away on holiday. Our long-awaited post-War gratuities had just been released, and I spent mine on a delightful and much needed holiday for both of us in Spain.

We spent a further idyllic two months awaiting my next appointment. By this time my ration-cards had expired and I urgently needed to apply for more. Only when I did so did the Admiralty wake up to the fact that I was still on leave. The Assistant Hydrographer (who was in charge of all officers' appointments) ruefully admitted that he had forgotten about me, and straightway appointed me as Navigator to H.M.S. *Seagull*, a home-based Survey Ship.

I joined *Seagull* on the west coast of Scotland in August. I had obtained permission beforehand from the Captain (Commander K. St.B. Collins) to keep a dog on board, and my mother had travelled down to King's Cross to hand over a six-months-old puppy to me, which she had bred herself from her two Cocker Spaniels, Jock and Sally. It was a black and white bitch called Jill. With Jill in tow, I caught the night sleeper from Euston to Glasgow and she slept alongside me throughout the journey. She was the first dog I had ever owned, and once aboard *Seagull*, she became a firm favourite of officers and sailors alike.

From our surveys off the west coast of Scotland we moved south to

Milford Haven. Things had changed in the realms of navigation, and we now had electronic aids to work with – not only radar, but a system called 'QH' (known in the R.A.F. as 'Gee'). I soon got the hang of this and found it extremely useful, We had a very congenial lot in the Wardroom: Bobby Griffiths as No.1, 'Snooze' Berncastle, Richard Green, 'Pay' Goodall, 'Bo' O'Grady and others. Our main survey that autumn was in the Bristol Channel, off the south coast of Wales, after which we moved round to Dartmouth.

During the winter lie-up and refit of 1947-8 Commander 'Kitchie' (Ketchil) Collins was relieved in command of *Seagull* by Commander 'Sid' Hennessey, and I relieved 'Bobby' Griffiths as First Lieutenant. We spent the first part of the season on surveys off the west coast of England and Wales, with occasional visits to Liverpool, Swansea and Portishead, but in the summer we moved round to the east coast and were based at Sheerness. Here I found reasonable 'digs' for the family on the sea-front and at week-ends we would link up with Bryan O'Neill (who was Assistant King's Harbour Master at Sheerness) and his wife, Alison. Collins and Hennessey were both delightful C.O.s and I found it easy to serve as the latter's 'No.1'. It was while doing so that I found myself 'rated up' (rather to my surprise) to Assistant Surveyor 1st. Class. Having so much leeway to make up in the hydrographic field, I hardly felt qualified for this higher status and the responsibilities that went with it.

At the end of November *Seagull* returned again to Devonport for the winter 'lie-up' and refit, and the drawing of Fair Charts. Mary and I had taken a little bungalow, 'Natterne', between Yelverton and Horrobridge and during the working week I used to commute by car between there and Devonport.

As *Seagull's* refit and lie-up at Devonport were drawing to a close, we acquired a new Captain. He was Colin Lowry, a man who lived for surveying. It was he who, as a young Sub-Lieutenant in *Challenger* at Bermuda in 1936, had largely aroused my own interest in the Surveying Service, having shown us midshipmen over the ship and explained some of the mysteries of hydrography to us. *Seagull* was his first command. He sent for me and announced his wish to mess in the Wardroom. 'I like company,' he said, 'and I feel very lonely up here. Is that O.K.?' It was the very last thing I wanted, and I was sure the other officers would feel the same. So I said I would consult them and let him know.

It was extremely embarrassing. One did not wish to offend one's Captain, however insensitive he might be. But his presence in the Wardroom would utterly inhibit the atmosphere of frankness and relaxation which was essential for the happiness of the officers, and hence for the whole ship. We resolved on a compromise, which I could present to the Captain with tact.

When reporting 'Rounds' to him that very evening, I said: 'Sir, the Wardroom would be delighted if you would join them for drinks before dinner on weekdays, and if you would dine in the Mess on Guest Nights.' The Captain saw through this veiled rebuff, but accepted it with reasonably good grace.

Colin Lowry had spent many of his past years as Executive Officer (1st. Lieut.) of Survey Ships, and had developed his own methods of performing most of the standard seamanship operations (laying and weighing beacons and dan-buoys, wreck-sweeping and so on), which, though often complicated, were dealt with straightforwardly in the Admiralty Manuals of Seamanship and of Hydrographic Surveying – based on well-tried procedures that had stood the test of time. Not, myself, being any too familiar with these procedures, I was anxious to try them before attempting any improvements or short-cuts, but the Captain wanted me to move straight to his own pet methods. This (and one or two other disagreements) gave rise to a bit of an altercation between us in the 'Cuddy'.

It was early on in the season, and he said to me (quite good-naturedly): 'Number One, I've had a lot of experience as a First Lieutenant, and I just hope I'm not going to be a bloody nuisance to you.' It was all I could do to restrain myself from responding in similar vein: 'Well, sir, I've had quite a bit of experience myself as a Commanding Officer, and I hope I'm not going to be a bloody nuisance to *you*.'

Unlike 'Kitchie' Collins and 'Sid' Hennessey, his two predecessors, who were competent professionals with a sense of proportion and outside interests, Colin Lowry had no sense of proportion and no outside interests. For him surveying was not so much a profession as an obsession. It was his only topic of conversation and socially, he was a bore. *Seagull* being a 'West Country' ship, we spent the whole of the 1949 season surveying off the west coast, mainly, as far as I can remember, in the Bristol Channel. We encountered all sorts of interesting problems, due to the great range of the tide and the strength of the tidal streams in the upper reaches of the Channel on both the English and Welsh sides. For much of our work we were based at Swansea, and I remember several pleasant weekends spent exploring the delights of the Gower Peninsula.

One afternoon, while we were ship-sounding off the south coast of Wales and I was working aft in the Chartroom, the telephone from the bridge rang and I answered it. It was the Captain. He said: 'Congratulations, Number One, you've got a son!' It was 17th August, and a signal had come through for me from Dr. and Mrs. Carlisle in Heswall to say that Mary had given birth to a baby boy and that both were well. As I was due for a spot of summer leave, I pushed off from Swansea that weekend.

It was about this time that the Hydrographer of the Navy called for volunteers from the ranks of Lieutenant-Commanders (1st Class) for a loan appointment to New Zealand. As the appointment was 'accompanied' (i.e. the New Zealand Government was prepared to pay travel expenses for the family) and as I was clearly eligible for it, I lost no time in volunteering. Apart from the fact that I had never been to New Zealand – and was rather intrigued by the thought of working there, I felt that a two-year overseas assignment would be nice for Mary, who, in all conscience, had so far derived little in the way of 'perks' from her naval marriage. It was therefore with some elation that later in the season I was told that the Hydrographer had selected me for the job.

Early in September, after more than two years in *Seagull*, I turned over my duties as First Lieutenant (to whom I can't remember), and pushed off on a fortnight's pre-embarkation leave.

It was still September when I sailed from Southampton in the Shaw Savill liner, M.S. *Dominion Monarch*. Among other passengers was a Captain Ruck-Keene, R.N., the new Senior Officer, New Zealand Squadron (an appointment carrying the rank of Commodore), who was on his way out to take up the post. I introduced myself and he immediately invited me to sit at his table for meals. I accepted the invitation gracefully and he replied: 'Good – otherwise I shall find myself sitting with a lot of Jews or Plymouth Brethren!' (A back-handed compliment, I felt, and I was later to find that Ruck-Keene prided himself on being the rudest man in the Navy!)

We set course for Las Palmas in the Canary Isles. At breakfast on the first day out Captain Ruck-Keene told me that the previous evening the Captain's steward had come to his cabin with an invitation saying that the Captain would be delighted if Ruck-Keene would join his table after Cape Town. I murmured 'How nice,' or words to that effect. 'And what do you think I replied?' asked Ruck-Keene. 'Well, sir,' I answered, 'I imagine you accepted with gratitude.' 'Certainly not,' replied Ruck-Keene, 'I told the steward to tell the Captain that nothing would give me less pleasure!' It was only after this that I realized that Ruck-Keene had been fuming from the moment he boarded the ship on finding that he, the Commodore-designate of His Majesty's Navy, had not been placed at the Captain's table (the reason being that the Captain, a Plymouth Brother, had filled his table with Plymouth Brethren).

We stopped only briefly at Las Palmas, and then resumed the voyage to

Cape Town. Captain Ruck-Keene continued both to amuse and to astonish me with his outbursts of vituperation and his general cantankerousness, but he was certainly an entertaining character. He seemed to take to me — presumably as the only other naval officer on board, and a relatively junior one at that. I was 'fair game' as a sounding board for his highly robust views on life. He had heard something of Sharpey (my old ship-mate of 1941), the officer who was to command the R.N.Z.N.'s Survey Ship, and wanted to know a good deal more, and I was able to enlighten him. At Cape Town he took me to lunch at the delightful Vineyard Hotel, some way outside the city. It was my first visit to South Africa, but we didn't stay long. We were soon on our way eastward across the Indian Ocean, and my main recollection of that voyage was the constant vibration caused by *Dominion Monarch's* diesel motors.

CHAPTER XII

New Zealand, H.M.N.Z.S. *Lachlan*, 1949-51

W E REACHED FREMANTLE, Western Australia, in mid–October. I had orders to take temporary command of an Australian frigate which had been converted for surveying, and which had been loaned to the Royal New Zealand Navy for that purpose. H.M.A.S. *Lachlan* was basically a River–class A/S frigate, which had most of her guns and anti–submarine armament still in place, her conversion for survey work being pretty superficial. She was still painted grey. After my experience in command of *Bigbury Bay*, I had no qualms whatever about taking command of her and sailing her round to Sydney as instructed. *Lachlan*'s crew was a mixture of Australians and New Zealanders, with the latter predominating. There were six officers, three R.A.N and three R.N.Z.N. They were all Lieutenants: Reg Hardstaff, Ian Mackintosh and 'Sandy' Sanderson from Australia, and Bill Smith, Frank Doole and Brian Bary (our Oceanographer, who joined later) from New Zealand. Our Engineer Officer and Paymaster were also New Zealanders. I took over the command from Reg Hardstaff and reported the fact to the Australian Commonwealth Naval Board and to the New Zealand Naval Board.

There then ensued an exchange of elaborately 'flowery' signals between N.Z.B. and A.C.N.B. to mark the handing over of *Lachlan* from the R.A.N. to the R.N.Z.N., and I was instructed to hoist the New Zealand flag at the jackstaff, in place of the Australian flag, at 0800 next morning. Somewhat to my surprise, I also received instructions from the A.C.N.B. to carry out an extensive off–shore survey in the Rottnest Island area, westward of Fremantle, and an endorsement from N.Z.N.B. to the effect that it was thought entirely appropriate that, on transfer of *Lachlan* from Australia to New Zealand, her first survey should be for the Australians! (I never saw the logic of this).

More to the point, however, was the fact that the ship carried hardly any hydrographic stores, equipment or instruments. These, I understood, were to be embarked 'on loan' from the R.A.N. when we got round to Sydney. We were in something of a quandary, therefore, as to how we were to carry out this first survey off Western Australia. I decided to signal A.C.N.B. (repeated to N.Z.N.B.) that my proposals for implementing their Hydrographic

Instruction would be signalled after due consideration. This evidently 'rang a bell' in the Sydney Hydrographic Office, for shortly afterwards I received a signal from the Australian Hydrographer which said, quite simply: 'Survey is to be based on D.R.'

'My God,' I thought, 'Is this the way they do things out here?' 'D.R.' means 'Dead Reckoning' – and this was the first time I'd ever heard of a hydrographic survey being controlled by so primitive and inaccurate a method. However, there it was and who was I to argue with the Hydrographer R.A.N.? So we settled down to do the job, and we did it 'flat out' at full speed, the whole survey being completed within a week. And, be it said, the result looked remarkably persuasive.

Well, with that behind us, we set off for Sydney. There was a south-westerly gale blowing, so I kept a prudent distance off-shore – which was just as well, because, while we were rounding Cape Leeuwin (the S.W. point of Australia), we had trouble with our boilers and had to stop engines. There we were, about five miles off a dead lee shore, and drifting steadily on to it, broadside on to a heavy sea. Seldom have I seen a more wicked-looking headland, dark and forbidding, studded with rocks, against which the full fury of the Southern Ocean was hurling itself, sending up huge spouts of white spume and spray. Closer and closer we got to it – and still the engineers could not get the boilers functioning. I began to get seriously alarmed and told the 'Chief' that he had half an hour to put things right, after which it would be too late. Another ten minutes, and he came up sweating to report steam back on the engines, and we were off again. It was a pretty close thing, but after that there were no more 'alarms or excursions' and we made an uninterrupted passage eastward through the Bass Strait and round to Sydney.

I berthed the ship (quite expertly) at Garden Island, and there, on the jetty to meet us, was Sharpey, now a Commander. He lost no time in coming aboard, and within the hour I had turned over the command and assumed the role of First Lieutenant. It was to be a memorable experience! (In fact I could write a book about my two years as Sharpey's No.1 – but I won't!)

As soon as we reached Auckland, New Zealand (or rather, the naval dockyard at Devonport), Commander Sharpey got to work on the dockyard authorities, and the ship was taken in hand for 'essential modifications'. She was to be made into a proper Survey Ship as understood by the Royal Navy. No Australian half measures for us! Out went the guns and A/S weapons, a new C.O.'s cabin was constructed for'ard from the 'Hedgehog' compart-ment, and on to 'X' gun-deck went a magnificently spacious Surveying

Chartroom, complete with all modern fittings ('Splendid for entertaining' said Commander Sharpey). The dockyard worked like beavers to make H.M.N.Z.S. *Lachlan* perhaps the most up-to-date Survey Ship anywhere.

All the time the pretence was being kept up that, in accordance with the Terms of Agreement covering the ship's loan to New Zealand, everything could be replaced and the ship returned to her original state within 48 hours!

When all was complete, and the ship had been painted white with buff funnel and masts in traditional style, we sailed for Wellington, the capital, which was to be our main base.

In the middle of Cook Strait (which separates N.Z.'s North Island from South Island) lies a dangerous rock (Cook's Rock?) whose position on the charts was at that time marked 'P.A.', i.e. 'Position Approximate'.

Our very first task in *Lachlan* was to find this rock, measure the least depth of water over it, and fix its position accurately. This was easier said than done, because, apart from the stormy weather frequently prevailing there even in November, a strong current flows through the Strait. Moreover, as the rock lies far out from the land, and the visibility is often low, it was often impossible to pick up the landmarks on either side of the Strait and measure the angles subtended by them with sextants, thereby plotting the rock's real position.

We spent the rest of the year surveying the Eastern approaches to the Cook Strait and the entrance channels to Wellington Harbour, as well as the huge, almost land-locked harbour itself, and came in to berth at Aotea Quay for most week-ends. We had arranged for our families to join us as soon as practicable, and before leaving U.K. had bought ourselves new cars on 'export licences' (thereby avoiding a heavy tax). During December I had arranged the two-year lease of a nice little one-storey house in Karori, one of the rural suburbs of the city up in the hills to the west. By this time our families had already sailed from U.K. and were steaming across the Atlantic and Pacific Oceans to join us.

Meanwhile, by means of meetings, conferences and presentations, Commander Sharpey was tirelessly promoting his own 'image' and at the same time endeavouring – not without success – to keep *Lachlan* in the public eye and place her activities squarely 'on the map'. These efforts included an inordinate amount of work for the surveyors in the Chartroom, even preparing (in 1950) an elaborately 'glossy' ship's Christmas card (incorporating photo-reductions of each of our surveys to date.) Hundreds of these were sent to every important authority Commander Sharpey could think of in N.Z. and U.K. – including Lord Louis Mountbatten!

The great day came on 3rd January when S.S. *Rangitiki* arrived in Wellington from U.K., bringing out our families to join us. I was there on Aotea Quay to meet them, but must have presented a rather sorry sight because I was hobbling about on sticks with my right foot in plaster. (A few days earlier I had stumbled over a 4-cwt. beacon anchor on the fo'c'sle, which had 'tripped' on to my little toe and broken it!). As soon as *Rangitiki* had berthed, I boarded her and greeted my family (including a new 'nanny') with enthusiasm. Jill, our Cocker Spaniel, arrived separately soon afterwards.

Lachlan spent the next three months till Easter surveying both the Cook Strait and the waters off the east coast of South Island. For the former we paid periodic visits to the Marlborough Sounds – particularly Queen Charlotte Sound – on the north coast of South Island, and for the latter work we were based mainly at Dunedin.

In the course of this a traumatic incident occurred while we were surveying the stormy Foveaux Strait in March. For this part of the work *Lachlan* had based herself at Bluff, at the southern extremity of South Island, ideally placed on one side of the Strait which separates South Island from Stewart Island to the southward.

We were recovering beacons – a tricky business at the best of times, but much more so in heavy seas. It calls for a high degree of skill on the part of the officer handling the ship (normally the Captain) and a certain deftness

Lachlan, *Queen Charlotte Sound, New Zealand, 1950.*

from the recovery party on the fo'c'sle. We had come up to a beacon, head to wind and sea at dead slow speed, and the ship was pitching heavily to the high swell driving in from the west, the ship's stem rising and falling 30 to 40 feet. I was in charge of operations on the fo'c'sle, standing more or less 'in the eyes' of the ship, and as close as I could get to the beacon, with its 30-ft. bamboo flagpole surmounted by a radar-reflector. One gets used to the rhythm of the ship's motion, but occasionally it falters and the ship suddenly plunges downwards or soars skywards quite unexpectedly. The trick is to snatch the spring-hook of the picking-up rope on to the loop of the beacon's wire recovery-strop at a moment when ship and beacon are relatively motionless – i.e. when both are in the trough or on the crest of the swell. The moment came – on the crest – and I grabbed the recovery-strop with my left hand to bring it to the spring-hook. Suddenly and unpredictably the beacon shot upwards, wrenching the wire strop from my hand and almost carrying me up with it as the ship's head dropped under my feet. My hand, mercifully, was unharmed, but the gold-crested signet ring had gone from my little finger and my wrist-watch had also vanished. I was fortunate indeed not to have had my arm wrenched out of its socket!

After Easter, Mary and I spent a week's leave exploring up-country. On my return to *Lachlan* we spent the next three months mainly on the Cook Strait Survey, coming in to Wellington for week-ends. Brian Bary had joined as our Oceanographer, with the rank of Lieutenant (Special), R.N.Z.N., and our bathymetric work was thenceforward punctuated with copious oceanographic observations, samples of every kind being catalogued, analysed and retained by scientists ashore.

In July, when well into the southern winter, *Lachlan* moved up to Auckland for her annual refit and lie-up in Devonport Dockyard. After the refit, we resumed surveying in the Cook Strait and along the east coast of South Island. Commander Sharpey's technique for the latter work was to ship-sound parallel to the shore and, as often as not, with one or more sounding-boats keeping station abeam of the ship. This had the great advantage (from Sharpey's point of view) of covering the ground much more rapidly than by the orthodox method of sounding at right-angles to the shore, but was open to much criticism from those of us who knew what we were about. (In fairness to Sharpey, however, it must be said that he was under considerable pressure from the Chamber of Shipping and other authorities to produce charts quickly).

After spending Christmas in Wellington in blissful summery weather, we embarked in the New Year, 1951 on a fresh round of surveys, concentrating once more on South Island waters – in the Foveaux Strait and along the east coast – and we were based at intervals at Bluff, Dunedin, Timaru and Port Chalmers. This coincided with a very kind offer from the parents of my old friend, Denis Mackay, to lend us their home at Tahunanui, near Nelson, for the summer. At this point, therefore, I took a spot of leave and spent a marvellous holiday there.

At one point Mary joined me for a while at Port Lyttleton, where I was based ashore, observing the tides and measuring the strength of the stream in the river-mouth. She took turns at reading the off-shore tide-pole and timing the passage of glass bottles as they flowed down-river to the sea.

At about this time a national 'waterfront' strike had broken out, involving all the ports in New Zealand, and since the country's coal-mines were located in South Island, this meant that the more industrially developed North Island was immediately deprived of its energy source. The Government therefore declared a State of Emergency, and directed the Army and Navy to work the inter-island ports. This measure so incensed the coal-mining unions that they too declared a national strike. The upshot of this, so far as we were concerned, was that *Lachlan* was ordered to suspend her survey work and proceed to Westport (on the west coast of South Island) to take over from another frigate which had been loading coal from trains into colliers, and not only to continue with this work, but to operate the coal-mines as well! In effect we were ordered to break the strike and see that North Island was supplied with the coal that it needed.

This was a challenge indeed – and a novel one at that – and *Lachlan*'s complement of 150 men rose to it splendidly. Much of the coal was excavated from open-cast 'pits' cut into the mountainsides above Westport and Greymouth, and the problem facing us was less of a mining than a transportation one, though all kinds of mechanisms were involved. Most of our engine-room staff were deployed on operating steam and electric winches, some on driving railway engines, and all those with lorry-driving experience on operating bulldozers, mechanical excavators and huge articulated trucks. Many of the seamen were assigned to working complicated conveyor 'ropeways', tipping-trucks, cranes and hoppers, and in building improvised bridges and ramps from which the fleets of trucks could tip their loads, while the ship's electricians and stokers operated the all-important power stations. Practically the whole of the ship's company was deployed ashore every day on these and related tasks, and the ship herself became little more than a dormitory rest-home.

As Executive Officer, it was my job to allocate appropriate manpower on a daily basis to each of the dozen or more tasks with which the ship was contending, at Millerton, Stockton, Downer's, Ngakawau, the 'Burma

Road', the three gravity-ropeway stations, the Westport waterfront, colliery loading, transport-driving etc., and also to provide hot evening meals from the galley and maintain essential communications. I would do this by promulgating, last thing at night, Daily Orders for the morrow. This meant keeping consistent tabs on progress as it developed, and because in these unfamiliar operations casualties were an inevitable – almost daily – occurrence, men had to be changed round and replaced as necessary. Some casualties were serious. One Petty Officer was crushed between coal trucks on the railway, and several were sent to hospital with broken limbs. The P.O. died from his injuries, and we had to lay on a full-scale ceremonial funeral, with firing party etc. On the whole, however, my policy was to keep every fit man 'in the field' and employ the 'walking wounded' on essential ship's duties. The result of this was that after a few weeks there was hardly a single quartermaster, diesel-watchkeeper, galley-hand or signalman on board who was not swathed in bandages or hobbling around on crutches!

As the organizational work fell to me late in the evenings, I was able to spend most days going round in my staff car to observe the different operations and judge the suitability or otherwise of the personnel I had assigned to them. I found this extremely interesting, and was amazed at the sailors' versatility in so quickly mastering so many unfamiliar and often complicated tasks.

I made several visits to the various coal-faces up in the mountains, and in some cases I was intrigued to see that the coal, instead of being cut from the earth, was simply being washed out of it by high-pressure hoses, the resultant flood of coal and water then being sluiced down the mountain side through specially built channels and tunnels. But undoubtedly the most intriguing of all the different systems was the operation of the long Stockton-Ngakawau ropeway, whereby coal excavated by enormous mechanical shovels was transported in chains of tipper-trucks down miles of steep railtracks and through several tunnels, via intermediate changeover points (where they were manhandled), to discharge into huge articulated lorries and thence to the cranes and hoppers on the quayside.

We knew that the rank-and-file of the Miners' Union were far from being enthusiastic about the strike, and were suffering considerable hardship, so I spent one day touring through the mining villages in my staff-car (flying the white ensign), and knocking at the doors of houses telling the miners to go back to work. Most of them were delighted, and said it was the best news they'd had for months. Some asked me whether the Union had sanctioned a return to work, and I replied that my instruction could be interpreted as an Order from the Navy! That was good enough for them. Next day many of them flocked back to the mines. However, it was a short-lived reprieve because when the Union heard what had happened, they lost no time in re-asserting their authority and countermanding my 'Order'. Gradually, under firm Government action, the strike began to peter out and in July, after we'd been at it for three months, our work started to ease off.

It must have been later on in July, when *Lachlan* was back on her east coast surveys between Dunedin and Timaru, that the Commodore, New Zealand Squadron, finally lost patience with our Captain. There had already been disagreements and altercations between Ruck-Keene and Commander Sharpey on a number of issues. The Commodore was an iron disciplinarian, who administered his squadron with a pretty heavy hand, standing no nonsense from anyone. Commander Sharpey, on the other hand, was an improviser, with a certain disregard for orthodoxy and regulations. Discipline was maintained in *Lachlan* on a somewhat 'ad hoc' basis, punishments tending to be fairly light and fairly few. In fact, we had a reasonably happy ship's company, who worked well together and seldom 'kicked over the traces'. The result was that our Quarterly Punishment Report recorded fewer offences than any of the frigates, and lighter punishments than regulations required.

We were steaming along the coast on one of our closely-spaced sounding lines off Timaru one afternoon when we received a signal from C.N.Z.S. stating that our last Punishment Return was unsatisfactory, and ordering our Commanding Officer to present himself in No.1 Dress (sword and medals) on board the flagship with all despatch! I really felt sorry for Commander Sharpey, and went up and told him that he had my full support, and that in my judgement discipline was a means to an end and not an end in itself. This, I suggested, was his obvious defence. He seemed quite moved. We agreed that nothing should be said about the signal to anyone else – but that the Officer of the Watch should simply discontinue sounding and fall out the survey-parties on reaching the northern end of the line we were on. Then we would set course for Auckland. We got there (to the surprise of the ship's company) early in the morning and Commander Sharpey duly presented himself to the Commodore, who (so he told me) 'tore him off a strip'. There was certainly no love lost between those two!

On another occasion we were lying at anchor off Nelson and Commander Sharpey was polishing up his image with the local authorities there, and generally 'doing his P.R.' He had invited the Mayor and five other civic dignitaries to dine with him on board, together with our Medical Officer. (I had been excused from attending due to pressure of work!). The dinner party got under way about 8 p.m. and all seemed to be going well

when, about 9.30, the M.O. emerged and asked me to get the motor-boat
alongside. He said that one of the Captain's guests had been ordered off the
ship! Apparently Commander Sharpey had taken exception to something
this guest had said, a blazing row had ensued, and Commander Sharpey had
stood up at the table and said: 'Sir, I must ask you to leave my ship
immediately.' My recollection is that the other guests were so embarrassed
that the whole lot decided to leave together – and did so. (So much for our
P.R. at Nelson!)

In October, after her annual refit and lie-up, *Lachlan* was back on the
survey grounds, and this time Commander Sharpey handed over command
of the ship – temporarily – to me, to progress a survey off the west coast of
North Island. Why he absented himself I cannot recall (perhaps he was
taking some leave with his family?), but I certainly relished being my own
man once more. However, it was while we were working off South Island
again that we received a signal from U.K. that I was to be relieved at the end
of my two years' Loan Service and was to return home. I was not at all
happy about this as frankly I was rather enjoying life in N.Z. As a matter of
fact I had seriously considered transferring permanently to the R.N.Z.N., a
step which would almost certainly have resulted in my becoming, eventually,
New Zealand's Hydrographer. But Mary had been against it. 'I'm
thoroughly enjoying my time out here, as long as I know we're going home
after two years,' she had said. But we had not yet been out there two years
(though my actual appointment had certainly run that long), and to leave
now would cause domestic problems (interruption of Virginia's school term,
lease of our house and so on), and I asked for an extension.

However, the wheels had been set in motion. My relief (Sam Mercer) was
already on his way out, a qualified navigator (David Watts?) had joined – and
it transpired that I had been earmarked for a command in home waters. I
was ordered to embark for U.K. with the family in November.

At last the great day came when we embarked in S.S. *Monowai* for the
passage across the Tasman Sea to Sydney. In a way we were really quite sorry
to leave New Zealand, but it was exciting too and we got a great send-off
from our friends on the quayside. During the first afternoon, when we were
clear of the land, the ship's motion began to tell on those who had yet to
find their 'sea-legs', which included Mary (who decided to 'take a stretch off
the land'). I took the two children up to the boat-deck, where I thought
they could come to no harm, and settled down to read my book while they
played about. I glanced up from time to time, to check that all was well, and
suddenly sensed that Nick was absent. I then saw him across on the starboard
side, squeezing himself through a gap between the guard-rail and a boat's

davit, right at the ship's side. I flew across the deck, faster than I have ever moved in my life, and reached the child as he stood, right at the very edge of the deck, peering down at the waves some thirty feet below. Without a word I seized him by the collar and drew him back.

It was only then, when the danger had passed, that the full enormity of it swept over me, and I was shaking like a leaf as I led little Nicky to safety. The whole incident had been witnessed by the Officer of the Watch, who happened to be looking aft from the bridge at that moment. As a result, action was taken to have the guard-rails modified to close off these dangerous gaps. It had been a very close thing and a nasty shock, but apart from that the voyage was completed without incident, and on 20th November we duly arrived in Sydney. On 23rd November we all embarked on the great white P & O liner, S.S. *Stratheden* to continue our homeward voyage.

A further episode marred the tranquillity of that voyage. I think it was in the Red Sea that tragedy struck. We had recently made the acquaintance of a pleasant middle-aged English couple, who seemed to have a nice sense of humour. The husband's name was Ramsay and he gave the impression of being something of a 'bon viveur'. We had bade them goodnight after dinner one evening and had ourselves turned in for the night when there was a frantic knocking at our cabin door and shouts of 'Come quickly, Geoffrey, something's happened to Ramsay!' I threw on a dressing-gown and rushed along the corridor to their cabin. On opening the door I saw Ramsay, his face almost black and his eyes staring, immobile. I knew at once that he was dead, and there was absolutely nothing that I could do. So I sped off in search of the ship's doctor and left the rest to him. They buried him at sea a day or two later. His widow was so distraught that she had to be restrained forcibly to prevent her from following him in. We did our best to comfort her during the rest of the voyage, and kept in touch with her for weeks after we got home.

As the year drew to its close, we duly arrived at Tilbury. Waiting to greet us was Mary's mother and also her brother Iain. Then on entering the hotel where we were to stay the night, who should be there to meet me but my mother! It was indeed a happy reunion, and a fitting end to perhaps the most memorable two years of our lives. After all, Mary and the children had sailed round the world (something which I never achieved!).

CHAPTER XIII

Lieutenant Commander (& C.O.), H.M.S. *Franklin*, 1952 and H.M.S. *Scott*, 1953

I HAD BEEN APPOINTED to command H.M.S. *Franklin*, the first surveying ship I ever served in, as Sub-Lieutenant in 1938, when she was brand new. Now, in middle age, she was to be my first surveying command. I joined her at Chatham in February, as she approached the end of her refit and lie-up, taking over from Lt.-Cdr. 'Micky' Royds, who was to be my First Lieutenant.

We were to work out of Sheerness, a dismal place if ever there was one. Our main tasks lay among the shifting sands and important shipping channels of the Thames Estuary, which were in constant need of re-survey and re-charting, and I could see that this work would keep us busy for many months. That being the case, it seemed sensible to look for a home for the family not too far from our base. Eastward of Sheerness, the Isle of Sheppey was not unattractive – in its way, and I spent one or two week-ends exploring and house-hunting. Minster, with its ancient church up on the hill, had its points, and on the edge of the cliffs overlooking the sea stood an empty four-bedroomed house which was for sale.

After discussions with Mary, I borrowed the money and bought the house, which we re-named 'The Cliff House'. I think it was towards the end of March that we moved in, and it remained a pleasant family home for us for the next ten years.

During the spring and early summer *Franklin* spent most of her time in the outer parts of the Thames Estuary, coming in to Sheerness for week-ends. Out in the Estuary, we often had to contend with a good deal of fog, and though we were able to complete the all-important large-scale re-survey of the Edinburgh Channels by visual-fixing methods, I decided that some of the smaller-scale surveys of other channels could be carried out by using the Decca-Navigator system (which was unaffected by fog). It was quite an eerie business, steaming back and forth in thick fog among the sandbanks, our fog-siren blaring away every two minutes, our echo-sounders continuously recording the depths, our radar displaying the movement of other shipping, and the Decca-dials constantly providing the co-ordinates for plotting our position.

Franklin, *Thames Estuary, 1952. (*Seagull *and* Scott *were similar.)*

This was progress indeed – a new experience for us to exploit advancing technology so as to press ahead with a hydrographical survey in totally 'blind' conditions – something which would have been quite unheard of a few years earlier. I was so impressed that I wrote a graphic report on it to the Commander-in-Chief entitled 'An Electronic Survey', on which he congratulated me!

In August I took the ship up to the west coast of Scotland, where we had been given several tasks, including a survey near the notorious whirlpool of Corrievrechan, and another demanding job measuring the tidal streams through the Corran Narrows, at the head of Loch Linnhe. I can no longer remember the particular reasons for these tasks, but they were interesting and taxed our ingenuity. At that time the Hydrographer of the Navy (Vice-Admiral Sir Archibald Day), was 'swanning' round the Outer and Inner Hebrides in another survey ship, H.M.S. *Cook*, commanded by Captain 'Buck' Baker, and he decreed that the two ships should meet one evening in a sheltered loch. *Cook* was already at anchor as I approached in *Franklin*, and I was ordered to berth alongside her. The heels of our big davits projected well beyond the ship's side, and though both ships had plenty of fenders out, I was anxious to berth gently so as not to cause damage. Moreover, with the eyes of the mighty upon me, I was naturally keen to show off my ship-handling skills, and as *Cook* was slowly swinging to her anchor and *Franklin*, with her turbine propulsion, had very poor 'brakes', I came in at dead slow speed and made a near-perfect 'alongside'. All to no avail, however, as shortly afterwards the Hydrographer told me that he thought I had been much too cautious!

Next day we were back on our survey-ground, and the Hydrographer came to watch our tidal-stream operations from the shore. He complimented me on the thoroughness of our organization and announced that he would make a formal visit to my ship on the morrow. I decided that on such an occasion it would be appropriate to hoist a Vice-Admiral's flag at the fore-truck (though in those days it was irregular to do so, since the Hydrographer did not exercise direct command of his ships). Archie Day, as he was piped aboard, saw the flag – but turned a blind eye to it. He was the soul of charm and obviously enjoyed a good gossip – not least about Commander Sharpey (for whom he clearly had no time at all). I was able to reel off a few of the choicer anecdotes about him from my recent experience in New Zealand, and also from our wartime experience in Gambia. From this time onwards it began to dawn on me that 'Droggy' had quite a warm spot for me (which was to have its effects later on).

Our major task in the autumn was to carry out a clearance-sweep, using double-Oropesa, of the waters between Islay and the north coast of Ireland, i.e. the western approaches to the North Channel, to prove a safe depth of 12 fathoms for our submarines transitting submerged between the Atlantic and their bases in the Clyde. We were to be based at Londonderry, and for that we now had available the splendid new chart of Lough Foyle and the River which we had made with so much toil and sweat 11 years before in *Challenger*.

This sweeping operation turned out to be about the most frustrating thing I've ever had to do in my life. The sea-bed in this area is extremely irregular, with numerous rocky outcrops, the tidal streams are swift, and at full flood and full ebb the sea breaks in over-falls where the outcrops occur, and the weather is notoriously fickle. Visibility was seldom adequate for fixing from shore-marks and, to control the sweep, we had to lay floating beacons – which, as often as not, would drag under and disappear in the strong streams. Added to that, with our sweeps set to 12 fathoms, the otters and kite – and sometimes the sweep-wire itself, would frequently snag the rocky bottom, necessitating quick work on the sweep-winches and immediate action on the bridge to stop engines. After a couple of weeks of this sort of thing, we had lost a lot of valuable gear, but we persisted for a full month and lost a lot more. Finally I had to report that the required passage could not be cleared to 12 fathoms (or even, in my view, to 10 fathoms), and to our intense relief, the whole operation was then called off.

We returned to Chatham for the winter. Being a Lincolnshire man, I was interested in the fact that during the War *Franklin* had been 'adopted' by the town of Spilsby, birthplace and home town of Sir John Franklin, the famous Arctic explorer, after whom the ship was named. It occurred to me to suggest to the Town Council of Spilsby that it might be appreciated if the ship's company of *Franklin* were to make an official visit to the town to thank the people of Spilsby for all the support they had given in the form of gift-parcels of winter knitwear etc. to the ship during the War, and that a suitable occasion for this might be Remembrance Day (which, in 1952, fell on November 8th).

Spilsby reacted with enthusiasm, and we set to to make all the necessary arrangements. I appointed one of my more personable officers, Lieutenant Nicholas, as Liaison Officer, and sent him up to Spilsby to work out a mutually acceptable programme with the local authorities, having first obtained clearance from my own authorities to take the ship up to Boston (which was the nearest port) for the occasion.

Several buses were hired to take the ship's company from the dockside to Spilsby, where, in the market-place, they were formed up on parade in No.1 uniform, the officers with swords. Flanked by my officers, I then led the parade in column-of-threes up the street to the church, where rows of pews had been reserved for us. The church was packed, and the Remembrance Day service was conducted with impressive ceremony, I having to say the immortal words of remembrance: 'At the going down of the sun . . .' etc. Afterwards there was a wreath-laying ceremony at the War Memorial (or cenotaph, as they called it) at which I 'did the honours', and then, with band playing, we marched back into the town and took up formation round the statue of Sir John Franklin. There was a goodly crowd of onlookers, some of whom (including my mother and my Aunt Sylvia) had been in the church congregation, so I had quite an audience for the oration which I then delivered. My speech, as far as I can remember, was to explain the link between town and ship, extol the fame of Sir John, and thank the good people of Spilsby for their support and generosity to the ship during the War. It seemed to go down well, judging by the applause.

After handing the parade over to the First Lieutenant (who dismissed it so that the sailors could accept the hospitality of the townsfolk in the neighbouring pubs), I joined up with my 'folks' and we motored off to have lunch with friends. That was about the end of the episode (a well worthwhile one, we all thought), and on the Monday morning we sailed back south to the Medway.

It was during that winter that we had to implement another of the perennial 'cuts' in naval manpower by paying-off one of the Survey Ships, and, despite fierce resistance from me, it was decreed that *Franklin* should be paid off. It would have been more sensible, in my view, to have paid off David Penfold's ship, *Sharpshooter*, which was a 'convert' to the Surveying Service, whereas *Franklin* was purpose-built. However, I had to take comfort from the Hydrographer's acceptance of my submission that *Sharpshooter* should be re-named *Shackleton*, and from the announcement that I was to be re-appointed to command *Franklin's* sister ship, H.M.S. *Scott*. It was nevertheless sad to see the last of H.M.S. *Franklin*.

I took over command of *Scott* early in the New Year from Lieutenant-Commander Charles Grattan. I had to admit that in some respects she was the better ship, her builders having gratuitously provided quite a number of 'luxury extras' which *Franklin* had lacked. Anyway, with the the refit over, and all the previous season's Fair Charts and so on despatched into the Office, I was all set for another year's work in Home Waters, and quite happy with my lot.

Early the previous year Queen Elizabeth II had ascended the throne on the death of her father, King George VI. The Coronation took place in June, and on the 15th of that month the Navy celebrated the event with a Review of the Fleet by Her Majesty the Queen at Spithead. While the Coronation itself was proceeding, *Scott* took time off from her surveys to spruce herself up in the shelter of Dartmouth Harbour (every ship in the Fleet was doing much the same), and on June 11th she took up her allotted berth in the review lines at Spithead. Over the next few days these lines filled up with a most impressive array of aircraft-carriers, cruisers, destroyers, sloops, frigates, minesweepers and submarines, including many foreign warships, as well as a number of large liners and dozens of yachts of various sizes. It was a huge armada, though probably not so great as at the Coronation Review of 1937, and significantly smaller than at the Silver Jubilee Review of 1935. I think the only battleship present was H.M.S. *Vanguard*, Flagship of the C-in-C, Home Fleet.

There were three Survey Ships present: *Cook*, *Sharpshooter* and *Scott*, and each of these had been designated as vantage-points and entertainment centres for certain Admirals and their guests. They were to be, virtually, Admirals' yachts — a role for which, at least, their white hulls and buff upperworks appeared to suit them. *Cook*, the largest of the three, was assigned to the Hydrographer of the Navy, while *Scott* was appropriated to the Admiral Superintendent, Portsmouth. In addition to the Admiral's guests, the ship's officers were permitted a number of guests of their own. (I was refused permission to allow any of the Lower Deck to invite a guest). While the Admiral and his party were to occupy the Wardroom, Chartroom and quarterdeck, the officers and their guests would have the Captain's Cabin and the bridge. My personal guests were my wife, my mother, my father-in-law and my mother-in-law.

We had to embark the guests in Portsmouth dockyard and steam out to our berth several hours before the review. We were quite close to the Soviet Union's cruiser *Sverdlov*, which was an object lesson in smartness. The Review itself took the usual form, being followed by a Fly-Past by the Fleet Air Arm and, in the evening, illuminations and a firework display – all very spectacular. But before that the Queen held a Reception on board H.M.S. *Surprise* (there being no Royal Yacht as such at that time) for the Commanding Officers of the assembled warships. She also gave a dinner party, in the Flagship *Vanguard*, for her Senior Officers, to which all Flag Officers and Captains were summoned.

The absence from their ships of so many Commanding Officers played havoc with the disembarkation of the thousands of other guests still aboard the ships of the Fleet, for a carefully timed programme of movements into the dockyard had been drawn up to off-load them. Some ships weighed anchor on time and were taken inshore by their Executive Officers, while others thought they should await the return of their Captains before moving. As each ship-movement was dependent on the previous one, the result was somewhat chaotic, and when *Scott* was scheduled to move, I found I had both the Hydrographer and Captain Baker on board (*Cook* having already weighed) but no Admiral Superintendent. The passage into Portsmouth Harbour at about one o'clock in the morning – with a myriad of confusing lights flashing and winking from every direction, and with pinnaces, launches and ferries criss-crossing the channel – was a veritable nightmare. We were all tired, including our guests, and I felt an enormous sense of responsibility, with so many distinguished passengers on board, to get them safely ashore. It was after two a.m. by the time we were secured alongside and they were all disembarked, and I was mighty thankful to be able to accompany my own guests to a hotel in Chichester for the rest of the night!

Our attention now turned to a new task. NATO had decided that a new base for destroyers was needed, and their eyes lighted upon a promising stretch of sheltered water in Northern Ireland: Strangford Lough. There were two possible snags; firstly, it had not been properly surveyed, and secondly, very strong tidal streams were known to run in and out of its narrow entrance, which might prohibit its use by destroyers. *Scott* was therefore required both to test the feasibility of navigating the Narrows and to carry out a comprehensive survey of the island-studded Lough. It was quite a challenge, and it appealed to me.

The name 'Strangford' derived from the Norse, and the Norsemen knew what they were about. The streams through the Narrows ran at up to 9 knots, causing a great deal of turbulence in the constricted channel between rocks on both sides. I decided that the best time to effect an entrance for the first time would be just after the start of the ebb-stream, so that the ship would be stemming the tide with plenty of water under her, and with a relatively weak stream to contend with.

In these circumstances there were no problems – it was all plain sailing. Similarly it was a simple matter to make an exit from the Lough shortly after low water, as the flood stream was just starting and most of the rocks were visible. But it was a different story when I took the ship in through the Narrows against a full ebb-stream. not only was the turbulence itself quite alarming, but the stream tended to split – and at one point, while creeping forward against the full strength of the current, the ship's head suddenly paid off to starboard while a counter-eddy caught the stern and carried it forward. We found ourselves almost beam-on to the channel, and heading rapidly for the rocks to starboard, the rudder ineffective and full speed astern the only remedy! I resolved not try that sort of thing again.

Once into the Lough, it was a scene of pleasant tranquillity, gently rippling waters bounded in the south by green wooded hills, opening northward into an expanse of clear blue lake studded with dozens of little green islands, the whole surrounded by gently sloping fields of pasture. It seemed an idyllic site for a hydrographic survey, and so it turned out. The task was to take us right through the summer and into October. It was an interesting job but, as surveys go, a somewhat unorthodox one. We had been supplied by the Hydrographic Department with a plotting-sheet of the area which had been constructed for the purpose by irregular methods (photo-reductions of large-scale Ordnance Survey sheets came into it somewhere), and though this saved us a lot of triangulation, it had its shortcomings, as we were to discover.

Most of the sounding was carried out by the boats, the Lough being too restricted for ship-work, and there were usually at least six separate survey-parties out 'in the field' every day, the ship at anchor serving as a floating base for them. As the survey progressed, berth was shifted to keep pace. As so often in fjords, lochs and loughs, the holding ground in Strangford Lough was not good, and whenever a gale was threatened, I had to find a lee. One spot revealed by the survey was a relatively deep depression between several small islets, and on the assumption that the anchor would stay put at the bottom of it, we tended to anchor there in bad weather. It is now marked on the chart as 'Scott's Hole'.

I was very conscious that summer (and more than a little concerned) that my naval career was in the balance. I was approaching the end of my time in the 'promotion-zone' from the rank of Lieutenant-Commander. In fact if, by the end of June, I had not been picked for promotion to Commander, I could say 'goodbye' to my further prospects, and continue to serve (probably ashore) as a 'Passed-over Two-and-a-half' till I reached the age of 45 in eight years' time. It was a gloomy outlook, and as the deadline approached I was on tenterhooks.

I knew that Mary and my mother were counting on it, and the thought of letting them down was bad enough, but it would also be a bitter blow to my own pride if I failed to 'make the grade'. Mary had been particularly helpful and supportive in the critical years, and I felt that, if I were promoted, it would be due more to her than to any merit on my part. All I could do at this stage, however, was to offer up some silent prayers (a nearby church came in handy for that) and hope for the best.

I knew that on the last day of June the promotion lists would come through about 10.30 a.m. on the naval broadcast, and I was damned if I was going to hang about the ship, waiting for the fateful decision. I went off in the motor-skiff with a few sailors to do some useful surveying, and took my mind off the whole business for several hours. As we headed back to the ship for lunch, I noticed unusual activity on the quarterdeck and on approaching the gangway, I saw that the Officer of the Day was wreathed in smiles and carrying a cap whose peak had been covered in gold foil. I knew at once that all was well. 'Congratulations on your brass hat, sir,' said the O.O.D. as I came up the gangway, handing me the appalling-looking object as well as the signalled promotion list. 'Miracles will never cease' was all I could say, but my heart was leaping with joy, relief and excitement.

So — now I was a Commander! I had cleared the first (and worst) of the hurdles strewn across the career-path of all naval officers, and now I could afford to relax a little. I had much to be thankful for. On our next week-end jaunt to Liverpool I got my uniform suitably altered and acquired my 'brass hat'. I have no recollection of what we did during the last few weeks of the season after completing the Strangford Lough survey, but I received word at that time that I was to be relieved of my command during the winter at Chatham, and appointed to a shore post in the Hydrographic Department early in the New Year.

CHAPTER XIV

Commander, Admiralty Hydrographic Department, Cricklewood, 1954-6

M<small>Y APPOINTMENT WAS TO</small> H.M.S. *President*, the name-ship of the Admiralty, on whose 'books' were borne the names of all naval personnel serving in that establishment. I was appointed to the Hydrographic Department as 'Superintendent of the Oceanographical Branch' (short title: S.O.B.). Apart from nine months of courses as a Sub-Lieutenant and a few short courses later on, it was the first shore appointment I had ever had – in almost twenty years at sea.

At that time the Hydrographic Department occupied three locations: Whitehall, Cricklewood and Taunton. 'Chart Branch', which embraced the chart-compilation processes, and included most of the 'brains' of the Department, was located at Cricklewood, in a relatively large and modern building. It was here that I had my office, just above the main entrance. The distance was too great for me to commute daily from home, and I had to settle for 'digs' in Dollis Hill and week-ends at home.

Up to 1952 the Oceanographical Branch (such as it was) had been run by a civilian scientist, Dr. J.N. Carruthers, whose interest was geared to basic research, the operational needs of the Fleet being largely neglected. This was not the proper function of the Department (whose role was to serve the needs of the mariner-at-large), and Admiral Day decided to rectify matters by replacing the civilian scientist with an active-service naval officer as Superintendent, thereby creating a new H.Q. post for a Commander (H). The change was facilitated by the recently formed National Institute of Oceanography at Wormley in Surrey.

The first incumbent of the new post was Commander G.S. Ritchie (who had commanded H.M.S. *Challenger* during her two-year round-the-world oceanographical cruise, 1950-52), and it was from him that I took over the job. My knowledge of oceanography was minimal, and I found it difficult to grasp the full purpose of my task. What I needed, I felt, was 'Terms of Reference' to guide the work of the Branch, and I said so – but there were none. (That comment, however, was to bear fruit in later years – so much so, in fact, that in due course Terms of Reference for every responsible post in the Department were drawn up, where none had existed before.)

The main subjects with which I had to deal were bathythermographs, ocean soundings, ocean bathymetry, ocean currents and magnetic variation, and the various offshoots and applications of these fields of study. Because, however, I was the only active-service Commander at Cricklewood, I became (in a sense) the right-hand man of the Assistant Hydrographer (1), who was a Captain (H) and Superintendent of Charts. One of his functions was to task the Surveying Fleet, a function which he tended increasingly to delegate to me. Thus, in addition to supervising the work of the Oceanographic Branch, I soon found myself virtually running all the Survey Ships as well! It was hard work but extremely interesting, and it gave me my first real insight into the workings of the Hydrographic Department.

Early in June, it was decided that our newest Survey Ship, H.M.S. *Vidal*, should pay an official visit to Washington, D.C., to liaise with the Hydrographer of the U.S. Navy, and that I and our Chief Civil Hydrographic Officer, Mr. Atherton, should take passage in her. She was commanded by Captain K. St. B. Collins, who was designated as the next Hydrographer of the Navy. We duly sailed up the Potomac River, and were given a great reception by the Americans. When the junketings (and serious discussions) were over, *Vidal* resumed her outward passage to the West Indies, but I was left in the tender care of the U.S. Hydrographer (Rear Admiral Waters). He had decided to visit the Oceanographic Institute at Woods Hole (which included a Naval Laboratory), and the idea was that he should take me up there with him. That, in fact, was the ostensible reason for my whole trip.

We set off in the Admiral's official car and drove up to New London, Connecticut, where we stayed the night in the U.S. Navy's Submarine Base (which I had last seen as a midshipman 16 years before). Next day we motored through some beautiful New England coastal scenery and out on to the Cape Cod peninsula, on the southern tip of which is Woods Hole, looking across to Martha's Vineyard. The difference in climate between hot and humid Washington and cool, fresh Cape Cod was hardly believable. An Atlantic breeze blew over clear blue seas dotted with the white sails of yachts and fishing boats. It was an interesting visit and I was duly impressed.

I had arranged to return by sea in R.M.S. *Queen Mary* (on the grounds that my study of oceanography could be better served while travelling at sea-level rather than by air, 30,000 feet above the ocean.) However, I found myself seated at meals with a party of English fellow passengers, and in particular a delightful American girl travelling on her own. These proved so congenial that any thoughts of sea-level oceanographical studies became occluded by a light-hearted Anglo-American flirtation, leading to a lasting friendship and eventual god-motherhood on Barbara's part.

As Superintendent of the Oceanographical Branch, I found myself an 'ex-officio' member of the British National Committee on the Nomenclature of Ocean Bottom Features (short title: N.O.B. Committee). This committee met at the British Museum of Natural History and was chaired by Professor John Wiseman, with whom I had had dealings in connection with sea-bed samples and deep soundings. An international conference on the nomenclature aspects had been arranged at Monte Carlo, and as Wiseman was to chair it, he felt it would be helpful to our cause if I were to attend. Never having visited the Riviera, I needed no persuasion, and, the Admiralty kindly agreeing to defray my expenses, in September I set off with Mary by train to Monte Carlo.

The conference took place in the International Hydrographic Bureau, alongside the picturesque spectacle of the yacht-filled harbour. From our hotel too, we had a glorious view of the harbour. The work of the conference was not very demanding, and it put us in touch with some interesting people. We were also able to try our hands at the roulette-tables in the fabulous Casino, an experience to be relished, though we never had any luck.

Basic oceanographic research at this time was being pursued by the N.I.O., using the Royal Research Ship *Discovery*, and it was thought expedient that I should obtain first-hand experience of the work being done by her. It was therefore arranged that I should join her at Thorshavn, in the Faeroe Islands (which I had always wanted to visit). So in April, 1955 I set off across the North Sea in the Danish ferry *Kronprinzesse Ingrid* from Harwich to Esbjerg and thence by train to Copenhagen where I continued my journey on the *Dronning Alexandrine*, an aged steamer used for the weekly mail service between Denmark and the Faeroes. It seemed a round-about way to get there, but there was no other, and it certainly suited me!

After joining *Discovery* at Thorshavn, I spent an interesting and instructive week in her, observing and participating in various scientific experiments and activities: measuring surface and sub-surface currents, obtaining water samples and temperatures from surface to sea-bed, measuring wave heights, trawling for plankton and dredging for marine life on the ocean floor of the North Atlantic. I was disembarked at Lerwick, in the Shetlands, and flew back to London from Sumburgh.

By the summer of 1956 I had done more than two years as Superintendent of the Oceanographical Branch at Cricklewood, and the time was approaching for me to take up another sea-appointment. I turned over my job to Commander J.S.N. Pryor in mid-summer, and so arranged things that I was able to take a full month's leave between appointments, spending a highly successful holiday with the family in Ireland, and visiting relatives there.

CHAPTER XV

Commander, H.M.S. *Owen*
(Indian Ocean Deployments), 1956-8

I HAD BEEN APPOINTED to the command of H.M.S. *Owen*, one of our larger, post-war Survey-Ships, and I took over from Cmdr. C.R.K. Roe at Chatham (where *Owen* was based) shortly after we got back from our holiday in Ireland. I had enjoyed my shore-appointment at Cricklewood, in particular my function in tasking our ships all over the world by drafting their Hydrographic Instructions, and, when unforeseen tasks arose, by switching them from one job to another by means of Supplementary H.I.s Knowing that *Owen* was to be my next command, I had paid rather more attention than usual to her H.I.s and the effect that they would have on my first season's programme. *Owen* was one of the first ships to be fitted with the new Two-Range Decca radio-location system, and it was important that we should try it out on a survey in home waters before proceeding overseas. The Thames Estuary provided an ideal testing-ground, and after re-commissioning the ship, working her up and shaking down the ship's company, we set to in September to erect the two 100-ft. 'Slave' stations, one at Leysdown on the Isle of Sheppey and the other across the Estuary in Essex. These operations, involving a fair number of officers and men at each site, took the best part of a week to complete, and several more days were required to calibrate the system and construct the latticed plotting sheet which was to control the survey. From then on, it was virtually all 'plain sailing', and by mid-October the survey was completed.

The time came to say our farewells and set out for our overseas surveys. We were bound, ultimately, for the Indian Ocean, but as Colonel Nasser had just nationalized the Suez Canal and virtually closed it, we were to sail round the Cape. I had invited my old colleague, Dr. John Wiseman (from the British Museum of Natural History) to accompany me for the first part of the voyage, with a view to obtaining some deep-sea cores and to try out some of his equipment. We spent a few days at Gibraltar, and then headed south to Freetown in Sierra Leone. We came in primarily to fuel, but were nevertheless well entertained.

We had various tasks to perform off the Gold Coast (now Ghana), both at

Takoradi, where a new harbour was to be built, and off Elmina and Cape Coast Castle. At Elmina was an old Portuguese-built fort, a castellated whitewashed structure standing just above the beach. In it lived the British Chief of Police, a lonely character whose only company was a pet monkey. He showed me over the fort, complete with portcullis and drawbridge and immaculately maintained inside, and I rather fell for his chosen lifestyle!

Meanwhile the Shell Oil Company had begun prospecting off the coast of Nigeria, where the presence of an off-shore oilfield was suspected, and where the Admiralty charts were singularly lacking in up-to-date bathymetry. Shell had approached the Hydrographer of the Navy with a request that the charts be up-dated and an offer to assist in the geodetic control of a re-survey, together with helicopter lifts as required. *Owen* had been assigned to the task, so we put in to Lagos.

An old shipmate of mine, Lieut-Cdr. 'Bobby' Griffiths, was now running the Nigerian Navy (such as it was), and he had laid on a strenuous social programme to cover the few days of our initial visit. This included cocktail parties with Sir Ralph Grey, the Chief Secretary, entertainment by Shell and beach parties at Tarkwa, together with a good deal of private hospitality at the hands of Griffiths himself. I agreed to embark a number of Nigerian Navy trainees for hydrographic experience during the course of the survey.

The suspected off-shore oilfield lay just within sight of the low-lying coast forming the Niger delta, between Akasa and Bonny, which was utterly devoid of landmarks of any description. We decided to lay a long line of floating beacons, about three miles apart and parallel to the shore, and get Shell to intersect at least one of them by theodolite observations from some of their geodetic stations inshore, over which they had built towers. The technique, then, was to fix the beacons in relation to one another by running Taut Wire Measuring Gear along the line in both directions, and observe the orientation of the line by taking sun-azimuths by sextant at the first and last beacon. When this was completed, we had established adequate control for ship- and boat-sounding to commence. We were also required to obtain a high density of sea-bed samples and a few cores.

This work – and a larger-scale survey of the Bonny River Estuary – occupied us for the whole of November. The latter task was to establish the exact extent and depth of the Bar which tankers had to cross in order to get in and out of Port Harcourt (up the Bonny River), where oil was being piped from the inshore oilfields of the Niger delta. I took the ship up to Port Harcourt after completing the survey, and we paid a final visit to Lagos before leaving the area. *Owen* continued her passage south to the Cape, 'crossing the line' with the usual ceremony on December 4th, and entering

Simonstown Naval Dockyard about a week later. Towards the end of December we left Simonstown (having really fallen for the Cape) and headed eastward into the Indian Ocean. On our way up through the Mozambique Channel, running a line of ocean soundings, we suddenly encountered relatively shallow depths – which, after steadily rising, then eased off at around 250 fathoms, before gradually plunging back towards the ocean floor. This uncharted feature looked remarkably like what the Committee on the Nomenclature of the Ocean Bottom was pleased to term a 'seamount' or 'tablemount', the remains of an antediluvian volcano. Its exact nature, however, could only be established by means of a regular survey, and this seemed a golden opportunity to do it.

We laid a floating beacon (with flag and radar-reflector) as close to the feature's summit as we could, and for the next 24 hours we ran lines of soundings radiating out from the beacon into deep water on all sides, fixing the ship's position at regular intervals by radar ranges and visual bearings. As the survey developed, the feature was clearly revealed as a classic example of a tablemount, and we had been fortunate enough to lay our beacon almost at the centre of its flat top. Having accurately fixed the position of the beacon by several sets of independently observed star-sights, and having recovered a sizeable chunk of the sea-bed on the beacon anchor, we drew out the results of the survey and I wrote up the report. I was gratified to note, several years later, that the feature had been incorporated in the latest editions of the Admiralty Chart, and was named 'Hall Tablemount'! (At least my name would go down to posterity somewhere – if only in the Mozambique Channel!)

We continued up to Mombasa to fuel and make contact with the local authorities before setting out to take in hand our main task of the season, a survey of Chake Chake Bay in Pemba (the Isle of Cloves), which belonged to the Sultan of Zanzibar.

It was early January by the time we reached Kenya and a few days later we anchored off Zanzibar. I had to 'make my number' with the Sultan before proceeding to Pemba. We gave him a 21-gun salute, and he received me with great courtesy in the Palace. He spoke perfect English and while regaling me with soft drinks and sweetmeats, took enormous pride in showing me photographs, treasures and mementoes of his links with Queen Victoria. I had time before sailing to have a good look round Zanzibar itself, a city belonging to a past age, with a fascinating collection of beautiful old Arab buildings. Zanzibar was still a thoroughly feudal community.

One of the reasons for our survey of Chake Chake Bay was its possible suitability as a protected Fleet anchorage. It was an enormous stretch of calm water almost enclosed by coral reefs and low-lying, sparsely inhabited islets, but little was known about its depths and it was virtually uncharted. Quite what Fleet might use it, or for what purpose, was not vouchsafed to us! Anyway, we had to start from scratch by measuring a base and setting up an all-embracing triangulation. This was a slow and painstaking, but extremely interesting, business. We were working practically on the Equator and there was seldom much of a breeze to cool us down. The ship lay idly at anchor and we were away all day in boats, marking, observing and extending the triangulation. Once a month I took the ship back to Mombasa to give everyone a bit of a break.

Communication between Mombasa and Pemba was infrequent and irregular, and *Owen* provided a supplementary service for mails etc. The day before we were due to return to Pemba, some of my officers informed me that there was a young English nurse who wished to return to the hospital at Wete where she worked, and would be glad of a lift. King's Regulations and Admiralty Instructions, however, prohibited the passage of women in H.M. Ships except with the approval of the Commander-in-Chief. As we were to make the passage in daylight, I thought it fair enough to explain the circumstances and signal the C-in-C East Indies for approval to take the nurse. Approval came through the next morning so I duly embarked her – in my quarters (to the chagrin of the Wardroom!) – and she was ferried across to Pemba. That, however, was not quite the end of the story. About a year later I met up with the Flagship, H.M.S. *Jamaica*, somewhere in the Indian Ocean and felt I should call on the C-in-C, whom I had never met. He met me at the top of the gangway as I was piped aboard and as we shook hands, he said: 'Ah, Hall! You're the man who gave passage in your ship to a woman, aren't you?' Although he had received copies of every one of my Reports of Proceedings for months on end, that, apparently, was the only thing he remembered about me or the ship!

After three months of arduous work at Pemba, the time came for us to start the long trek home again, and early in April, as the Suez Canal was still closed, we set course back to the Cape. While running south-westward off the coast of S.E. Africa, we suddenly hit enormous head-seas, which broke over the fo'c'sle and did considerable damage, sweeping our Land-Rover overboard. After calling at Simonstown, we went up to Saldanha Bay for a few days out of the limelight, to paint ship in readiness for our forthcoming visit to Monaco in May.

Every five years the Hydrographers (and senior members of their staffs) of some fifty countries would converge on Monaco for a fortnight's Conference at the International Hydrographic Bureau. A great many professional, technical and general matters of mutual interest would be discussed, there would be a lot of social activity attended by delegates' wives, and the three officers to comprise the Directing Committee of the I.H.B. for the next five years would be elected by the whole Conference. A degree of international prestige was involved in this election, and there was always considerable competition and much lobbying beforehand for these important posts. *Owen's* presence was intended largely to enhance the prospects of the British candidate, who on this occasion was none other than Captain C.S. Lowry, Royal Navy.

We made an impressive entry to Monte Carlo Harbour, with a tight turn to starboard to bring us portside-to immediately in front of the Bureau building, and there, waving to welcome us, was Mary (not to mention Rear Admiral Collins, Hydrographer of the Navy, and many other distinguished officers and wives).

It was marvellous to have Mary with me again after almost eight months' absence. She had been on holiday in Italy and had come on from there. We stayed at Monaco for a full week – the only Survey Ship present – and did our best to maintain the prestige of the British delegation by giving formal receptions and a lunch party for Captain Lowry, and taking most of the foreign delegates to sea to demonstrate our latest equipment and techniques.

Owen arriving in Monte Carlo, 1957.

When the time came to leave, we felt we had been a distinct asset to the Conference (though in fact Colin Lowry did not get elected to the Directing Committee).

To the best of my memory, *Owen* re-fitted that summer at Sheerness, which could hardly have been more convenient for me! It was a good summer and I was able to see a lot of the family.

Meanwhile in July I had re-commissioned *Owen* for another season in the Indian Ocean, but by this time the Suez Canal had been re-opened, so we would be going out through the Mediterranean, with various surveys en route. The first of these was a re-survey of Gibraltar Harbour, which would take us about a month. This presented a golden opportunity for Mary to come out with our small son Adrian for the duration of our stay there. As it happened, I was able to arrange for them to take an 'Indulgence Passage' (at virtually no cost) in the Royal Fleet Auxiliary stores-ship *Port Dunvegan*, and after we had taken the two elder children to their new schools and seen them safely settled in, Mary and Adrian duly embarked at Chatham in late September. *Port Dunvegan* sailed a day or two before *Owen*, so they were waiting for me at the Rock Hotel when we reached Gibraltar early in October.

We spent the whole of October on the re-survey of Gibraltar Harbour. It was a pretty straightforward job and I was able to spend most evenings with the family ashore. But our month there ended all too soon and, with the survey complete, *Owen* headed eastward to Malta. We didn't stay long there, because we had a survey to do off the north coast of Cyprus, after which we put into Limassol for a break. Passing through the Suez Canal, now under Egyptian ownership and control, we were interested to note that it seemed to be as efficiently run as it ever had been. (So much for all the arguments put forward on our behalf against its nationalisation the previous year!)

Halfway down the Red Sea we had another survey to do in the vicinity of Jebel Zuqar, which took us a few days, and we then continued on to Aden to prepare for our next big task off the Hadhramaut coast. This had a dual purpose and was something of a joint effort. The south coast of Arabia had not been accurately tied-in geodetically with the over-all triangulation of the Middle East and its extension into Africa and Asia, and the Director of Military Surveys was anxious to establish a series of stations along the coast at which astronomical observations could be made to determine their geographical positions. Not only were these points virtually inaccessible from landward, but they lay in territory over which British jurisdiction was at best nominal (known, at that time, as the East Aden Protectorate). Our task, therefore, in addition to carrying out a much-needed hydrographic survey off the Mahra Coast, was to land and support small R.E. survey teams at the points in question.

It turned out to be a most interesting operation. Because the natives were known to be unfriendly, we were provided with an armed contingent of the Hadhramaut Bedouin Legion under a British colonel, whose task was to protect the R.E. surveyors while ashore. We started off with a visit to Mukalla, some 200 miles east of Aden, early in December. The Sappers and their escorts were landed further along the coast in the evenings and picked up at dawn, while the ship sounded during the day. As we moved further eastward, a complication arose. I was informed that the Mahra Coast was part of the historic domain of the Sultan of Socotra, and that it would be necessary to obtain his consent before putting anyone ashore there. I was therefore to proceed to Socotra, some 200 miles to the southward, to call on the Sultan.

Socotra, a large island strategically placed off the Horn of Africa and guarding access to the Gulf of Aden, had been a British Protectorate for many years, though as far as I know, there was no British presence on the island, which was ruled, quite independently, by the Sultan himself. He resided at the island's capital, Hadibo, on the north coast, and we anchored there about a mile off-shore. I sent a boat in to find out if the Sultan would receive me, and was informed that he was very ill. I therefore sent our Medical Officer to offer assistance, and he reported that the Sultan had a temperature of 104. Treatment was given, however, and the next day I was informed that he was much better and would be delighted to receive me.

I took with me the Arabic-speaking H.B.L. Colonel (Colonel Snell), both of us in 'full regalia' with swords and medals, and we were hospitably received at the rather pathetic little whitewashed 'Palace' in which we sat down to talk with the somewhat unprepossessing Sultan. He was traditionally attired in Arabic royal dress, with burnous, long curved scimitar and with a bejewelled dagger in his belt, and though looking pretty frail, seemed quite spry. He was highly impressed by the medical attention he had received, so I offered him the Doctor's services for anyone in his entourage who might be in need of them. From then on the M.O. was kept extremely busy! The Colonel then explained the purpose of our visit, and after much discussion and innumerable cups of coffee, the Sultan gave his consent. It transpired that his claims to the Mahra Coast, on the Arabian mainland, were of an ancestral nature, and that there had been virtually no contact with its people for many years. Our mission, however, was an opportunity for the Sultan to re-assert his authority in a distant part of his ancestral domain. Not only would he give his consent to our landings, but he would provide us with two emissaries carrying copies of his 'Royal Edict', which would ensure safe-conduct for the Survey parties and their escorts. Well pleased with the outcome of our deliberations, I thanked the Sultan profusely and offered to fire a Royal gun-salute for him when we took our departure on the morrow.

With our two Socotran emissaries aboard, we weighed anchor, fired the promised gun-salute, and headed back across the Gulf to Ras Fartak on the Mahra Coast. As dusk fell, we moved close inshore towards the next observation point, lowered a motor-boat and whaler, disembarked the R.E. surveyors, their armed H.B.L. escort and the two emissaries, and cast them off. We watched the boats as they made their way inshore and saw the whaler run up on to the beach with the landing-party. As they made their way inland, they were soon accosted by a fairly large gathering of armed natives, and a protracted 'parley' ensued. This we were unable to observe from the ship, and could only await the return of the boats with growing impatience. Night had fallen when they eventually returned, apparently bringing with them, to our surprise, the whole landing-party – but not the emissaries!

The Colonel explained what had happened. The party had been surrounded and outnumbered. The two emissaries had stepped forward and, unrolling their scrolls, had proceeded to read out the Royal Edict calling upon the Mahra people, in the name of their Sultan, to provide safe-conduct – 'without let or hindrance' – to the landing-party. No sooner had the Edict been promulgated, with the announcement of the Sultan's name, than the two emissaries were promptly seized and captured! The ensuing protests from Colonel Snell and his Legionaries were then drowned by the natives, shouting that they were in no way vassals of the Sultan of Socotra and would have no truck with him whatsoever. In the circumstances, and to avoid what looked like being a bloody incident, the Colonel, reckoning that discretion was the better part of valour, ordered the whole party to withdraw.

For this operation I was reporting direct to H.E. The Governor of Aden (Sir William Luce), repeating my signals to C-in-C East Indies, Admiralty (for Hydrographer) and D.Mil. Survey. I was fairly sure that an immediate report of the evening's incident, involving the capture of the Sultan's emissaries, would cause the Governor to cancel the remainder of the operation, since he had quite enough on his mind in Aden, without a potential flare-up in the Protectorate. As a cancellation at this stage was the last thing we wanted (there being only one or two more points to be observed at), I therefore decided to delay my report and to press on to complete the job by subterfuge.

We realised that the natives were now aware of our tactics and had organized themselves to congregate on the shore at the spot to which they could see the ship was heading in the evening, so we decided to turn this to our advantage with a game of bluff. With all lights blazing as usual, we steamed in towards a point on the coast some ten miles to the eastward of our next intended landing, drawing the watching natives along the beach in the desired direction. Then, as soon as it was really dark, all lights were suddenly extinguished, the ship was blacked-out, speed was increased and the ship turned abruptly to seaward. We then doubled back at high speed to the westward and approached the actual observation-point in complete silence and pitch darkness, veering the heavily-greased anchor-cable slowly to the bottom and lowering the whaler. The landing-party was then silently rowed in, with muffled oars, to the beach, which was deserted. All went well and the observations were completed shortly after midnight, the landing-party returning to the ship in triumph during the Middle Watch. Back we went to the survey-ground, to continue sounding during the day. We repeated the whole process the following night. The operation was now complete – and my report could be signalled in a less alarming context. (As John Roberts, my First Lieutenant, remarked at the time, this operation was certainly 'One for the Book')!

We spent Christmas at Aden, with various other units of the Fleet and were quite glad when it was over and we could sail for our main task of the season on the vast Seychelles Bank in the middle of the Indian Ocean.

The only regular communication for passengers and freight between the British Crown Colony of the Seychelles and the outside world was the fortnightly mail service run (I think) by the B. & I. Line between Mombasa and Port Victoria, about 1,000 miles apart. Otherwise all communication was by Arab and Indian dhows sailing to and from East Africa, Mauritius, Arabia, the Persian Gulf, Pakistan and India. There was no air service whatever, because there was no airfield in the islands. The Seychelles consisted of a group of about half a dozen tropical islets standing in the middle of a huge, relatively shallow, coral bank, the edges of which tended to curve upwards like a saucer, and sometimes broke the surface to form outer islets. The largest of the Seychelles Islands was Mahé, beautiful and mountainous, on which stands the capital and only port, Port Victoria. To reach it from Mombasa, ships had to cross the shallow western edge of the bank, and then traverse about 150 miles of slightly deeper, but barely surveyed, water, in which a fair number of shoals had been charted, many of which were marked 'Position Approximate' or 'Position Doubtful', and some 'Existence Doubtful'. This passage was, therefore, something of a nightmare to the Masters of the B. & I. mail-ships, and a proper survey of the route had long been called for.

My plan was to concentrate initially on the outer two-thirds of the area, and to control the survey with Two-Range Decca. To provide the best possible angles of 'cut' throughout the survey-area, and to ensure that we were well within range at all times, I decided to place the Green 'Slave' on the western side of Silhouette Island and the Red 'Slave' as far up to the north as possible. Fortunately, on the northern rim of the bank there were two small islands: Bird Island and Denis Island. Bird I. was the more westerly of the two, and should provide an ideal site for the Red station. Having established the two 'Slaves', we then had to locate them accurately and to 'connect' them geodetically – no mean task as they lay over 80 miles apart. While observing the geographical position of the Red station by star-sights with an astrolabe, we proceeded to use our recently acquired Tellurometer system to measure the exact distance between it and the Green station on Silhouette I., as well as measuring, by theodolite, the True Bearing of Red from Green. It was a process fraught with difficulties, and it took us the best part of two weeks. The Tellurometer distance was, at that time, the longest that had ever been measured.

With the two 'Slaves' now established, with a crew of four men in camp at each site who were in radio communication with each other, and with the whole system calibrated and tested, I decided to run a single line of soundings out to the western end of the area, and then continue towards East Africa. There was still a great deal to be done to complete the Pemba survey which we had abandoned the year before, and I had decided that this could best be done by detaching a camp-party with the two Survey motor-boats and letting them get on with it while the ship progressed the Seychelles survey. We billeted the party (two officers and eight men) at a place called Mkoani, and after spending several days erecting marks and observing an extension of the triangulation for them, Owen refuelled at Mombasa and returned to the Seychelles.

We were now into February and for the next six weeks, in generally superb weather conditions, we systematically sounded out a ten-mile wide swathe covering the first hundred miles of the shipping-route across the Seychelles Bank, anchoring out on the survey-ground each night and inking in the day's work. We had to break off at intervals in order to visit one or other of the two 'Slave' camps, to replenish provisions and change round personnel, and occasionally I would take the ship into Port Victoria to give the men a well-earned 'run ashore' and spend a night or two myself at the lovely Beau Vallon Hotel.

I shall never forget the gloriously clear sea-water which enabled one to see every feature of the sea-bed in depths of 40 to 50 feet and the brilliantly white sand which contributed to this clarity. It was almost uncanny, sometimes, as the ship moved steadily through the water, with the echo-sounders showing seven or eight fathoms, and one looked down from the bridge to see stones and pebbles, boulders and seaweed harmlessly sliding beneath her. I remember one time, while I was turning the ship off Bird Island, when the transparency was such that there seemed to be no water under her at all – and I thought we were certain to go aground! The beautifully sandy beaches on all the islands, fringed by graceful palm-trees, were another unforgettable feature of the Seychelles.

It was while reconnoitring a site for the Green 'Slave' on Silhouette Island that I fell in with a quite extraordinary character, the almost legendary 'Uncrowned King of Silhouette'. Descended, as were almost all the white land-owners, from the original French colonists, his name was M. Dupont, and he owned the whole of this beautiful, mountainous and isolated island, which he ran as a benevolent aristocrat on an unashamedly feudal basis. He knew every member of his community by name and they all loved him.

M. Dupont was a most interesting man and a great story-teller, some of whose yarns were barely credible. In the early 1920s he had apparently represented Britain in the javelin-throwing contest of the Olympic Games – and won it! His expertise, he said, had derived from youthful experience in spearing and harpooning sharks and whales in the waters surrounding his island. A few miles off-shore there was a dangerous rock marked on the chart 'E.D.' Dupont swore it existed, and said that he had once touched it with an oar We made a thorough search for it, but never found it. (Could he have touched a whale or a shark?). His tales were legion, and one night, when we were anchored near Silhouette, I invited him off to dine with me. It was a thoroughly entertaining evening. I had apologized for the weakness of my 'chilli-wine' (of which I always added a few drops to the soup) and next morning, after the ship had got under way, a boat was observed vainly trying to overtake us, with six men at the oars and a solitary, be-hatted figure perched up in the stern-sheets holding something aloft. I stopped the ship and the boat drew alongside. A bottle was passed inboard and brought to me on the bridge with a message attached. 'To fortify your chilli-wine', it said. The bottle contained the most powerful lot of fresh chillis I have ever experienced, and they have lasted me to this day!

One Friday afternoon I took the ship in through the reefs to Port Victoria to give week-end leave. There were no alongside berths and very little swinging room, so I moored with two anchors and mooring-swivel, shut down the boilers and reverted to four hours' notice for steam. I shoved off across the island to spend an evening at the Beau Vallon Hotel. Half the ship's company also pushed off for the week-end. On my return, the ship's siren was blaring and our patrols were out on the streets. I was informed that an 'Operational-Immediate' signal had been received which the Paymaster and another officer were attempting to decipher. Meanwhile the First Lieutenant had taken steps to recall all libertymen. The signal was from C-in-C East Indies and addressed to *Owen*. It was enciphered in a code which we apparently did not carry. Nevertheless, the Cypher Officers had somehow succeeded in unravelling the first bit of it — which read: 'Proceed forthwith to . . .' — but they could get no further. I told the Chief to start raising steam and we began the slow process of unmooring. Libertymen began trickling back in twos and threes. Within an hour we were ready to move, but at least a dozen of the crew — including the Coxswain — were still ashore, and no further progress had been made in deciphering the signal.

I signalled the C-in-C to the effect that I was moving, that his signal was undecipherable (and possibly corrupt), and requested instructions in Plain Language as to whether, on leaving Port Victoria, I should turn east or west. We hauled out through the reefs and into the bay, and a boat with two more libertymen caught us up. As we cleared the islands, a P/L signal came through ordering me to proceed at full speed to Male in the Maldive Islands. (They lay a thousand miles to the north-eastward!)

From then on an absolute spate of signals flooded into the W/T Office — in a code that we did carry. *Owen* was to assume the role of a floating 'British Residency' for our High Commissioner in Ceylon at Male, capital of the Maldives (a dependency of Ceylon), during critical political negotiations with the new Sultan, who had apparently abrogated a Treaty of Defence under which Britain held the vital air-base at Gan. The ship was also to act as a W/T link with Whitehall, for which our small Communications Staff would be augmented by C-in-C. Meanwhile I was in communication with the Governor of the Seychelles regarding the support of my stranded libertymen and the crews of our 'Slave' stations on Silhouette and Bird Islands.

It was now mid-March, the weather was superb, the sea a deep blue, glassy calm with a low, lazy swell. The ship throbbed from stem to stern as she worked up to full power, and we forged ahead to this new venture feeling somewhat depleted but rather elated. I was concerned about the thirty or so men we had left behind in Pemba and the Seychelles, and sent off a stream of administrative signals to ensure their welfare and support in our absence, which might well be for a month or more. (The Governor of the Seychelles assured me he would make good use of the stranded libertymen on Mahé, and would charter an island-schooner to replenish the camps on Silhouette and Bird Island.)

It took us about three days to reach Male at full speed, and on arrival we felt our way in to the lagoon, through reefs and with some caution, neither the charts nor the Sailing Directions being particularly helpful. We anchored about a mile off the capital, put down all the boats, spread our awnings, and set to to chamfer up the ship. For a diplomatic assignment of this sort, I felt, we ought to be looking our best. Meanwhile, and while awaiting developments, we might as well carry out a local survey of the lagoon and the entrance-channel.

Signals now started coming in from Colombo. I was told to expect the arrival of the High Commissioner by air on the morrow. He would be coming in an R.A.F. Sunderland flying-boat, and (if I had no objection) would be bringing his lady secretary (!) On that point I at first demurred. It would cause complications and was against Regulations. The High Commissioner then appealed to the C–in–C, saying he couldn't perform without his secretary. The C–in–C approved and told me to make the best of a bad job (so to speak), so we prepared for a bit of an upheaval. I moved out to the Chart-house to make way for H.E., and the Doctor moved out of his cabin to the Sick Bay to make way for the lady secretary. We all wondered what she would be like.

As the flying-boat alighted on the lagoon in a smother of foam and spray, all eyes (and every pair of binoculars) were trained on it, and when the door opened and two figures emerged, an audible sigh wafted through the ship. 'She's a blonde' was the word whispered along the guard-rails as the launch approached. And up the ladder came first, a heavily-built, rather florid, paunchy gentleman, dark-haired and heavy-jowled (who reminded me immediately of the actor Robert Morley), and following him a sprightly short-haired damsel in a flowing summery dress, a blonde, to be sure, but hardly the 'glamourpuss' of the sailors' over-heated imaginations! Certainly Nancy Elwood was no oil-painting – an efficient career girl, no doubt – but she was female and the object of all attention. It was astonishing really, and rather amusing, to witness the scene on the quarterdeck that evening: Nancy seated on a deckchair 'holding court' in the centre of a circle of officers hanging on her every word ('like bees round a honey-pot', as someone remarked at the time).

We soon settled down to a comfortable routine. Each morning H.E. would be ferried in to the Sultan's palace for a round of long-drawn-out negotiations, and each evening he would return to dictate a long report to

Nancy for the Foreign and Commonwealth Office. When typed, these reports would be sent down for ciphering and transmission by radio to Whitehall, usually about midnight, so as to be ready on the Civil Service desks for action next morning. I was concerned at the inordinate length of these reports and the amount of work they entailed for the cypher and communications staffs, and got H.E. to agree to let me vet them in draft form. Brevity is a vital attribute of naval signalling, and drastic condensation of H.E.'s meandering drafts seemed imperative. But the Royal Navy and the Diplomatic Corps are entirely different breeds, and in this matter we could find little common ground.

One example sticks in my memory. Four or five pages had been handed to me one night (which would take hours to encipher and transmit) and I did my best to condense it – in naval style. It was H.E.'s draft report on the day's negotiations with the Sultan, and one paragraph opened with the words: 'As I was lying in my bath this evening, it occurred to me that . . .'! I had become rather less than enchanted with 'Robert Morley' by this time. He tended to spread himself all over my cabin and behaved very much as if he owned the place. And this latest 'blurb' really added insult to injury – '*my* bath' indeed!). So I struck the whole thing out and substituted the one word 'Consider', which entirely preserved the sense of the paragraph and was, I felt, an object-lesson in the merits of conciseness. But H.E. would have none of it. 'No, no,' he said, 'The chap in Whitehall who's dealing with this business knows me quite well and those words will convey a subtle nuance to the contentious assertion which follows. I insist they remain in.' After that I rather gave up, and reflected that this, presumably, was what 'being a W/T link with Whitehall' was all about!

Apparently the young Sultan had quarrelled with his father (whom he had succeeded) and, having somewhat revolutionary and anti-imperialist ideas, had set the cat among the pigeons by tearing up most of his father's internal and external measures – including the Defence Treaty concerning Gan. However, by early April, H.E. had managed sufficient arm-twisting of one sort or another to bring the negotiations to a successful conclusion and to fly back to Ceylon. *Owen* was thus released and lost no time in sailing back to the Seychelles.

But time was now getting short. We had to recover the two camps and all their equipment, re-embark the stranded libertymen, call on the Governor – to thank him for all his help – and set off for Pemba to recover Jack Cooper's survey-party from there. Fortunately the Pemba survey was virtually complete, so, by the end of April, we were once more heading home towards the Suez Canal, though calling at Aden, where Maurice Heath was

now the A.O.C. and well able to entertain me! It took us a month to get
home, via Aden, Malta and Gib, and we reached Chatham early in June. It
was the end of my first overseas surveying Command, which, on the whole,
I had thoroughly enjoyed. At the end of the summer I was due for another
shore job.

CHAPTER XVI

The Citadel, Admiralty, 1958-60 and H.M.S. *Owen* (Atlantic Deployment), 1960-61

I THINK IT WAS IN SEPTEMBER, 1958 that I took up my next appointment – in Whitehall. My post was officially designated 'Officer in Charge of Staff Charts' (O.C.S.C.), but in fact that title in no way reflected the range of my duties and responsibilities. My office was underground, in the massive wartime 'Citadel' projecting from the north corner of the Admiralty into Horse Guards Parade. There were no windows and we worked entirely in artificial light, fresh air being blown through the office from ship-type ventilation trunks. Though responsible for the only completely up-to-date set of some 4,000 Admiralty Charts for use, as required, by the Naval Staff, I had a multitude of other duties barely connected with that, including Radio Navigational Warnings, NATO Standardization, War-time Light Lists and aspects of charting policy, Territorial Waters etc. I worked with a small staff of three naval officers and two civil servants.

Mary and I had decided that another two years of weekly or daily commuting from Sheppey to London was simply 'not on', so we let our house at Minster to another naval officer and found ourselves a 'Service Letting' at Farnborough in Kent, which was within easy travelling distance of Whitehall.

By 1960 it had become clear to me that my time ashore was running out. I was to be appointed again to command H.M.S. *Owen* for another two years. I had long hankered for the old days, when our ships had pioneered the exploration of distant lands, particularly the polar regions, and on occasion I had been instrumental in arranging for them to co-operate in the transport and landing of University and other scientific expeditions to the Arctic. I felt that the Navy had a potential long-term interest in these areas, and in ice-navigation generally, and was concerned that over the years our experience in that type of work had dwindled to virtually nil. When a plea from the Governor of the Falkland Islands Dependencies reached us for urgent surveys to be undertaken in South Georgia on behalf of the whaling industry, I made strong representations to the Hydrographer that we should respond positively and that the task should fall to *Owen*. After much discussion and argument this was agreed, and it fell to me to initiate the necessary planning. *Owen* had been re-fitting in Gibraltar, with Roy Benson, her First Lieutenant, in temporary command. She was due to complete in May, and it was decided that I should fly out there to take over from him and bring the ship back to U.K.

Having drawn up an outline programme for our first 'season' (which included visits to many exotic and seldom-visited places), I thought it sensible to equip myself with a 16mm. colour ciné-camera, so I bought one before setting out. That camera was to be the source of many hundreds of feet of colour-film that I was to send home from far-away places over the next two years, and which helped to keep us in touch with each other during long months of separation.

When I got out to Gibraltar, I found *Owen* beginning to emerge from her re-fit, though there was still much to be done to make her ready for sea. It was brought to my notice that we had a suspected thief on board, several of the sailors having had money stolen from their lockers. A few days later, one of the seamen was caught red-handed with marked notes in his possession. He had a highly blemished Service Record and the case cried out for exemplary punishment. I proposed to the Flag Officer, Gibraltar, that the culprit should be dismissed from Her Majesty's Service. He agreed, and I read the Warrant to the assembled sailors on the quarterdeck that evening. It had the desired effect, because I had very little further trouble throughout the commission.

I commissioned the ship on May 17th, 1960 and we sailed a fortnight later. Our first commitment was an official visit to the Spanish Hydrographer at Cadiz, and this was followed a few days later by a similar visit at Lisbon to the Portuguese Hydrographer. Both visits involved much protocol, gun-salutes, calls, demonstrations, receptions and entertainment, and both went extremely well, the ship, newly re-fitted and freshly painted, doing credit to the R.N. and making a very good impression on our Iberian hosts.

Our first port of call in U.K. was Dartmouth, where we had a survey to do for the rest of June. There was a good deal of liaison, of course with the Royal Naval College – and with the Training Flotilla – most of the cadets visiting the ship in groups for indoctrination, their first introduction to the Surveying Service.

In July we moved up to Scotland and Northern Ireland to carry out a survey in the Western Approaches, using the new improved Two-Range Decca system known as Lambda (Low Ambiguity Decca). Using Londonderry as our base, we established one Slave on the Island of Tiree and the other at Saligo Bay on Islay. The area we were concerned with, embracing the Stanton Banks, lay towards the edge of the Continental Shelf. It was of vital importance to our submarines, and had never been surveyed. As an alternative to Londonderry, we sometimes used Oban as a base, but from a logistical point of view it was less satisfactory. Our Survey covered a thousand square miles, and weather conditions were consistently adverse, enabling us to acclimatize ourselves to what might be in store for us in Antarctic waters. At the end of August *Owen* returned to her home port, Devonport, to grant leave and prepare for her long Atlantic Cruise.

On 20th September, after an Inspection by the Hydrographer of the Navy (Rear Admiral E.G.Irving), the ship sailed for a protracted oceanographic cruise in the Atlantic, laden with special stores and equipment, and with three civilian scientists embarked. We were to carry out a programme of scientific research drawn up by the British Museum of Natural History and the Imperial College of Science and Technology, Dr. J.D. Wiseman of the B.M.N.H. and Dr. C. Evans of the I.C.S.T. directing the work. Our third 'scientist' had been rather 'wished' on us by the Hydrographer as a passenger. This was the redoubtable Mr. Duncan Carse (who, as a one-time Radio Personality playing 'Dick Barton − Special Agent', had been something of a household name). His mission was to be marooned on the most inaccessible part of South Georgia for two years in order to carry out what he described as 'An Experiment in Loneliness'. Our job was to land him and leave him.

By the time we reached the Azores, a week later, we had occupied nine oceanographical 'stations', at each of which we had sampled the water-column (from seabed to surface), measured its temperatures, trawled for plankton and other forms of marine life, and obtained a core of sediment from the ocean floor, while taking continuous records of the depth along our track. We put in to Punta Delgada to fuel, and there, on the quay to meet us, was a presentable young lady called Venetia. She had come to collect Duncan Carse and they disappeared into the hills together.

We stayed three days in the Azores, and as we were about to continue the cruise, the Engineer Officer reported to me that our starboard engine was out of action. One of the E.R.A.s had somehow succeeded in jamming the propeller-shaft and the combined efforts of the engine-room staff had failed to free it. This was indeed a 'facer', as Dockyard assistance was clearly needed. I was very loath to return to Devonport, so proposed instead to make for Gibraltar on one engine. This was approved. It was a distinct setback for our plans, but handling the ship with only one engine was a challenge which I was ready to accept. Making good use of the wind on our starboard quarter, I took the ship out stern first and set off to the eastward.

We reached Gibraltar on 5th October, and as it was obvious that we'd be there for at least a fortnight, I wired to Mary to join me, which she did very quickly. Almost by magic we found a delightful house and excellent car within 24 hours of her arrival!

Gibraltar was a pleasant interlude, marred by the death of our Chief Stoker, whose family flew out to the Naval Funeral ceremony and were greatly comforted and befriended by Mary. The Ice Patrol Ship, H.M.S. *Protector*, came in on her way down to the Antarctic, and I took the opportunity to transfer a survey detachment under Lieutenant Barry Dixon, with one of our Surveying Motor-boats, to take passage in her to South Georgia as an Advance Party, pending our own arrival.

Repairs to our starboard shaft were eventually completed, and we sailed again on 23rd October, a new Chief Stoker being brought out to us by helicopter from one of our aircraft-carriers off the Portuguese coast. After topping up with fuel once again at Punta Delgada, we continued the oceanographical cruise, paying particular attention to the Mid-Atlantic Ridge. Early in November we investigated the Nares Deep and the Puerto Rico Trench, from which we obtained a sediment core from a depth of almost five miles! It was certainly the deepest core ever obtained by the Navy, and it took us about seven hours to get it.

From the Puerto Rico Trench, we continued the cruise southwards through the islands of the Antilles, calling briefly at Antigua and St. Lucia, making surveys of some of the inter-island passages, saluting the Diamond Rock, and bringing the score of oceanographical stations up to 25. At some of these 'stations' we lowered our under-water camera down to the ocean floor and obtained astonishing photographs of marine creatures in their pitch-dark oozy environment.

An important objective of our scientists was the tiny group of islets known as St. Paul's Rocks, an isolated peak of the Mid-Atlantic Ridge which breaks surface just north of the Equator. The rocks form an arc which shelters a bay from the effect of the easterly Trade Winds, and in the 1870s H.M.S. *Challenger* had moored in that bay, with hawsers out to the rocks on three sides. I was not prepared to do the same with *Owen* but I sent in a strong landing-party, including our scientists, in the ship's two whalers, and they spent a profitable and interesting day there, while the ship did a systematic survey all round the Rocks. A major point of interest for geologists and geophysicists is the fact that these rocks have been exuded from the earth's core, and a determination of their age will give them the age of the Earth. Needless to say, samples of rock were brought back to the ship, and because the islets are hardly ever visited, we left behind a 'Time Capsule' (for the edification of posterity).

Having 'crossed the line' with the usual ceremony, we put in to the Brazilian port of Recife (Pernambuco), where two rather embarrassing incidents occurred. We were to berth alongside a promenade in the centre of the city, so I asked for floating fenders to keep the ship clear of the wall. They were not available. As the tide fell, our starboard bilge-keel caught a projecting 'step' on the wall, and the ship took a growing, and quite alarming, list to port (which was made much of by the local news media)! And, when the time came to leave, I swung the stern out into the stream and held on for'ard, and as the ship turned, her port anchor caught on the stone balustrade and knocked a section of it over. (It was many months before I heard the last of that episode, because the city lodged a claim for damage against the Admiralty!)

Our next objective was the island of Martin Vaz, terminal point of the Trinidad Seamount Chain, some 600 miles off the Brazilian coast. It was described in the Sailing Directions as 'inaccessible' and that posed an irresistible challenge. The island is claimed by Brazil, but we had obtained clearance to visit it (and had actually embarked a Brazilian naval officer for hydrographic experience and liaison duties), so on 4th December we anchored close under its precipitous shores and sent in a landing-party. One officer and a seaman scaled the cliffs to reach the summit, while the scientists investigated the island and a sketch-survey was made by the boats. I reported the landing by signal and it brought us some good publicity in the national press, while the Brazilian authorities found it hard to believe. Apparently it was the first recorded landing on Martin Vaz.

Rio de Janeiro was as beautiful and colourful as ever, but its intoxicating music and general zest for life seemed somehow to have evaporated over the quarter-century since my last visit. (Or could it simply have been that I had grown older?). Anyway, we were excellently cared for by the Brazilian Hydrographer over the four days that we were there, and it was indeed a memorable visit. We moved on from Rio to spend Christmas with our counterparts in Montevideo, where the Uruguayan Navy did all they could to entertain us.

This brought to an end the first phase of our oceanographical cruise, and our scientists packed their bags and flew home to join their loved ones. We had run a continuous line of oceanic soundings 10,000 miles in length, occupied 67 oceanographical 'stations' and obtained 50 deep-sea cores, as well as making many other types of scientific observation, including photographs of the ocean floor. As *Owen* was the first British Survey Ship to visit South America since Captain Fitzroy's voyage with Charles Darwin in H.M.S. *Beagle* 130 years before, the Argentine Navy sent a special aircraft down to Montevideo to collect me and three of my officers for a 24-hour visit to Buenos Aires. Both their Hydrographic and Antarctic Institutes were anxious to consult us as to our forthcoming surveys in South Georgia, and our projected visit to what they were pleased to call the 'Islas Malvinas'.

On 27th December *Owen* left Montevideo and headed east across the South Atlantic, on a Great Circle course to Tristan da Cunha. My original plan had been to go straight down to South Georgia, but while in Rio, we had unfortunately developed trouble with one of the boilers – a severe case of something akin to 'condenseritis' – and its tubes had been badly damaged. Docking in South America had been considered, but the Admiralty had directed me to proceed to Simonstown instead. By this time, evidence had emerged which gave grounds for suspecting that negligence had contributed to the damage, so, after leaving Montevideo, I ordered a Board of Inquiry to be convened on board. Its Report showed conclusively that normal vigilance on the part of the Stoker Petty Officer of the Watch would have prevented the damage to the boiler tubes, and disciplinary action had to be taken against him. Meanwhile we continued steadily eastwards, sounding as before, and continuing with our oceanographical observations.

CHAPTER XVII

H.M.S. *Owen*, South Georgia, 1961

TRISTAN DA CUNHA, which we reached on 4th January, is probably the loneliest of all our colonies, and our visit was of enormous interest to the inhabitants. Various sporting and social activities were arranged (including a cricket-match), but we had to keep a very close eye on the islanders when they came aboard, their pilfering activities being notorious. While the boats made a hydrographic survey of the anchorage and approaches to the pier, scientific observations were carried out ashore – including measurement of the Earth's magnetic field on the slopes of the volcano. Little did we think, then, that in a few months' time that volcano was to erupt with devastating consequences, not only vitiating our survey-work, but leading to the total evacuation of the island.

What worried me at the time was the fact that our Medical Officer was in great demand ashore, where a number of cases were causing anxiety, and the fact that the island had no resident doctor – which, in my view, was an extraordinary state of affairs. The obvious answer was to put the M.O. ashore and leave him there while we continued on to South Africa. As he was also the ship's Naturalist, he would be able to 'kill two birds with one stone' during our absence, and, despite his understandable reservations at missing the fleshpots of the Cape, that is what I did.

Simonstown had lost none of its charm and my friends and relations there were as hospitable as ever. While repairs were effected to our boiler, the Commander-in-Chief, South Africa and South Atlantic (under whom I was operating) announced his intention of carrying out our Annual Inspection. This certainly put the pressure on us, and involved us all in a great deal of hard work for the first week, but we came through the Admiral's inspection with flying colours and a period of relaxation followed.

At the end of January, with repairs completed, we were ready to resume the season's work, with attention now directed towards South Georgia (where our Advance Party had already been landed by *Protector* six weeks earlier). First, however, we had a job to do on Gough Island, which lies 250 miles south-eastward of Tristan da Cunha. Apart from the scientific observations which we were to make on the island, I had arranged to re-embark our Medical Officer, who had made his way there by fishing boat.

Gough Island, a British possession, is uninhabited – except by a small team of South African meteorologists. *Owen* arrived there on Accession Day (February 6th), and to make ownership perfectly clear to the occupants, I decided, on anchoring, to fire a Royal Salute and to Dress Ship Over-all. The island is steep and precipitous, with lush vegetation in the valleys, and dominated by the very striking 'Nag's Tooth' peak. It was in the lee of this peak that Hugh Vaughan, the First Lieutenant, and Mike Wright, another of my (H) officers, spent much of the day measuring the Earth's magnetism. Meanwhile Duncan Carse, who had a personal interest in weather conditions in the Southern Ocean, hobnobbed with the meteorologists.

As we entered the Roaring Forties, our oceanographical work came to a virtual halt. Weather and sea conditions became too severe to occupy more 'stations', and with No.77 under our belt, we had not done too badly. A few days later, we entered the Antarctic Convergence, where sea and air became much colder and fog descended. The main hazard now was drifting icebergs. Look-outs were permanently posted, and radar and asdic were operated continuously.

The first icebergs were sighted quite close on 11th February, 1961, in daylight but in low visibility. I was disturbed that they had not been detected by radar, although assured that the radar was working properly (and it did pick up some of the larger bergs). I became very uneasy about continuing in these conditions after dark, and decided to heave-to till dawn. When dawn broke, I found the ship literally surrounded by icebergs of all shapes and sizes, some a few cables away, others stretching away to the horizon on all sides.

I must say, it was an amazing sight – awe-inspiring indeed. But just then I was less concerned with the aesthetics of the scene than with the fact that none of these icebergs had been reported by the radar. I called the radar operator to the bridge to take a look. 'Why have none of these contacts been reported?' I asked, 'Is the radar working?' 'Oh yes, sir, it's been working perfectly all night, but the screen is clear,' replied the operator. 'Well, it can't bloody well be working then, can it?' I countered, 'Use your eyes, man!' And I silently thanked my lucky stars that I'd had the intuition to stop the ship overnight. If we'd continued our passage, relying on radar, we would certainly have struck one of those icebergs – and that would have been the end of us. *Owen* was not strengthened for ice-navigation, and her thin plating would have crumpled like paper on impact. The ship would have foundered, and in those latitudes the chance of rescue for survivors was nil. (Eventually the Senior Radio Electrical Mechanic rather sheepishly reported to me that the radar had been 'off tune')! We had all learnt a valuable lesson.

It took us 24 hours to thread our way through this 200-mile-wide belt of icebergs, some of them so enormous that we had to make drastic detours to get round them, and all of them drifting slowly northward from their birthplace in Antarctica. Beautiful in the sunshine they certainly were, glistening white, with greens, blues and deep purples streaking their sides in the shadows, but it was a great relief to break out at last into open water again.

The first sight of South Georgia is truly breath-taking: a great range of snow-clad peaks rising straight out of the sea, a hundred miles long, and stretching right across the southern horizon. The isolated mountain peaks gradually joined up and the land beneath steadily took shape as we approached from the north-eastward, and in the evening we cautiously felt our way into the bleak inlet of Elsehul, where we anchored.

There in front of us, just inland from the beach, were the two tents, and lying at her moorings a short way from the camp was our surveying motor-boat. As we came to anchor, there was a sudden bustle of activity ashore, the tents (or what remained of them) were struck, a dinghy put out from the beach, and a few minutes later the motor-boat came alongside us. Barry Dixon, leader of our Advance Party, came up the ladders with a roll of charts and plotting-sheets under his arm, followed by his merry men, one of them carrying a baby seal which flip-flopped about on the upper deck.

They had been ashore there for two months and had done splendidly,

Owen *surveying off South Georgia, 1961.*

establishing an invaluable geodetic framework on which to base our coming surveys in the north-west part of the island, and, despite the near-disintegration of their tents from the frequent storms, they had apparently enjoyed the experience. I must say, I was relieved to find them in good health and in good spirits after what must have been quite an ordeal.

That night a storm blew up (the first of many we were to contend with over the next two months) and we had to set anchor watch, with steam at immediate notice. Next morning was bright and clear with little wind, and we set off along the coast to the south-eastward. A glorious panorama of snowy mountains and glistening glaciers unfolded before our eyes, and armed with binoculars, sextants and station-pointers (and with Duncan Carse to help with identification of peaks and headlands), we plotted the features for use in the coming coastal survey.

Leith Harbour was the only whaling station still in use, and here we had arranged to fuel. In places the water was red with the blood of slaughtered whales, while the huge carcasses of others lay lashed alongside anchored whale-catchers, waiting to be flensed.

Apart from the surrounding scenery, which was wild and superb, Leith Harbour, with its atmosphere of commercialized death, slaughter and gore, was not an attractive haven. But it represented, for us, the only source of succour in South Georgia, if we should ever need it, so we had to establish a friendly liaison with the local management. On their part, of course, we were more than welcome, as they realized our work was largely for their benefit (if rather late in the day).

We next had to 'make our number' with the Administrator at the Island's 'capital', King Edward Point. This lies in a secluded bay inside one of the largest inlets about halfway down the coast, surrounded by snowy mountains and completely sheltered from the ocean. Here we berthed on the end of the small wooden pier projecting from the low-lying spit of land on which stands the Administrator's house and a few other wooden buildings. Across the bay lay Grytviken, another run-down whaling station, and on a low hill opposite the Point was situated the grave and stone monument to Sir Ernest Shackleton, whose exploits are legendary.

We were now free to start work in earnest. Our first task was to establish a boat-camp on Bird Island in the north, from which a strong detachment could progress a large-scale survey of Stewart Strait, the rock-studded passage leading to the whaling-grounds in the west. It was the hazards of this passage that had stimulated the repeated requests from the whaling community for proper up-to-date charts of the area, so the Stewart Strait survey was, in a sense, the most important of our objectives.

Mindful of the extreme conditions, we set up a really well-found encampment. Much thought and energy went into its construction – and siting. There was a perfect harbour for the boats in Jordan's Cove, opening on to Bird Sound, and, just inland from the cove, on fairly high tussocky ground, we set up a number of specially strengthened tents to house two officers and three boats' crews (about sixteen men in all) together with a veritable mountain of provisions and other equipment. There we left them, in the company of huge numbers of penguins and seals, to get on with the inshore sounding.

We had meanwhile embarked several civilian botanists, who were intent on seeking out certain rare species of exotic flora suspected of growing only in South Georgia. Some of these they had located on Bird Island, but their real 'mecca' lay further south, in Royal Bay and Moltke Harbour. As we would be passing that area anyway, I agreed to put them ashore there on our way round to the other side of the island, much to their delight.

Each time we made a coastal passage, we ran a fresh line of soundings, close to, and parallel with, the previous one, and to seaward of it, thus gradually building up a useful survey of the coastal waters of the island.

We had already run several lines between the north-west tip and the coastal area, but now, on passing the entrance to Cumberland Bay, we were breaking new ground, with drifting icebergs to contend with. Royal Bay, into which the vast Ross and Weddell Glaciers debouched, was full of small ice-floes as we came to anchor, but the motor-boat threaded her way through these as she took the botanists in to their hunting-grounds behind Moltke Harbour. Once rid of them, we were at last free to concentrate on the next challenge, which came to be known as 'The Saga of Duncan Carse'.

I had got to know Duncan fairly well during the months that we'd had him on board. Whenever we carried civilians, scientists or otherwise, I made a point of having them to dine with me, usually with one or two of the officers, and during the long Atlantic cruise I had one of these dinner-parties practically every week. Duncan was an interesting man, with some extraordinary experiences behind him, but he had problems.

While we were in South Africa, the lady named Venetia arrived and swept Duncan off. We didn't see him again till he rejoined us on sailing. He seemed moodier than before. So it was that, as we headed south to take him to his chosen abode on the other side of the island, our W/T office was kept unusually busy with the transmission and reception of radio-messages between him and Venetia. I gathered that he had proposed to her and was persuading her to accept his proposal, and, furthermore, that his whole

long-prepared 'Experiment in Loneliness', for which we had brought him all
these thousands of miles across the ocean, now depended on the outcome of
these private negotiations! The general assumption, not unnaturally, was that
if Venetia said 'Yes', Duncan would call off his self-imposed two-year exile,
and that would be that, whereas if she said 'No', the whole thing would go
ahead as planned.

Anyway, I was damned if one of Her Majesty's ships was going to hang
around awaiting the outcome of a romantic affair involving a civilian
passenger, and one, moreover, who had had five months to reconsider his
plans. My orders from the Admiralty were to land Duncan Carse in an
isolated cove near Ducloz Head on the desolate south-west coast of South
Georgia, together with his ten-ton load of hut, instruments, stores and
equipment, and provisions for a two-year sojourn. The sooner that was
done, the sooner I could get on with our surveys. If he was to call it off at
the last minute, so be it. In that case I would discharge him into the care of
the Administrator at King Edward Point, to find his own way home as best
he could.

Weather conditions looked distinctly ominous as we approached Cape
Vahsel and Cooper Island, with great banks of dense cloud pouring over the
lofty summits of the Salvesen Range, and when we turned to the
southwestward we met the full force of a mounting gale. It looked anything
but promising, but I carried on to Cape Disappointment, the southern
extremity of South Georgia, to see what lay round the corner. Out of the
lee of the land, as we poked our nose round the Cape, conditions rapidly
deteriorated, with heavy head-seas, a ferocious gale, driving sleet and the sea
studded with 'growlers' and 'bergy-bits'. Discretion, I felt, was quite
definitely the better part of valour in these circumstances, so I put the ship
about and we headed back eastward.

We would simply have to wait till conditions improved. I decided to seek
shelter in Larsen Harbour, of which we had a chart of sorts, and which
opened off the much larger and deeper Drygalski Fjord. We anchored just
inside its entrance, in good shelter, and I took several of the officers in the
motor-skiff as far up the 'harbour' (it was really a small, steep-sided fjord) as
we could penetrate, and we were able to stretch our legs ashore for a while.
When we got back to the ship, I heard that Duncan had received his long-
awaited message from Venetia, and that she had accepted him. 'Well,' I
thought, 'that takes care of that.' The projected landing (Operation
'Castaway') was presumably 'off'. But I was quite wrong. It was now
definitely 'on'. Apparently, if Venetia had rejected Duncan, he would have
called the whole thing off and gone home to press his suit. Now that the

two of them were formally 'engaged', his mind was at rest – and he could hardly wait to get started!

Next morning the gale had abated and we re-traced our course of the previous day. Rounding Cape Disappointment, we headed up along the desolate west coast, feeling our way through barely charted waters, past the Pickersgill Islands, to Ducloz Head. The wind blew steadily from the north-westward, parallel to the shore, and up towards Annenkov Island I noticed several large icebergs. We anchored about a mile off shore and immediately got down to the business of landing Duncan Carse and his mountain of stores. The moment we had waited for so long had at last arrived. Every available boat, motor-boat, motor-cutter, whalers, skiffs and dories, were pressed into service, loaded to the gunwhales with stores and provisions. The large wooden hut which was to be Duncan's home for the next two years, and which we had carried all this way in flat sections on the fo'c'sle, was stacked on to a huge square raft (built by our shipwrights) and hoisted over the side and into the water by one of our main derricks. Then it was laboriously towed ashore by the motor-cutter.

Duncan, with a fairly large party of sailors to man-handle the stores up the beach, had already gone in to select the exact site for the hut and to supervise its erection. Boats plied back and forth between ship and shore, ferrying in everything that was needed. There was no lack of willing helpers to carry the stuff up from the beach, to hold the hut sections while they were screwed into place, and to pile up the hundreds of cases and boxes where Duncan wanted them. It seemed to take ages and I was getting impatient.

I was also apprehensive, because the barometer was falling and the wind was rising. With extraordinary suddenness the gale struck. Within minutes the sea was being lashed to a frenzy, vicious white horses and towering waves appearing all round us. We hoisted the Black Flag at the masthead, the signal recalling all boats, and we started shortening-in the cable, while steaming ahead to the anchor. I had to get out of this as we were on a lee shore. To my utter dismay, I then realised that the huge icebergs which we had assumed to be stranded near Annenkov Island were rapidly bearing down upon us, driven headlong down-wind by the rising gale.

The very last thing I wanted, at that juncture, was a collision with an iceberg, but what could I do? We still had several shackles of cable out, and though the windlass was heaving it in at full blast, the icebergs would be upon us before we could weigh. Two of them, the size of houses, were but half a cable away already. Using the screws and rudder, but with our forefoot still tethered to the bottom, I was able to point the ship between the icebergs, and they both slithered past us, one on each side, only a few feet away. That danger at least was past, but it had been a close thing.

Meanwhile the boats, several of them in tow, were battling with the seas to get back to us. The motor-cutter, towing the huge empty raft, was making no headway at all. If anything, it was losing ground, being driven back towards the rocks. Then, thank God, the tow parted; the motor-cutter leapt ahead and the raft was a 'write-off'. All the boats got back somehow, half-swamped, and several half-unloaded. Stores and gear of all sorts had been left on the shore where they lay, and the hut was only half erected. We had been well and truly 'caught with our pants down', but had just managed to get away with it.

Steaming into the teeth of the gale, we ran a long line of soundings all the way up the west coast to Bird Island, then, in the night, we reversed course and ran a second line down-wind and parallel to the first. Peering ahead through the murk as dawn broke, I saw a great upheaval of water rising into the air and cascading back in a smother of stormy spray – only a few cables away and right in our path. 'Breakers ahead! Stop both engines!' I yelled, and then, 'Half astern!'. We stood and watched as the seas ahead seethed and boiled in turmoil, flinging aloft great spouts of spume and spray. It was an uncharted reef, which we there and then (and with good reason!) dubbed 'Horror Rock'.

We rode out the rest of the gale at anchor in the lee of Annenkov Island, and it wasn't till the following day that the wind abated and we could resume the landing operation. Back we went to Ducroz Head, and this time we were in luck.

We finally got Duncan and all his paraphernalia safely ashore, with his hut securely roofed and screwed together, and all stores and provisions stowed under cover. He came off to the ship to report all well, to thank us for our efforts and to take his leave of us. It was a dramatic moment, and I was determined to lay on a little ceremony – if only for the photographers and ciné enthusiasts. A whole crowd of us gathered on the quarterdeck, and as I shook hands with Duncan and bade him a last farewell, I handed him a carved and gilded plaque of the ship's crest to hang in his hut, to remind him of *Owen* during his long and lonely vigil. Off he went, and the last we saw of him as we steamed away was a lonely figure standing on the beach, waving forlornly against a vast back-drop of glacier-laden mountains.

Duncan had certainly chosen quite the most isolated spot imaginable in which to pursue his 'experiment'. Behind his bleak little cove the land rose steeply through ice and snow to the towering peaks of the Allardyce Range, with the (as yet unclimbed) Mount Paget dominating the scene. Access overland was virtually impossible, while to reach human habitation by the coastal route would involve a hazardous journey of at least a hundred miles. What a challenge he had set himself!

Anyway, we were at last free to get on with our own pressing tasks and without more ado, we set off on another line of soundings up the dreaded west coast. This time I decided to take the ship through the unsurveyed Hauge Strait, between Annenkov Island and the mainland, and all the way up to Bird Island we had the most stupendous views of the daunting panorama unfolding to starboard, with clearly identifiable peaks and tangents for regular visual fixing.

We were now into the last days of February and the southern summer was on the wane. We had a lot of leeway to make up. Anchoring in Bird Sound, we called in on our camp-party at Jordan's Cove to check on their progress and welfare and to replenish their stores, before making ready to start our own work in the Stewart Strait. The whole area had been divided up between the ship and the three sounding-boats, two of which were camp-based. Before we could make a start, however, we were struck by yet another storm, a storm of such unparalleled ferocity that I hope never to see its like again. Despite having both anchors down with ten shackles out on each, and steaming into the wind to ease the strain, we dragged halfway out of the sound during the night. I have never seen anything like the state of the sea: its whole surface white with spume and spray being blown clean off the water by katabatic winds of incredible fury as they roared down from the Paryadin Ridge. 'Williwaws' spiralled past in endless procession as they were swept seaward and into the air, to dissipate in clouds of spray. All day we struggled to hold our ground, and then during the night it suddenly stopped. Glorious pink light on the snowy peaks heralded the dawn of a perfect day, and in lovely conditions we got down to work.

CHAPTER XVIII

H.M.S. *Owen*, The South Georgia Surveys & Return to UK, 1961

ALL THROUGH THE MONTH of March we plugged away at the Stewart Strait survey, the boats working inshore among the rocks and islands, and the ship out in the open sea. The Strait, two miles wide and studded with shoals, ran north and south between Bird Island to the east and the Willis Islands in the west. Great masses of dark brown kelp marked the shallower shoals, and made it difficult to sound over them, while wildlife of all kinds abounded in sea and air: whales, porpoises, seals and penguins (often mistaken for shoals of fish), with seagulls and gannets wheeling above them, and always a great white albatross or two gliding peacefully round us. There was no lack of interest in this survey – whether on our part or on theirs!

Storms were frequent and usually sudden, quite often accompanied by blinding snow and 'white-out' conditions. The boats would have to run for shelter, and when all marks were obscured, the ship would heave-to and wait for a clearance. Sometimes these storms would last for days, and to make up for lost time, the boats' crews would put in very long hours when the weather subsided, even then being generally soaked to the skin by spray.

During one of these storms we lost the motor-cutter. I had insisted that the boats should always work in pairs, to provide mutual support in case of emergencies. On this occasion the motor-cutter was following up one of the camp-based sounding boats which had developed trouble with her steering-gear, when suddenly, in the middle of Bird Sound, she buried her bows in an enormous wave and stood on end. The sounding-boat, despite the trouble with her 'kitchin'-rudders, managed to turn about and rescue the motor-cutter's crew, but could do nothing, in those conditions, to salvage the boat herself. We lost a lot of valuable gear in that incident (apart from what we were able to 'write-off' from earlier 'losses', under this heading!).

Sometimes the ship would break off from the Stewart Strait survey to make a dash down the north-east coast to Leith or King Edward Cove (on one occasion to land an emergency appendicitis case) and to build up the coastal survey. Great care had to be taken on these sounding-lines to avoid the icebergs drifting along the coast from the south. Most of them had calved from the numerous South Georgian glaciers (the ones from Antarctica drifting much further to seaward), and they were of all shapes and sizes. The largest — some of them vast and irregular from several capsizes, others like huge flat-topped sugary wedding-cakes, all of them stunningly beautiful — were easy to avoid, though often interrupting our lines. It was the smaller ones, some barely breaking the surface and hardly visible, that were the main hazard. At night, and in low visibility, they were a constant anxiety despite a continuous radar and asdic watch, but though we had to shoulder some of them aside, we never accidentally hit one.

Except when on passage, I would normally anchor overnight, particularly while we were engaged on the Stewart Strait survey, which was visually controlled. The problem was that one never knew what the night would hold in store as regards the weather. It could blow up very suddenly from any quarter, and if one anchored in the lee of the land in the evening, one sometimes found oneself on a dead lee shore by midnight, with a rising gale springing up from seaward. Furthermore, good shelter could only be found close inshore, where there was little room for manoeuvre, and where the holding-ground was frequently poor. I soon learnt that it was better to set a full anchor-watch, with an officer on the bridge and steam on the engines, as a matter of routine, rather than to have to do so in the middle of the night when awakened by the Quartermaster (on whose judgement I could rarely rely). Constant watchkeeping by day, and constant anchor-watch by night, certainly imposed a strain on all of us, but it was the price we had to pay for never being able to relax. Constant vigilance was absolutely vital for our survival in those treacherous waters.

By the end of March, though feeling tired and worn from many sleepless nights and constant anxiety, I was, nevertheless, stimulated by the challenge and spiritually uplifted by the elemental forces we were contending with, as well as by the wild magnificence of our surroundings. I was not in the least downcast, therefore, when the Commander-in-Chief announced his impending arrival from Antarctica, and his desire that *Owen* should join him in King Edward Cove. He was flying his flag in H.M.S. *Protector*, the Ice-Patrol ship, and we happened to be in Stromness Bay as she passed along the coast outside.

As *Protector* hove in sight, *Owen* got under way and steamed out of the Bay at 15 knots to meet her. Passing down her side on an opposite course, we fired a gun-salute to the C-in-C's flag, and then fell in astern of the flagship and followed her down to anchor in King Edward Cove. The Admiral was in an affable mood, having clearly enjoyed his time down south, and was interested in the progress of our work. I accepted his invitation to dine on board that night, after which we sat through a rather indifferent cinema show in the Wardroom. It was a pleasant change to meet some new faces, and to compare notes with the flagship's C.O., Captain Forbes, whom I had known of old.

After the Flagship's departure to continue her homeward passage via the Falklands, we suffered a series of breakdowns which obliged us to remain at anchor in King Edward Cove. To add to our frustration, the weather was superb, ideal for progressing our surveys. As Easter was approaching, I felt justified in invoking the Synod of Whitby to bring it forward and to celebrate it there and then, instead of taking time off (which we could ill spare) on the Day itself. So we rigged Church on the quarterdeck, held an appropriate service, with prayers, lessons and hymns, and I declared a Make and Mend for all except those engaged in the repairs.

We were now into April and autumn was upon us. The whaling season was over and we were out on a limb, the only sea-going ship in the entire area. It was essential that we work flat out now to complete the surveys before conditions took a real turn for the worse and made further progress impossible. We returned to the Stewart Strait area to size up the situation with the camp party. They had really done marvels. The large-scale surveys of Elsehul, Undine and Bird Sound were complete, but there were still several gaps in the medium-scale survey of Stewart Strait. I called a 'Council of War'. We had a week at the most to finish everything. The most difficult area lay at the outer extremity of the Willis Islands, rock-strewn and totally devoid of shelter. Every attempt to sound it so far had failed. I would take all the boats out there together and lie off while they made a supreme effort jointly to complete it. And, despite appalling weather, that is what we did.

There remained only one more area outstanding, plus a number of important examinations of newly-found shoals, and these the boats could do on their own. We had three more days, and I was determined to fit in two more jobs if I possibly could. One was to detach Peter Cardno, my Navigator, to make a survey of Right Whale Bay, in which we had once anchored, and which he had implored me to agree to, and the other was to look in again on Duncan Carse before we finally departed. We landed Cardno and his party with one boat at Right Whale Bay, and then set off on our third circumnavigation of South Georgia, this time in an anti-clockwise direction. Anchoring once more off Ducloz Head, I sent a small party, including the Medical Officer, to check on Duncan's welfare. They found him in his bunk, laid up with a leg injury.

'How bad is it?' I asked by signal. 'Nothing broken – a bad sprain,' replied the doctor. 'Does he want to be brought off?' I inquired. 'Definitely not, but can we spare another case of whisky?' said the doctor, We sent in the required medicine. 'Can you treat the injury?' I asked the doctor. 'I have prescribed self-massage and complete rest,' was the answer, 'Duncan has his own pain-killers.' On return to the ship, the M.O. told me that Duncan had slipped on a rock a few days previously and had been laid up ever since. 'I think he has a very low pain-threshold,' he added.

And so we finally abandoned Duncan Carse, with many felicitous good wishes and farewells, though one couldn't help having some misgivings, considering his self-willed predicament. We continued southward, rounded Cape Disappointment and Cape Vahsel (avoiding Cooper Sound, which we had felt our way through with considerable trepidation in February), and then put in for the last time to King Edward Point. Here, as previously agreed, I embarked the Administrator and his wife, who had asked for a lift to Montevideo.

Our next stop was at Right Whale Bay, to pick up Pete Cardno and his party. Despite wretched conditions, they'd made good use of their three days there, and brought off a very presentable survey of the bay and anchorage (which has since been incorporated with the other new Plans on Chart 3585). Next day was April 10th, my deadline for final departure, and it only remained now to recover the main camp party from Jordan's Cove.

At this juncture we became enveloped in fog and, to make matters worse, more and more icebergs seemed to be crowding in on us. Moreover, the wind was rising steadily and things looked ominous. It was clear that autumn was upon us. I took the ship round Bird Island and anchored, without any kind of a lee, half a mile off the Cove. The camp-party, forewarned by radio of our arrival, had struck their tents and dismantled their two metal 'Uniport' huts, and were assembled on the beach with a veritable mountain of stores and equipment, their boats already loaded up with other gear.

Roger Morris, my Senior Watchkeeper (later to become Hydrographer of the Navy), had been standing in as Navigator since Cardno's detachment and he was on the bridge with me for this final evolution. It was now blowing a gale, and we were on a lee shore. He was distinctly nervous, continuously checking the anchor-bearings. The boats started to come off, battling their way out through stormy seas. Hugh Vaughan, my First Lieutenant, assisted by the Boatswain, was in charge down aft, where sea conditions were prohibitive for the boats. As they approached, they were immediately 'hooked on', hoisted to deck-level, and rapidly unloaded. Then back inshore to pick up another load. 'I think we're dragging, sir,' said Morris, squinting

over the Pelorus. Start weighing,' I yelled down to the cable-party on the
fo'c'sle, and rang down 'Slow Ahead' to the engine-room.

Our hearts were in our mouths by this time. It was touch and go whether
we'd get the last load off or whether we'd have to abandon everything and
'get to hell out of it' if we were not to be driven on to the rocks. Even as the
shout from the Cable Officer, 'Aweigh!' reached my ears, screamed above
the gale, the last two boats were on their way out. I pointed the ship into the
wind and held her steady. Vaughan and the Boatswain, with every
conceivable seaman, got the boats hooked on and, as I watched them clear
the water, with only seconds to spare, I gave the order: 'Half Ahead, Both
Engines!'. Whew! A great sigh of relief – almost audible – swept through the
ship. We had done it, and we were safe. I offered up a silent prayer of thanks
to the Almighty, set course to the westward, and went below for a double
rum-and-lime.

A general euphoria pervaded the ship as we headed up towards the
Falkland Islands. It resulted largely from the knowledge that we were at last
on our way home, but partly also from a sense of relief, a sense of
satisfaction, and a sense of achievement on the part of all concerned. For my
own part, I certainly felt a tremendous sense of achievement – that we had
done all that we set out to do, and that we had come through it practically
unscathed.

After a brief call at Port Stanley to fuel and to report to the Governor on
our surveys, we headed up to the Rio de la Plata, continuing with our
oceanographical observations with a further six 'stations'. We combined this
with a line of soundings from the Falklands to the Argentine continental
shelf (particularly asked for by their Hydrographer). In retrospect, I have no
doubt that the request was motivated to support Argentina's claim, on
geophysical grounds at least, to sovereignty over 'Las Islas Malvinas' –
though, at the time, their claim was dormant and did not enter our minds.

At Montevideo we landed the Administrator of South Georgia and his
wife before steaming up river to Buenos Aires, where, at the invitation of
their Hydrographer, we spent five days on an official visit, hosted by the
Argentine Navy. Those days were action packed with sport, entertainment
and hospitality – and did much to relieve us all from the stress of the past
three months.

In late April we resumed the oceanographical cruise with a wide sweep
south-eastward across the Atlantic and up to West Africa, via Ascension
Island (virtually a huge volcanic slag-heap thrown up from the Mid-Atlantic
Ridge). After replenishing our almost empty fuel tanks at Freetown in mid-
May, we pushed on northward past Cap Blanc, disproving the existence of

several doubtful shoals en route to Tenerife – where we enjoyed an excellent Whitsun week-end.

At our 100th oceanographical station we found a new seamount (and took a rock-sample from its summit), and on entering the Channel, we were welcomed home by the Hydrographer – who made a precarious descent from a helicopter, narrowly missing our bridge. Next day (31st May) we arrived at Devonport, to a tremendous welcome from one and all – and congratulations from the C-in-C Plymouth, who had kept a watching brief on our progress. The oceanographical cruise had been an epic in itself – for the quantity of valuable data obtained, the inordinate amount of sea-time, and perhaps the sheer endurance off South Georgia.

The Dockyard had much work to do on the ship during her summer lie-up, which would take at least four months. This meant we could all take our full entitlement of leave – and Mary and I took a long holiday in Scandinavia. I had now reached the end of the Commanders' promotion zone, so I had plenty of time to contemplate what could well be rather a bleak future. But when we reached Stockholm early in July, news arrived that I had been selected for promotion to Captain – which put a rosier complexion on the rest of our holiday.

Towards the end of September, as the ship was emerging from re-fit and we were preparing for our next task, in the Indian Ocean, the local press carried a headline: 'Navy Abandons Injured Man On Desert Island' – followed by a report that after six months of loneliness at Ducloz Cove, our castaway's encampment had been totally swamped in the middle of the night by a tidal wave. It demolished his hut and swept away practically all his stores, leaving him to salvage only the bare minimum for survival. Somehow he had managed to attract the attention of a passing sealer, which picked him up and brought him to safety. So ended the Saga of Duncan Carse.

CHAPTER XIX

Captain, H.M.S. *Owen* (International Indian Ocean Expedition), 1961-2

T HE SECOND HALF OF *Owen's* commission was the Indian Ocean Cruise. Though I was not actually to be promoted to Captain till the end of the year, I had been 'selected', and felt myself a 'four-striper' in all but name.

The ship had been extensively modified during the summer refit, to equip her for action as the British contribution to the International Indian Ocean Expedition. A great deal of special equipment had been installed, including a new type of deep-sea echo-sounder, a Precision Depth Recorder, a magnetometer and a gravity-meter, with automatic recording equipment. Our main task was to make a comprehensive reconnaissance of the western part of the Indian Ocean – between Africa and India – under the guidance of scientists from the Department of Geodesy and Geophysics at Cambridge University. With about half a dozen of these scientists embarked, we sailed from Devonport on 11th October, 1961.

Our outward passage, via Gibraltar and the Suez Canal, consisted of continuous bathymetric, gravimetric and magnetic traverses, the main one running straight along the axis of the Mediterranean, with checks on the gravimeter at each end. One man fell overboard off the Algerian Coast, but we managed to pick him up, and when we reached Port Said on October 29th, we found the Egyptians remarkably uncooperative, which was hardly surprising considering they were commemorating the fifth anniversary of our abortive invasion!

We ran a zigzag traverse down the Red Sea, which, as an extension of Africa's Great Rift Valley, was of particular interest to our geologists and geophysicists, and then embarked on a survey among the Haycock Islands, where a reef had been reported across the main shipping channel. When halfway through this survey, we received an urgent signal requiring our immediate presence at Perim Island, where the inhabitants had suddenly run out of fresh water and were parched.

Rain falls on Perim about once in five years, and the island is hot and arid. Fresh water for its three hundred inhabitants has therefore to be distilled from the sea, the distillation plant being powered by oil fuel.

Through gross mismanagement, it had run out of fuel and come to a grinding halt. Could we please let them have 3,000 gallons of fresh water before they all died of thirst? As we could not anchor closer than a mile from the settlement, that would not be easy – quite apart from the lack of suitable containers. On the other hand, the islanders had plenty of oil-drums, so getting some local dhows to bring these out to us in relays, we spent the day pumping oil into them by hand, and thus got the local distillery functioning by nightfall.

We spent two days at Aden, and after refuelling and checking the gravimeter, set off on 8th November to run the first of our exploratory traverses for the I.I.O.E., from a point eastward of Socotra and south-westward towards the Kenya coast.

It may surprise some people to hear that the force of gravity is a variable, and that things do not weigh the same everywhere. For instance, a brick weighing 2lb. in England would weigh less on the Equator and more at the Pole, due to the centrifugal force of the Earth's rotation, though latitude is not the only factor. Composition of the sub-surface rocks and their depth below the sea-bed will also affect the Earth's gravitational 'pull', so that by continually measuring the strength of this force (and allowing for the change in latitude) some indication of the sub-surface structure is derived.

Another variable is the strength of the Earth's magnetic field. While its horizontal and vertical components obviously depend on the magnetic latitude (i.e. the distance from the magnetic poles), the total intensity is affected by the composition of the Earth's crust, parts of which may themselves be magnetic. By continuously measuring the total intensity of the magnetic field, by means of a magnetometer towed well astern of the ship (and therefore outside her own magnetic field), further indication is given of variations in the sub-structure.

Measurements of gravity and magnetism arising from the rocks beneath the sea-bed will obviously be affected by the vertical distance between them and the point of measurement – i.e. the depth of water – and this factor, together with the shape of the sea-bed, both of which we were continuously recording with the new Precision Depth Recorder (PDR), would need to be collated with the other measurements. *Owen* was thus pioneering a completely new technique, making simultaneous measurements of bathymetry, magnetism and gravity continuously along pre-determined lines in an exploratory geophysical survey of the western basin of the Indian Ocean. The correlation between these three 'parameters' could best be appreciated when contoured tracings of each were superimposed on the others, but I remember a particularly telling instance of the relationship between the gravity and bathymetry. We were steaming along in very deep water over a flat and featureless sea-bed when the gravimeter started showing steadily increasing readings. The scientists became quite excited: what could be causing this steady rise in the force of gravity? The sea-bed remained as it had been for several hours — quite flat. 'We may be approaching a seamount,' they said. Up on the bridge, I was sceptical. 'The gravimeter's probably on the blink,' I thought as I watched the PDR trace giving a uniformly flat bottom. But suddenly, as I watched, it began climbing steeply. There was no doubt about it: we were running up the steep slopes of an uncharted feature rising abruptly from the abyssal plain, a newly discovered seamount, and the gravimeter had detected its proximity a mile or two before we reached it. From then on I had a new respect for that machine!

Our magnetometer, a cylindrical affair, towed through the water on the end of a long, insulated electrical cable, had been designed primarily for use in 'temperate' latitudes, where the vertical component of the Earth's magnetism exceeded the horizontal component (or was at least measurable). Though it measured total intensity. it needed this vertical component in some strength to produce any results when towed horizontally (as we were towing it). As we steamed steadily southward into lower magnetic latitudes, however, the vertical component became weaker and weaker, and the magnetometer gradually ceased to function. Some means had to be found, therefore, of towing it vertically, so that the strong horizontal component could be brought to bear on its sensitive mechanism in place of the vanishing vertical component. Our shipwrights rose to the occasion by building a sledge-like raft on which the instrument could be mounted in a vertical position, and once we had got this raft to tow satisfactorily, our magnetic problems were over.

We finished the first of these traverses in mid-November, and, on 16th, we entered the sleepy old Arab sea-port of Lamu, on the Kenya coast, not far from the borders of Somalia. Here we set up a large camp-party to progress a survey of the harbour and approaches, while the ship herself embarked on a more extensive survey off-shore, including the approaches to Lamu, Manda and Patta Bays. Towards the end of the month, we paid a quick visit to Mombasa for fuel before resuming work on the survey.

We broke off from the Kenya Banks survey on 11th December and, leaving the camp party ashore at the mouth of Lamu Harbour to progress the inshore surveys during our absence, we headed out towards the Seychelles. My purpose was to select sites for the Lamda radio-location stations which would be needed for our forthcoming surveys in that area, to mark them out on the ground and get the local authorities to clear them of trees before our return in March. As part of the I.I.O.E. programme, we also had to establish an automatic tide-gauge at Port Victoria, in order to obtain a year's continuous observations. We spent a bare week on this work, marking out excellent sites on Bird and Denis Islands, and giving the sailors and scientists a good run ashore on Mahé before heading back to East Africa.

Inasmuch as the Seychelles are an enormous lump of granite sticking up in the middle of the ocean, they are unique, and they were a source of endless wonder to our scientists. Are they a bit of Africa, dropped off and left behind during the era of Continental Drift? Why were some parts highly magnetic, others not? These and a host of other related questions had to await our forthcoming geophysical work next March. This brief visit was no more than a preliminary reconnaissance.

After Christmas at Mombasa we returned to Lamu to continue the Kenya Banks survey for a further week, and to re-embark the camp-party on completion of their surveys. Though there was plenty of scope to extend our surveys northwards, our programme at that stage did not permit us to spend any longer in that area, so, assuming we would not be returning, we recovered all our marks. While at Lamu on New Year's Eve, I decided to fill the famous 'Owen Bowl' and throw a party. 1961 had been an eventful year for all of us, and it deserved a proper send-off. My promotion to Captain had also come through, and the end of a survey had to be marked in traditional style. Furthermore, who knew what 1962 would hold in store? It was indeed a memorable party!

We returned to Mombasa on 6th January, and two days later commenced another long scientific traverse across the Indian Ocean, starting off in a south-easterly direction. We were making for the isle of tortoises and turtles, Aldabra. We had hydrographic, scientific and geodetic work to do there, and I planned to land a two-boat camp-party for 48 hours so as to free the ship for work among the other islands of the group. Aldabra is a low-lying atoll, almost enclosing a tidal lagoon (in which, during the First World War, the German commerce-raiding cruiser, *Königsberg* had sometimes hidden herself). As we drew near, we could see the light green water pouring out from the lagoon into the deep blue ocean as the tide fell, and I decided to take the ship in against this outflow. (If it was deep enough for the *Königsberg*, it would be deep enough for *Owen*, I reasoned). We got in all right, and anchored inside the narrow channel to disembark the camp-party, and this had to be done before the tide turned, as there was insufficient room to swing. At slack water, I was just able to turn the ship in time to steam out again against the incoming flood.

Aldabra Island was suspected of being incorrectly charted, so the camp-party were to observe its geographical position (by timing the transits of stars at 45° altitude), and carry out the groundwork for a subsequent mapping survey. They had also to establish an automatic tide-gauge for the I.I.O.E. Meanwhile, the ship was to determine the relative positions of the other islands (by running taut-wire measuring gear) and sketch in their size and shape by visual cross-bearings. Cosmoledo and Assumption were both wrongly charted, while Astove was found to be not only much larger than shown, but also no fewer than 4 miles out of position.

Continuing eastwards, past the Farquhar Islands, we got involved in a cyclone. Heavy seas and a rising wind caused much discomfort and anxiety, and seriously interfered with our next task, in the Agalega Islands. Our efforts here to set up another tide-gauge were thwarted by rough seas and a heavy surf, and we spent the whole afternoon trying to recover one of our officers who had managed to land but could not get back. Had it not been for the efforts of a local surf-boat's crew in fighting their way out at the third attempt, he would have been marooned on the island for six weeks, as I was determined not to hang around for the cyclone to hit us so close inshore. As it was, with the seas getting ever more ominous and a jet-black sky, we just got clear in time.

Setting course to the north-eastward, we commenced a 2,000-mile traverse, parallel to the first one, towards the coast of India, crossing the Equator for the fourth time. All our special scientific equipment functioned faultlessly, and we gleaned a great deal of valuable new information. The traverse finished just outside Bombay, which we entered on 25th January.

We received a great welcome – particularly by the I.N.'s Hydrographic Service, but Bombay itself was bedlam. We had arrived on one of India's national holidays, 'Republic Day', which covered the whole week-end, and the city was packed with holiday-makers in carnival mood.

However, we achieved our operational objectives, changed round some of our scientists, embarked the Co-ordinator of the International Indian Ocean Expedition, and set off to the southward on the easternmost of our long ocean traverses. This was to take us on a zigzag course through the maze of shoals, reefs, islands and atolls which make up the Laccadive and Maldive archipelagos, and somehow managing to keep the ship in safe water, we were able to show the Co-ordinator at first hand some of the problems that would later confront the I.I.O.E.

At the southernmost tip of this 800-mile-long chain of islands lies Addu Atoll, containing the strategically important air-base at Gan, and here we spent a week in February, surveying, observing, diving, establishing another automatic tide-gauge and making many other types of investigation. The ship herself spent much of the time locating, salvaging and repairing a broken submarine power cable. From there we continued the traverse from the Equator to the Tropic of Capricorn, skirting the Chagos Archipelago and the Saya de Malha Bank, rounding the Cargados Carajos reefs, and on down to Mauritius.

Mauritius, which I had not visited before, was quite an 'eye-opener', and I was struck by its mountainous scenery and lush vegetation, and also by the beautiful beaches at the north end of the island, from which some of us bathed.

Off we went again in a sweeping arc to the northward, via the tiny islet of Tomelin (on which the scientists landed to measure the gravity and study birds), and back to Agalega. Here we found a very different state of affairs to that which we had experienced in January, the weather being quite perfect, so that we were able to carry out all our tasks without hindrance. From Agalega we returned to the Aldabra-Cosmoledo group of islands to tie up a few loose ends from our earlier visit, and re-embark our three tide-watchers, as well as Government map-makers who had been using our geodetic data for their survey. The three sailors, who had spent six weeks leading a Robinson Crusoe existence, were quite fit and cheerful, complaining only of land-crabs, rats, mosquitoes and a shortage of beer.

The next leg of our traverse was aimed at the Amirante Bank, west of the Seychelles, which we reached early in March. There had been much communication with the Governor (the Earl of Oxford and Asquith, if I remember rightly) about the tree-clearance I had asked for for our Lamda sites, and what with labour costs and compensation for the land-owners, he had decided that it was more than the Colony's budget could bear. As it was going to take time to agree how these costs could be shared with Whitehall, I decided to defer the main Seychelles Surveys for another year, and restrict this season's work to a general scientific reconnaissance of the islands, and of the vast submarine plateau on which they stand.

A radial system of bathymetric, magnetic and gravity traverses was run from the centre of the plateau for about 100 miles, into abyssal depths, in all directions, and, in the course of this work, we were able to spend a day at anchor off Praslin Island, on which is located the famous Vallé de Mai (thought by some to be the original site of the Garden of Eden).

We spent a couple of days at Port Victoria, where many of us had friends from previous visits, and I remember a most embarrassing incident from that occasion. I had been asked to dine with H.E. the Governor, and to bring with me our senior scientist, a geophysicist of some repute (who shall be nameless). We dined and wined extremely well, and conversation was both scintillating and fascinating. An interesting discussion degenerated, over the port, into an argument between the Earl and our scientist, who, having imbibed not wisely but too well, became both voluble and vehement, and, if not exactly abusive, started addressing H.E. as 'Guv'. I was appalled, and took the first opportunity to bring the proceedings to a close. Next morning I made a special call on the Governor to apologize personally for the scientist's ill-mannered behaviour (which, I felt, reflected badly on the ship), and was much relieved that H.E. appeared to take it all in good part.

Having achieved our purpose in the Seychelles, we reluctantly returned to the Kenya coast. We put into Mombasa to fuel and to discharge our scientists (for a month), and then moved up the coast to pick up the threads of our surveys off Lamu. We had to re-mark the area, and extend the triangulation northwards to enable the ship and boats to work in and around Manda and Patta Bays, and we had to lay tautly-moored floating beacons to control the more distant work off-shore. But by 9th April, and after a farewell visit to Lamu, I reckoned the surveys were complete, and took the ship back to Mombasa.

Two days at Mombasa were enough to replenish stores, fuel and provisions, and to embark a fresh team of Cambridge scientists, and on 12th April we headed eastward once more, for the Seychelles. This visit was partly to make a fresh check on the gravimeter, but mainly to try to clarify policy for future surveys of the Bank. However, the islands also provided the right point of departure for the last of our geophysical traverses across the Arabian Sea, terminating at a point on the Indian coast between Bombay and Karachi. This traverse included our sixth crossing of the Equator – and on completion we put in to Karachi for a two-day 'Operational' visit to the Pakistani Hydrographer.

On 28th April we started the long homeward passage, running a continuous series of geophysical traverses similar to those on our outward passage, via Aden, the Haycock Islands (where we spent two days completing the survey broken off six months earlier), Suez, Malta and Gibraltar, and so back at last to our home port, Devonport, which we reached on 31st May, exactly a year since our home-coming from the Atlantic Cruise.

What a commission it had been! We had done so much! We had visited so many strange places; we had broken so many records. In the two years since commissioning, we had obtained 53,000 miles of new oceanic soundings, and had steamed the equivalent of three times round the world (75,000 miles). It had been such an epic that we all felt it should be properly written up, so we compiled and published a glossy magazine for distribution to all and sundry, including at least one copy for everyone who had participated in it. It was gratifying to hear later, from the local Naval Authorities, that in their opinion this was the best Ship's Magazine they had ever seen!

Two episodes stand out in my memory about that ensuing summer. Firstly, the Royal Geographical Society recognized our achievements by awarding me the 'Cuthbert Peek Grant' in the shape of a magnificent inscribed silver salver (which is one of my most treasured possessions). Secondly, I was deputed to present a paper to the Commonwealth Surveyors' Conference at Cambridge – on 'The Measurement of Gravity at Sea!' This was an ordeal I had not bargained for, and ought, in my view, to have been assigned to the Senior Cambridge Scientist. However, I duly wrote a pretty straightforward factual account of our work, for advance distribution to the conference, and went up to Cambridge to 'present' it in person. As I was virtually the only non-scientist present in the crowded hall, I decided on a light-hearted approach, speaking as 'a simple sailor'. This seemed to go down rather well, causing much friendly amusement, and when I rounded off my oration by saying 'The only thing I know about gravity is that without it I would not be able to drop any bricks,' the conference burst into spontaneous applause – and I sat down! (I was told afterwards by several of the delegates that it was the best speech of the whole conference!)

CHAPTER XX

Greenwich (War Course), 1962 and Assistant Hydrographer, Admiralty, 1963–5

I RELINQUISHED COMMAND OF H.M.S. *Owen* that summer, after working up the results of all our surveys and seeing the ship well into her annual refit. I was earmarked for another shore appointment, this time as Assistant Hydrographer at the Admiralty. However, as the post would not be vacant till the following spring, it was decided that I should fill in the time by undertaking the six-month Senior Officers' War Course at the Royal Naval College, Greenwich, starting towards the end of September, 1962. This would be the first time that an (H) officer had taken the course.

Mary and I went down to look for accommodation and found a suitable first-floor flat within reasonable walking distance of the College. Though most of the Senior Officers on our course were Captains, R.N., others were drawn from all three Services and included one or two Civil Servants. The Director was a Captain Northey, R.N., who had recently been the British Naval Attaché in Moscow.

The course was of a very 'general' nature, concerned largely with Current Affairs, but also with aspects of military, economic and industrial strategy. It was run on notoriously 'gentlemanly' lines (as befitting Senior Officers!), with fairly relaxed schedules and plenty of scope for self-expression and participation in discussion and debate. Eminent speakers from all sorts of national activity came down to address us, and we travelled about the country, visiting different establishments of national importance or general interest: Porton Down, an R.A.F. Bomber Base, the U.S.A.F. ICBM Base at Mildenhall, a Royal Dockyard, the Old Bailey, the House of Lords, the R.M. Commando Training Centre at Lympstone, the R.A.F. College of Air Warfare at Manby, etc., etc.

Amongst many other speakers was Vice-Admiral Sir Peter Gretton, at that time Controller of the Navy, on the future size and shape of the Fleet, with much emphasis on the projected nuclear-powered 'Polaris' submarines. This gave me an opportunity to point out to him that submarines of that sort could not be operated without a massive expansion of the Surveying Fleet to undertake the oceanographical surveys they would need – a remark which later reached the ears of the Hydrographer and earned me a 'pat on the back' from him.

The course ended shortly before Easter, 1963, with the Admiral President, Rear Admiral Morgan Giles, chairing a conference on some such subject as European Union or the Unification of Europe, which each of the 'syndicates' into which we had been divided had been studying in depth for about two weeks. Our syndicate had deputed me to write our paper, which I did, with a good deal of emotional enthusiasm included, as I felt rather strongly about it. It came under fire from one of the other syndicates, whose paper took quite a different line and was much more objective. When the Admiral President invited me to respond to this attack, I had to admit that the speaker had deployed some persuasive arguments, and that they had been 'dispassionate'. 'But, sir,' I went on, 'I don't think one ought to discount passion' – a remark which convulsed the Admiral and provoked gales of laughter all round!

In view of the fact that I was to spend the next two years in Whitehall as Assistant Hydrographer, and that all our family interests seemed to lie to the north of London, Mary and I felt that it would save a lot of trouble if we could find a house on that side of the metropolis. After looking in the Hampstead area, we found a delightful little house in a quiet cul-de-sac off Fitzroy Park in Highgate, which we bought and which turned out to be ideal for our purpose. It was in an entirely rural setting, yet only five miles from the Admiralty, which was easily reached by public transport.

It must have been in late spring or early summer that I became Assistant Hydrographer (A.H.) for the first time. My office was on the first floor of the main Admiralty building, alongside that of the Hydrographer of the Navy, Rear Admiral E.G. Irving. We had a connecting interior door between our offices, and there was always a good deal of to-ing and fro-ing from one to the other. I usually had more paper-work to deal with than the Admiral, and, by mid-morning, having cleared his in-tray, he would usually wander in to me for a general chat. Although this was welcome enough, as keeping me very much 'in' on his thoughts and outlook, it was also irritating and time-wasting for me, and usually meant that I was seldom clear of the day's work before 6 p.m. in the evenings.

My main field of responsibility as A.H. was Personnel, which embraced all (H) officers and Surveying Recorders, as well as the Schemes of Complement of all our ships. Every aspect of the officers' careers was dealt with by me: recruiting, training, appointment, advancement, promotion and retirement. Not only did all Confidential Reports on officers come to me, but I was also on the receiving end of all applications and requests affecting their careers, especially for particular appointments. Officers were encouraged to send in 'Preferences' for their next type of appointment, and twice a year I used to promulgate a Forecast of Officers' Movements. These would usually occur in January and August, during the winter lie-ups and summer leave periods, and my forecasts were timed to give all concerned several months' notice, while taking account of officers' expressed preferences. It was quite a chore, and, needless to say, it was seldom possible to please everyone.

One very interesting aspect of this planning work was the insight it gave me into the long-term career prospects of my own colleagues, having regard to their ages, ranks, seniorities, records, reports and promotion chances, together with projected retirement dates for their seniors. Poring over the big diagrammatic charts which my predecessors had constructed, showing the careers of all our captains, commanders and lieutenant-commanders projected through the next decade, it didn't take me long to tumble to the fact that I had at least a sporting chance of reaching the top of the tree myself!

I had taken over as A.H. from Captain R.H. ('Tim') Connell, and the last thing he had said to me was that 'Steve' Ritchie would be the next Hydrographer and David Haslam the one after that. David was considerably junior to me, and not yet a Captain, so I spent some time examining the evidence for Tim Connell's prediction. Since the end of the War, no officer had held the post of Hydrographer for more than five years, and that had become the established practice. Admiral Irving was expected to retire in 1965, after five years in the 'Chair', and if Steve Ritchie were to do likewise, he would retire at the end of 1970. By that time I would be the senior Captain, and, although I would then be 54, and due to retire on reaching nine years' seniority, I could see no reason why Steve should not hand over to me! I mentioned this privately to Steve one day, and said that whereas I was by no means sure that I wanted to become Hydrographer, I was certainly not going to stand for any 'jiggery-pokery' which would deny me that option. Steve saw the point and put it to Admiral Irving, who agreed. With enhanced prospects, my morale improved!

One really fascinating aspect of my work as A.H. was the enormous activity flowing from the decision of Government to transfer the strategic nuclear deterrent from the R.A.F. to the Royal Navy, in the shape of a new squadron of Polaris submarines, each of which would carry 16 intercontinental ballistic missiles with nuclear war-heads, and would be nuclear-powered. The implications of this decision, though foreseen by the Hydrographer and his staff (from their close contact with the American

Oceanographical Office), were slow to dawn on the Admiralty, particularly as they affected our own Hydrographic Service. As I had pointed out to the Controller during the War Course at Greenwich, 'Polaris' submarines could not be properly operated without a massive expansion of oceanographical effort on the part of the Surveying Service and the Hydrographic Department. The need for such expansion had already been brought home to us by our own Submarine Service when they started to build a new class of nuclear-powered 'hunter-killer' Fleet submarines, which, being 'True' submarines (as opposed to conventional ones, which were now referred to as 'submersibles'), could dive to great depths and remain there almost indefinitely. Alerted to this requirement, the Hydrographer had initiated a new construction programme for the replacement of our ageing Survey Ships with a new class of specially-designed 'Survey/Oceanographical Ships', and the 'Polaris' programme (which had been given priority over everything else) immediately added fresh impetus to the urgency of our requirements.

By working in close consultation with the Naval Staff, the Polaris Executive, Flag Officer Submarines, and the United States Naval Oceanographer, we were able to assess the size and extent of the task facing us, and it was a daunting one. From this, we could deduce and define the resources, in ships and manpower, that we would need to perform it. A whole new Survey Fleet, and a considerable increase in our civilian staff, would be necessary, and these urgent requirements now had to be argued through the elaborate and ponderous Whitehall 'establishment', right through to the Treasury and the Cabinet. The paper 'war' involved in this effort became a full-time task in itself, and absorbed much of my attention for months on end.

We set our sights on a balanced Survey Fleet of twelve ships, in three separate categories: four large ones for oceanic work, four medium-sized ones for coastal work, and four small ones for shallow-water work inshore (in addition to the civilian-manned motor-launch used by the South Coast of England Survey). In order to man this expanded fleet, we would have to pay off the four post-war frigate-conversions (*Dampier*, *Dalrymple*, *Owen* and *Cook*), which were costly in manpower, and which, by 1965, would be 20 years old. This would leave us with the more modern *Vidal* (for oceanic work) and the three vessels of the Inshore Survey Squadron, *Echo*, *Egeria* and *Enterprise* (for shallow water work).

To make up the new fleet of twelve ships, we would therefore have to order three in the first category, four in the second, and one in the third. These would have to be designed (by us) and built for the purpose. To clarify the different categories and functions of these vessels, I proposed a simple classification system. I did not like the clumsy expression, 'Survey/Oceanographical Ship', so proposed that these be classed as 'Ocean Survey Ships' (OSS). The medium-sized ones should be classed as 'Coastal Survey Vessels' (CSV) and the small ones as 'Inshore Survey Craft' (ISC). This classification was officially accepted without demur.

Having eventually got our new-construction programme approved in principle, it fell to me to propose names for the new ships. I was keen to resurrect some of the famous old survey-ship names from earlier centuries, and thoroughly enjoyed myself poring over the old lists. With my penchant for all things Icelandic, *Hecla* immediately took my fancy. Should the other ships of the OSS-class also be given 'volcano' names (*Aetna* and *Erebus*) or (as 'H' was Hydrographer's abbreviated title within the Admiralty) should their names also start with an 'H'? I pondered on this and finally went for the latter option, recommending the good old names *Hecate* and *Hydra*. Names for the CSVs were a bit of a problem. Now I come to think of it, we had originally asked for six of these, but they were later cut down to four. We had declared that these vessels would operate in pairs, which would scale down their Schemes of Complement. I felt that there should be a common factor in the choice of their names, and that each pair should be distinguished by a further common factor. The list of old survey-ships showed an abundance of 'animal' names, and from these I was able to select three pairs, each pair starting with the same letter, viz. *Bulldog* and *Beagle*, *Fox* and *Fawn* and *Penguin* and *Porcupine*. The last pair never materialized, but the other four names were accepted.

Finally, I came to the ISCs. We had been offered two Inshore Minesweepers for conversion to survey craft, and although we had only stated a requirement for one, we decided to accept them both, and to augment the three existing 'E'-class of the Inshore Survey Squadron with one, the other replacing the South Coast of England Survey's civilian-manned SML. As these ex-minesweepers differed somewhat from the three 'E'-class ISC, though of similar size, and as there were no suitable old names starting with 'E', I picked on another pair of names for them: *Woodlark* and *Waterwitch*, both of which were approved and accepted.

There were definite advantages in being Assistant Hydrographer! Not only did A.H. arrange the appointments of all our officers, but he was in the unique position of being able to arrange his own! Next summer I would have completed two years as A.H., so would be due for another sea-appointment. That would just about coincide with the delivery of the first of our new Ocean Survey Ships, H.M.S. *Hecla*. What could be more appropriate?

In my six-monthly 'Forecast of Officers' Movements', put out shortly before Christmas, I was shown as due for *Hecla*, in command during the ensuing summer (1965). Then on 21st December, Mary and I (as C.O.-designate) were invited up to Yarrow's yard at Scotstoun, on the Clyde, to attend the launching ceremony of H.M.S. *Hecla*, the first of our new class of Ocean Survey Ships. Margaret Irving, wife of the Hydrographer of the Navy, named and launched the ship, and became her 'Sponsor'. It was a very happy occasion, the first time either of us had witnessed the launching of a ship, but it was not to be the last!

Once it was established and recognized that I was to be the ship's first Commanding Officer, much of the planning for her first commission naturally came my way, so during the spring of 1965 a good deal of my time as A.H. was taken up in working out how best *Hecla* could contribute to the increasingly urgent survey task imposed on us by the 'Polaris' programme. As ever, the building programme had slipped, and it soon became obvious that the ship would not be ready before the late summer or early autumn. However, we had seen to it that these new ships would be equipped with helicopters, and I managed to arrange for *Hecla*'s Helicopter Flight to commission on schedule and be available for work independently during the summer. To prepare for this, I sent myself off for a C.O.'s Helicopter Course at Portland, which would give me the essential knowledge that any commanding officer would need if his ship was to operate these flying-machines.

One of the first tasks that 'Hecla' would be faced with after commissioning would be a survey to the north-west of Scotland, on the edge of the continental shelf, and this would require the siting of Lamda and Hi-fix stations on two remote islands: North Rona and St. Kilda. By means of our 'Wasp' helicopter, I could reconnoitre these islands, and select, mark and co-ordinate the four required sites well in advance of the ship's arrival, and so save valuable time. I therefore arranged to be relieved as A.H. fairly early in the summer, and appointed myself to *Hecla* in a supernumerary capacity, pending commissioning. As there was a temporary shortage of Captains (H), I managed to get an Acting-Captaincy for Johnny Pryor (who was a Commander) so that he could take over from me.

CHAPTER XXI

H.M.S. *Hecla* (and her helicopter), 1965

IT WAS MID-SUMMER when I left the Admiralty, and after taking some leave, I flew up to Stornoway to meet our Helicopter Flight (No.409), which was to be based there. The Flight Commander was a Lieutenant-Commander 'Pete' Spelling, and the Flight consisted of a Chief Petty Officer and four other Fleet Air Arm ratings. Their job was to service and maintain the 'Wasp' helicopter and ensure its operational readiness when required. Peter Spelling was an experienced and extremely competent pilot, though less than conscientious about paper work, and (as I was to discover later) anything but hidebound by Naval Regulations. I took to him immediately.

The island of Rona (commonly referred to as 'North Rona' to distinguish it from the other Rona in the Hebrides) lies in absolute isolation some 40 miles N.N.E. of the Butt of Lewis. It is uninhabited, except by thousands of seals and millions of sea birds, though there are traces of former habitation by Celtic monks in the shape of a few ruined stone cells. This tiny island was our first objective, but we needed fair weather to land on it and good visibility to find it! While waiting for the right conditions, Pete Spelling took me on several practice flights over the Outer Hebrides, and I soon developed complete confidence in his expertise as an aviator.

The day came when we could set out on our first operational sortie, with the helicopter loaded with all the surveying equipment that I would need. We took our departure from the Butt of Lewis and headed out into the blue. After half an hour's flying, there was still nothing in sight and one couldn't help feeling distinctly lonely out there, and a bit apprehensive too. What would happen if our engine failed and we had to ditch? However, peering ahead with my binoculars, I soon made out the misty summits of the island's three hills, right in front of us but still a long way off.

Pete Spelling put the 'Wasp' down gently near the grassy summit of the western hill and shut down the engine. We got out and I started the day's work, with theodolite, hand-bearing compass and hundred-foot tape. I had to select, mark and fix the exact sites for the various components of the Lambda station and its camp, so that we had an uninterrupted 'view' to the westward, and then do the same for the ancillary Hi-Fix station (whose performance was to be checked out against the Lambda system) several hundred yards down the southern slope of the hillside. The weather was lovely but the work took us most of the day. Afterwards we wandered round the north side of the island, which was low-lying, and on which hundreds of seals were basking, many of them with new-born pups. The baby seals are white and I was astonished at the number which appeared to have been abandoned by their mothers. I was both horrified and disgusted too to see how many of these had been attacked by the swarms of sea birds, some having had their eyes pecked out.

I think we spent about a month at Stornoway, and I'm sure we made more than one trip to North Rona. But our other objective was St. Kilda, 50 miles west of the Outer Hebrides. To make that trip, we needed not only settled weather, but also some form of stand-by rescue service, which would be provided – given adequate notice – by Flag Officer, Naval Air Command. We had to wait several days for the right conditions, and I must say that despite the invisible air support (somewhere back in Scotland), I felt more apprehensive when we set out for St. Kilda than I had on our first trip to Rona. It seemed to take hours of flying over empty ocean before we finally sighted it.

St. Kilda is a compact group of small, steep islands about 50 miles from the nearest land, of which the largest is Horta. When Pete Spelling and I arrived in our 'Wasp' helicopter, and alighted near the summit of Horta, there was a small Army communications unit stationed on the island, accommodated, as far as I can remember, in war-time Nissen huts some distance from the crumbling ruins of an old village. We were struck by the stark beauty of our surroundings and in particular by the immensely high cliffs on the north side of Horta, which fall 1100 feet sheer into the ocean.

Here on St. Kilda we had much the same task to perform as we had achieved earlier on North Rona. But first we had to make contact with the Army unit, to explain our mission, and to safeguard the pegs and markers which we would be leaving in the ground to identify the Lambda and Hi-Fix sites. This necessitated a long walk down to their encampment and a tedious climb back afterwards. We spent most of the day selecting, marking and fixing the positions of the various sites, and meticulously describing them for future recovery by the ship's survey parties. Meanwhile, the gale which had been forecast for the evening was beginning to warn us of its impending arrival. We had to hurry.

The helicopter had been parked, and securely 'anchored' to the ground, on the very edge of a high precipice, some distance above us. We toiled our way up to it and as we breasted the summit of the ridge, we were struck by the full force of a strong south-westerly sweeping the face of the precipice some distance above us. The gale had already arrived and the 'Wasp' was straining at the leash, its rotors flapping alarmingly in the violent up-draught. There was no time to lose. We piled ourselves into it, cast off the lashings, and virtually shot upwards as the rotors started to whirl. In seconds we were out over the edge of the precipice and climbing rapidly. It had been a pretty close shave, and we both breathed sighs of relief as we swung away to the eastward on the long haul back to Stornoway.

Our third objective was the Flannan Islands, some 15 miles west of Lewis, and our task there was relatively simple, though the islands hardly lent themselves to helicopter landings, there being hardly any flat land on them. A lighthouse and the keepers' cottages dominate the larger island, and I was able to arrange a measure of support in that quarter for our eventual camp-party. We were also able to find just enough space for the Lambda and Hi-Fix stations. This meant that I now had the basic information from which the plotting-sheets could be constructed for the control of our forthcoming surveys. The whole area could be covered by one or other of the two pairs of 'slave'-sites. Our helicopter had already proved its immense value.

I sent the Helicopter Flight back to Lee-on-Solent and flew down to London. Armed with all the required data from the three islands (of which aerial photographs had been specially taken for us by the R.A.F.), I was able to pin-point the exact positions to be occupied by the Lambda and Hi-Fix 'slaves', and from there it was a reasonably straightforward job for Chart Branch's Geodetic Section at Cricklewood to calculate their co-ordinates. That done, the necessary plotting-sheets could be constructed, and I was then in a position to start drawing the various sets of intersecting range-curves.

In August I went up to Scotstoun to look over *Hecla* as she was fitting out, and to meet the officers who had already joined, as well as key ratings of the pre-commissioning crew. The ship was most impressive, and although there seemed to be a great deal of work outstanding, the general consensus was that she would meet her scheduled commissioning date.

Meanwhile, up in Iceland, my daughter Virginia had commissioned the Professor of Art at Reykjavik University to paint a large water-colour picture of Mount Hekla for me to hang in the ship, and, quite independently, Petur Sigurdsson (the Icelandic Hydrographer) had also presented the ship with a picture of Hekla, already framed, as a Commissioning present. This one would be fixed in a prominent position in the Chartroom, while the water-colour (which I much preferred) would have a place of honour above the fireplace in the Captain's cabin.

The great day came on September 8th, when *Hecla* was commissioned.

The ceremony and religious service, conducted by three Naval Chaplains, and attended by much of the Navy's 'Top Brass' and their wives, was held on the dockside, with a Royal Marine Band to accompany the hymns and provide suitably stirring music for the occasion. I read out the Commissioning Warrant from a flag-bedecked dais, and afterwards the assembled company repaired to the ship's Flight Deck for the traditional reception. Using my sword, Margaret Irving (the ship's Sponsor) and I cut the Commissioning Cake, I made a light-hearted speech, and the champagne started flowing freely. There were other speeches too – by Sir Eric Yarrow (whose firm had built the ship) and by the Hydrographer of the Navy. It was a fitting start to an eventful commission.

That evening we sailed down the Clyde for Acceptance Trials, with the Commodore, Contract-Built Ships ('Basher' Watkins) and Yarrow's people embarked, but with an Admiralty Pilot (a retired Captain, R.N.) in temporary command. I was not impressed with the way he handled the ship – particularly with his use of the bow-thruster – and I told the Commodore that I could hardly wait to get my hands on the ship and take full command. All went reasonably well and the formal hand-over and signing of papers was finally completed that night. Extraneous personnel were disembarked at Greenock, after which I anchored the ship at Tail of the Bank. I was indeed a happy man.

We went south for a quick visit to Plymouth Sound, Spithead and Portland – where we embarked the Helicopter Flight – and then steamed back up the Irish Sea and round into Londonderry, which was to be our forward base for the immediate surveys up north. Naval Regulations would have us spend the first month on Trials and Work-Ups off Plymouth and Portsmouth, but I had managed to persuade the 'Powers that Be' that the 'Polaris' surveys were too urgent for that, and, furthermore, that the operations I had planned would constitute as good a Work-Up as any that they could devise. We were to go straight in at the deep end. With autumn upon us, we headed north for the survey grounds, all geared up to establish the Lambda and Hi-Fix camps at the three sites I had reconnoitred during the summer. This would be a major test for the helicopter.

We hove to close under the lee of the Flannan Islands, with all the masts and spars, electronic equipment and camp-gear made up into portable loads ready to be moved on to the Flight Deck. The helicopter took off and the first of these loads was then placed in the big carrying net. With the helicopter hovering low overhead, the wire-rope lifting-pendant dangling from it (with a heavy spring-hook at the end) was snatched on to the four corners of the net and the helicopter swooped into the air and away towards the islands. It seemed simple enough, but as the aircraft gathered speed, the heavy load slung beneath it began to swing, and the swing became steadily more pronounced and more alarming.

The net contained the five 20-ft. steel spars that made up the main Lambda mast, and as it swung backwards and forwards, ever closer to the horizontal, the long spars began to approach the blades of the 'Wasp's whirling rotor. It looked highly dangerous. Was Pete Spelling aware of the danger? Surely he must be, because the helicopter itself was now advancing in fits and starts, pulled backwards on the back-swing and forwards on the fore-swing, a motion that was actually aggravating the pendulum-effect that was so alarming. I called him up on the R/T and advised him to hover until the swing had subsided. I think he'd already worked that out for himself, and was actually doing so. The immediate danger was over, but it had been a near thing. Neither Pete Spelling nor any of the rest of us had had previous experience of helicopter load-lifting, and we learnt a valuable lesson. Henceforward, we used a much shorter lifting-pendant and, with enhanced vigilance from Spelling, we had little further trouble of that sort.

By the end of the day, and after some two dozen lifts by the 'Wasp', we had everything safely ashore on the islands, including the camp-party itself. We had to land another party of stalwart sailors by boat, to help with the erection of the Lambda mast and the Uniport huts, but the whole operation was completed within 24 hours. It would certainly have taken several days – even with good weather – if we had had to rely solely on the boats. Our helicopter was proving a veritable godsend.

We repeated the whole process at St. Kilda, and everything went swimmingly. For October in those parts, the weather was remarkably kind to us, and I could manoeuvre the ship quite easily, turning her with the wind fine on the starboard bow for the helicopter to take off and put down, and holding her there with our 'internal tug', the bow-thruster. We lay a comfortable distance between Horta and Boreray, while the 'Wasp' flitted back and forth all morning and all afternoon, carrying load after load inshore. With the St. Kilda 'slave'-camp finally established and in radio contact, and with the 'Wasp' safely back in the ship's hangar, we set course for North Rona.

Next morning, when we were nearly there, Pete Spelling reported to me that the helicopter was 'U/S' (i.e. unserviceable). Some part of its anatomy needed replacement, and we did not carry a spare. This was indeed a serious setback. Should I divert to Stornoway and wait for a replacement to be flown up to us (a delay of perhaps two days), or should we go ahead and land everything at North Rona by boat? Weather conditions were good, and if they held, we might finish the job within 48 hours. I decided to chance our luck and try.

There was only one conceivable landing-place on the island. It was a long cleft in the rocks on the west side of a low-lying promontory. This cleft, wide enough to take the boats, formed a natural 'dock' in which the water, though deep, was susceptible to the Atlantic swell. This, coupled with the high sheer side of the cleft, made unloading anything but simple – but that was only half the battle. Once each boat-load of stores had been carried up to the rocks with ropes, those stores had to be carried half a mile across country, uphill all the way. The two big sounding-boats ran a shuttle-service between ship and shore, the stores being lowered into them by the ship's crane. A day ashore, in fine weather, makes a welcome change for any sailor, so there was no lack of volunteers to do the portering. My recollection is that we lay at anchor that night and continued all next day. Nothing could have demonstrated more clearly what a tremendous asset the helicopter represented (when serviceable) in operations of this sort.

Having established our three widely-separated 'slave'-stations, all fully manned and provisioned, and all in radio contact with the ship and with one another, we were now able to start the survey. It was the first properly-controlled bathymetric survey that had ever been undertaken of these waters and it was full of interest. It was also the first test of the new ship in her designed role. *Hecla* had been fitted with a great deal of automated equipment – including the much-vaunted A.D.L (Automatic Data Logging) system – all of it virtually untried. Needless to say, we experienced our fair share of 'teething troubles', but on the whole everything worked splendidly. We plugged away at this survey throughout October and November, in steadily deteriorating weather conditions, sometimes having to break off to sort out a problem on one of the islands or to seek shelter from really severe storms.

The survey covered a large area on the edge of the continental shelf, between the Faeroe Islands and the Outer Hebrides, and in these notoriously stormy waters *Hecla* had ample opportunity to demonstrate her sea-keeping qualities and her behaviour in really rough seas. It quickly became apparent that her motion in a seaway was quite unacceptable. She rolled heavily – and sometimes violently – in a beam sea, and, due to her relatively short length, she pitched horribly in a head sea. On the other hand, she remained tolerably dry. There came a time in the course of replenishing the camp on North Rona by helicopter, when we received warning of a very deep depression, accompanied by winds of hurricane force, approaching from the south-westward. To run for shelter meant abandoning the job we were doing, so I decided instead to complete it, and then try to duck behind the centre of the depression and so avoid its full fury.

We steamed flat out into the Atlantic, with the epicentre fine on the starboard bow, and slowly drawing to the right. About midnight I altered course to the north-west and we began pitching heavily into a heavy head sea. I decided to heave-to, head to wind, and ride it out. When dawn broke, it was blowing Force 10-11, with truly mountainous seas bearing down upon us, the ship burying her head in the huge waves, and the screw racing as the stern came out of the water. I kept just enough way on the ship to prevent her head paying off, and closed up a second Officer of the Watch to operate the bow-thruster.

All day the storm raged and the seas thundered down upon us, huge breaking waves bigger than anything I'd seen before, and the ship soared into their crests and plunged into their troughs, shuddering from end to end under the impact of hundreds of tons of water sweeping over the fo'c'sle and crashing into her upperworks. We lay hove-to some 50 miles S.W. of the Faeroe Islands, with the engine at slow-ahead. To have given the ship any more power would have been to risk serious damage from the enormous waves, and because I lacked complete confidence in the ship's stability in such conditions, I was reluctant to turn her round. With these seas on her beam, I feared she might roll right over, and with the seas astern, she might well be 'pooped'.

On the other hand, with the storm showing no signs of slackening, we could lie there for days, wasting valuable time. As evening drew on, I resolved to risk everything – and get out of it. Warning all hands that the ship was about to alter course ('and may roll heavily') – so that everything movable could be secured – I put the engines to half ahead and ordered 'Starboard 35'. We all held our breath. She came round quickly, rolled hard over to starboard, then straightened up and, with the seas now right astern, ran smoothly before them. We breathed again. She had behaved better than I'd feared. Keeping her speed just a little slower than the speed of the great waves – so that they rolled smoothly under her, we ran down through the night towards the Flannan Islands, and out of the worst of the storm. That storm will remain forever etched in my memory. I think the date was the 10th November.

Towards the end of the month I took the ship into Loch Ewe – for a double purpose. In the first place, our A.D.L. had accumulated so much survey data that it had outstripped our ability to assess and digest it. We needed a few days' respite to portray it properly, consider it carefully, and work out which parts needed checking for further investigation. In the second place, we had to prepare the ship for our forthcoming official visit to the Icelandic Hydrographer in Reykjavik, a task involving re-painting the hull to eliminate the ravages of the past two months of continuous sea-time. It was now late in the season, and the country round Loch Ewe was under deep snow. Our passage to Iceland was bitterly cold. The sea-spray, curling over the fo'c'sle with every plunge, froze all over the decks and superstructure, blotting out all vision from the bridge windows (except through the rotating screens) and making normal movement on the upper decks extremely hazardous. The wind was in the north – straight off the icefields – and when we reached a lee in Eyrabakki Bay, we had to turn steam-jets on to the windlass and cables to un-freeze them. We lay there at anchor, in the shelter of the snow-clad land, and made final preparations for our arrival on the morrow and for the official visit.

The visit to Iceland was part of the trials and tests to which I was determined to put *Hecla* before the end of her first season, and to cross the Arctic Circle in December seemed a reasonable challenge. We sailed north, rounded the north-west 'horn' and continued to Eyjafjord, the long firth running down to Akureyri (Iceland's northern capital).

Eyjafjord was completely frozen over when we left Akureyri, and our passage through it to the open sea provided the first test of the ship's performance as an ice-breaker, though in fact the ice was pretty thin. Once through it, we headed east, so circumnavigating Iceland, and continued round to the southward, then on to pass close to the Faeroes, and so back to Scotland. I think it was during the passage back from Iceland, during which we were running an oceanographical traverse, that a memorable episode occurred. A beam sea was running and the ship, as usual, was rolling heavily. I was having my customary bath before dinner, and having a nice lazy soak, when, to my astonishment and dismay, the water just poured out of the bath on to the floor, leaving me 'high and dry'. After that, I made a strong recommendation to Their Lordships that *Hecla* – and her two sister-ships – should be fitted with stabilisers! On 17th December we entered our home port, Devonport, for the first time, and gave Christmas leave to all hands. I reckoned it had been well earned.

CHAPTER XXII

H.M.S. *Hecla*, South Africa and North Atlantic, 1966–7

WHEN THE NEW YEAR DAWNED, I saw Old Age staring me in the face. I would be 50 later that year. My mother would be 80. None of us were getting any younger, and I felt I had to come to terms with it and do something. Just then, however, I had other things on my mind. I had a new boss – Steve Ritchie had become the new Hydrographer – and a new project had been set for *Hecla*. I was told to take her down to South Africa. The purpose was twofold. In the first place, the South African Navy had expressed interest in ordering an Ocean Survey Ship of the same type as *Hecla*, to be built in U.K., and wanted to assess her at first hand. In the second place, scientists of the White Fish Authority were keen to investigate the potential of the Benguela Current as a source of hake for the British fish market.

We sailed from Devonport about 9th January, and made a direct passage down to Bathurst (now Banjul) in Gambia. We were running the customary bathymetric/magnetic/gravimetric traverse throughout the voyage, and our brief call at Bathurst was for the purpose of obtaining a check on the gravimeter. The place did not seem to have changed appreciably since my last visit, in *Challenger*, some 24 years previously, but at least we now had a decent chart to navigate on! The sticky heat of the Gambia made a pleasant change from wintry Britain, but it was a relief to get out into the breezy ocean again.

We rounded the Cape of Good Hope on 1st February – and ran straight into a south-easterly gale. Our visit to Simonstown was both 'Formal' and 'Operational', but the formalities were much in our thoughts as we shaped up to enter the Naval Base, with everything 'ship-shape and Bristol-fashion'. At that moment, as we started to turn, some 2–3 cables off the beach, there was a total power failure! The main engines stopped, the lights went out, the bridge instruments failed, and the 'inter-coms' packed up. I had no communication with the engine-room, or with any other part of the ship – and we were drifting straight down wind on to a rocky lee shore. 'Bloody hell!' I thought, then, dashing out to the bridge-wing, I yelled down to the

Cable Officer on the fo'c'sle: 'Let go port anchor!'. That held her, and she rounded up into the wind, about a cable off shore. Still no sign of power being restored, so I called up the naval tug which had been standing-by off the dockyard entrance, and requested assistance. Halfway over to us, the tug stopped and signalled that she had a steering breakdown. 'Ye Gods!' I muttered, 'What else?' It was hardly an auspicious start to our visit. (The South African Navy might well wonder if it was wise to order a new Survey Ship based on a design which was subject to total power failures like this!) But it might have been worse, I suppose. Before the anchor took hold, I could see in my mind's eye the sort of headlines that would be splashed across the front pages of *The Cape Argus*, had we fetched up on the rocks just in front of Admiralty House – which we very nearly did!

Apart from that inauspicious episode, however, the visit was a great success. There were the usual courtesies and formalities to be got through on the first day, and the next day was largely taken up with a thorough inspection by the South African Naval C-in-C and members of his staff. There was also much liaison and discussion with the S.A. Hydrographer, and between our scientists and those of the University of Cape Town, concerning the forthcoming Benguela project. We remained at Simonstown all that week.

With South African scientists and Naval officers embarked, we set off into the Benguela Current to start the hake-count, using special equipment designed for the purpose. The Current flows northwards along the west coast, and the relatively cold water is extremely rich in nutrients brought up from the Southern Ocean. There are numerous and frequent 'up-wellings' of this cold, plankton-bearing stream of Southern Ocean water, which, for the most part, flows underneath the warmer Atlantic surface water. Where these up-wellings occur, the sea abounds in fish and seals, porpoises, dolphins and whales, and a myriad of sea birds wheeling and diving on the creatures below. It is quite amazing to see such concentrations of wild-life activity, but it does not help the accurate measurement of water-depth, since sound-velocity varies with the temperature and density of the water-masses through which it has to travel. We spent virtually the whole of February on this fisheries-survey, which, in its way, was fascinating, particularly for the scientists. These we disembarked at Walvis Bay, heading home from there on the 1st March.

Our passage from there was fairly uneventful, though the following episode is worthy of mention. Shortly after leaving Walvis Bay, we found ourselves among a flotilla of whale-catchers which were busily hunting and harpooning a school of large whales, one of which, trailing a stream of blood, swam past the ship just below the surface. A whale-catcher, harpoon gun at the ready, was chasing it. My heart went out to the wounded whale, and I made myself extremely unpopular by turning the ship to cut across between the hunters and their quarry. I received a volley of abusive gestures from the catcher's bridge and fore-deck, but I reckoned the whale had escaped.

Our return passage was without further adventures, though useful from a scientific point of view, as our geophysical traverse brought some quite startling new data to light, particularly when we crossed the Gulf of Benin. We got back to Devonport towards the end of March, in good time to take some well-earned Easter leave.

We started the summer session early in May, with a traverse round the south and west of Ireland, and then, via Belfast Lough, to Loch Boisdale. From there we set out to re-establish the 'Green' Lambda station at Gob-na-h'Airde on St. Kilda, followed by the 'Red' station on North Rona, both operations being carried out faultlessly, this time by our 'Wasp' helicopter. With the preliminaries completed, we resumed work on the 'Polaris' survey.

Throughout the summer and autumn of 1966, Hecla worked continuously on this important survey between the Faeroe Islands and the Outer Hebrides, breaking off from time to time to visit places in the Orkneys, Shetlands, Faeroes, Hebrides and Ireland. An agreement had been reached with the Irish Government under which, in return for us undertaking to survey some of their ports, harbours and bays, they would permit us to erect our Lambda-stations on Irish territory in order to control our ocean surveys in future years. This agreement worked out to the mutual advantage of both countries. Thus, to provide inshore-survey experience for our people, and to relieve the monotony of the ship's work in remote waters, we were able to land a strong detachment, with two sounding-boats, at Killybegs, in County Donegal, and to survey the port and its approaches.

We set up this party in rented accommodation on 2nd June. We were delighted by the reception we got from the local populace and from their authorities. Killybegs was a thriving fishing-port, and the Irish Government was determined to expand its off-shore fisheries. The only charts were those of the British Admiralty – based on lead-line surveys of the 19th century, and a re-survey by modern methods was long overdue. The local community understood this, and regarded the arrangement as eminently sensible. But part of the agreement stipulated that, in order to keep a 'low profile' and avoid unwelcome attention from the I.R.A., Hecla was not to remain in an Irish port longer than was strictly necessary to disembark (and re-embark) shore-based detachments. Nor was she to anchor in Irish waters except under stress of bad weather. Thus, on this occasion, the limiting factor was the time it took to ferry the Land-Rover ashore in an inflatable raft: not more than two hours. (I had previously sent an officer in plain clothes to make advance arrangements for accommodation, logistics etc., so everything was ready for us when the ship arrived.)

The main survey proceeded on routine lines, working 'round the clock', day and night, for a fortnight at a time. For those not directly involved in the hydrographic and scientific aspects, it was tedious watch-keeping and day-work, with little diversion other than the ship's own entertainment programmes. For me, however, it was far from boring. Quite apart from the interest and fascination of the developing survey, and my daily stint at hand-contouring of the bathymetry in the Chartroom, the whole business was immensely satisfying. I was aware that *Hecla* would almost certainly be my last sea-going command, and I intended to make the most of it. Standing there on the bridge, or sitting in the Captain's chair, with nothing in sight except the vast blue ocean, the ship surging ahead on a steady course, engines throbbing and machinery humming in the background, officers and men quietly and efficiently performing their duties on all sides, I often thought what a marvellous job I had. With so much power at my finger-tips, lord of all I surveyed, my word virtually law, the sea and the sun and the sky my constant companions, what job on earth could compare with command of one of Her Majesty's ships? It was a privilege of which I was very proud, and the responsibilities I shouldered seemed a very fair price for the trust reposed in me. I counted myself a very lucky man.

Our re-entry to Killybegs happened to fall on 19th July, my 50th birthday, and I was determined to make the most of it. Peter Odling-Smee had been told to draw up a guest-list, to include all the local people who had befriended or helped his party in the course of the six weeks during which they'd been based there. *Hecla* anchored inside the harbour while the boats brought off all the stores and surveying gear, and the Boatswain supervised the re-embarkation of the Land-Rover by means of our inflatable raft. As soon as everything was re-stowed on board, I had no option but to take the ship out again. But I ordered the boats to remain inshore till 6 p.m. and to bring out my invited guests. I took the ship out – with ostentatious wavings of farewell and blasts on the siren, and anchored her well outside the harbour and out of sight of the port. About 6.15 p.m. the boats appeared, laden with 30 or 40 cheerful guests, and for the next two hours we celebrated both the completion of the survey and my 50th birthday, a process which, I felt, did much to cement Anglo-Irish relations!

A few days later we anchored in Lough Foyle, and exercised our organisation for military support of the Civil Powers by landing an armed platoon on Magilligan Point. We then went in to Londonderry for a long week-end's rest and recuperation.

In mid-September we undertook an exercise lasting for about a week, in which we were involved with a number of civil engineers and scientists in a geodetic survey to establish a 'proving-ground' or trials area centred on Dubh Artach. We aimed to 'evaluate' the accuracy of the new Hi-Fix radio-location system (which, as recounted earlier, we had tried out in 1965 in comparison with our Lambda system). The Dubh Artach project involved accurately fixing the ship's position in a number of 'stations' as she moved across the proving-ground, by tellurometer ranges observed simultaneously from National O.S. Triangulation Points on Iona, Tiree, Colonsay, Arran and Islay.

The work involved gave the sailors plenty of exercise, scrambling up the mountains, while the surveyors and scientists spent many hours with their mathematical calculations in the Chart Room.

Autumnal weather conditions in the North Atlantic were having the usual effect on the progress of our main survey, at which we continued to plug away throughout October, breaking off now and again to visit the camps on North Rona and St. Kilda, and to spend week-ends in Londonderry and Lerwick in the Shetlands. We had our fair share of storms to contend with, and just when the survey had reached completion, disaster struck at St. Kilda. Winds of hurricane force had struck the islands, wreaking havoc among our camp party, blowing away one of the Uniport huts, with most of its valuable equipment, and levelling the other one to the ground. It was a miracle that there were no serious casualties among the camp personnel, and incredible that the Lambda mast itself was left standing. But the place was a shambles and a great deal of expensive damage had been sustained. There was nothing for it but to call it a day and bring off everything by helicopter from both there and North Rona, and head south to less stormy regions.

November found us carrying out a seismic survey in the Celtic Sea, dropping 300-lb depth-charges all over the place and studying their subterranean reverberations for clues as to the possible existence of oil-bearing strata. This required a brief visit to Milford Haven to embark the scientists and their equipment, and, on completion, a longer sojourn in Falmouth Harbour at anchor. This was primarily to prepare the ship for her forthcoming role as the Hydrographer's Flagship during a Conference of the North Sea Hydrographic Commission in Hamburg. The N.S.H.C. had sprung up largely in response to the problems posed to national charting agencies in countries bordering the North Sea by the growing number of very large deep-draught tankers navigating the shallow waters of the southern North Sea. At that time, its membership comprised Norway, Sweden and Denmark, West Germany, Holland and the U.K., and its Chairman, in 1966, was Rear Admiral G.S. Ritchie. For such an assignment, we would obviously have to look our best.

All freshly painted and 'done up to the nines', we sailed from Falmouth on 15th November, called in at Dover, and arrived at Hamburg on 18th. *Hecla* was given an alongside berth at the main town jetty, very much in the public eye, and immediately ahead of the new German Survey Ship, *Meteor*. All kinds of protocol marked the first day, starting with the arrival on board of Rear Admiral Ritchie, and the hoisting of his flag at the fore truck. There were numerous calls and return calls, and, in the evening we gave a formal Reception on the Flight Deck for all the local dignitaries as well as the various delegations to the Conference, and, of course, their wives.

The North Sea Hydrographic Commission's conference was held on board the *Meteor*, Dr. Roll being the host. Apart from a pleasant little ceremony, at which he and I exchanged complimentary speeches (in English) and I presented him with a framed picture of *Hecla*, I was not directly involved in the conference proceedings.

Before we left Hamburg, with the Hydrographer embarked, I spent an hour in the *Meteor* with her Captain, comparing notes. She was fitted with every modern device, including 'active' stabilisers to reduce rolling. This sounded promising, as one of our big problems was heavy rolling. 'Do not fit them,' said the German Captain, 'they make the motion worse – quite unpredictable and most uncomfortable.' It was a useful tip, and we looked thereafter towards 'passive' stabilisers. *Hecla* returned to Devonport for her winter lie-up and refit on 25th November, after a long and successful season.

It must have been in the spring of 1967 that I went over to Ireland, accompanied by my son Nick and a school-friend, on a reconnaissance for some of the surveys *Hecla* was to undertake during the coming season. Next on the Irish Government's list of priorities for our surveys of their inshore waters was Killala Bay in County Mayo, and I wanted to investigate the facilities at Ballina and Killala for basing and supporting a detached boat-party there before the season actually started. I also had permission from the Irish authorities to establish a Lambda-station on Bloody Foreland, in County Donegal, for further surveys we were to undertake later in the season. We did quite a bit of motoring during that reconnaissance.

By this time all four of our Ocean Survey Ships, *Vidal*, *Hecla*, *Hecate* and *Hydra* were deployed on the vital work in support of the 'Polaris' programme in the North Atlantic. A survey of the ocean on such a massive scale had never been undertaken before, and because there was a great deal more in the surveys than met the eye, security had become a major consideration

The British National Nuclear Deterrent had been transferred from the Royal Air Force's 'V'-Bombers to the Royal Navy's nuclear-powered Ballistic Missile Submarines, the Polaris Force.

This switch represented perhaps the most expensive Defence project in our entire history. We were following the American lead in the development of strategic weaponry, and it was inevitable that we followed their lead in the massive Ocean Survey Programme. However, we did not follow it slavishly. We had our own independently-developed survey techniques, and, in some respects, our methods were superior to theirs. The O.S.P. provided an impetus for much closer liaison between the Royal Navy's Hydrographic Service and the U.S. Navy's Oceanographic Office than anything that had gone before, and we fed on each other's experience and results.

CHAPTER XXIII

H.M.S. *Hecla*, North Atlantic, Greenland, Iceland, Scotland and Ireland, 1967

OUR MAIN TASK (that is to say, *Hecla*'s main task) for the 1967 season was the survey of a huge area south-west of Iceland. Hitherto we had controlled our ocean surveys by means of the Lambda radio-location system, which had a range of about 200 nautical miles. To have approached the Icelandic Government for permission to set up our Lambda-stations on their territory would have been to risk unwelcome speculation in Iceland as to the purpose of our work, and, given the political sensitivity and strong neutralist sentiments of the Icelanders (despite the fact that they were one of our N.A.T.O. allies), would probably have resulted in a refusal. The Americans, however, already had a Long Range radio-location system covering the North Atlantic, known as Loran-'C', with one of its stations actually sited in Iceland. (Other stations of use to us were sited in the Faeroe Islands, in southern Greenland, and, if I remember rightly, in Nova Scotia). Unlike Lambda, an 'active' system requiring continuous transmissions from the ship, Loran-'C' was a 'passive' system which required reception only. *Hecla* had been fitted during the winter with the relevant Loran-'C' receivers, and we could use whichever pair of transmitting stations provided the best 'cut' in the particular area we were working in.

Before starting up on this survey, however, we made a sortie out to Rockall to check on what remained of H.M.S. *Vidal*'s 'Annexation-plaque', ring-bolt and flagstaff, secured there in 1955 as 'permanent' evidence of British ownership. My recollection is that they had all succumbed to 12 years of continuous battering by Atlantic seas, and I reported accordingly. From Rockall we made a traverse back to Londonderry, which was to be our main base for the season. Our next job, in mid-April, was to land a two-boat detachment at Portree, on the Isle of Skye, to carry out an extensive local survey which was expected to take three or four months to complete. That done, the ship was free to pursue her own work up north.

Apart from diversions (which were many and interesting), we spent the whole of that spring and summer surveying the ocean off Iceland. The first diversion occurred towards the end of April, when the Loran-'C' station near Cape Farewell, in Greenland, was blown down in a gale. It was a vital station for us (as we were using the Greenland/Iceland pair), so we had to stop work and return to Scotland. I found it most frustrating, lying idle and waiting for the station to 'come on the air', and decided, instead, to go and investigate. One of my ambitions had long been to visit Greenland, which I had never seen. So we weighed anchor and headed back to the survey-ground. My plan was to resume work if the station became operational, and if not, to continue westward to Greenland. The weather was absolutely superb, with cloudless blue skies, brilliant sunshine, high visibility and a flat calm (perfect for surveying!), but the station remained 'off the air'. So we continued westward all day. At the first sign of ice, I flew off the helicopter to scout ahead.

A cold current flows southward along the east coast of Greenland, bringing with it the Arctic pack-ice. Inshore, the pack is dense, becoming progressively looser away from the coast. We very soon became surrounded by loose pack-ice and small bergs as we continued towards the land, and I was concerned that we should keep open water behind us when the time came to withdraw. I told Pete Spelling, in the helicopter, to keep a careful watch to seaward to ensure that we did not become entrapped as we turned northward, parallel to the coast. Weaving our way between the ice-floes, we cruised steadily northward with ice on all sides. Away to the west we could see the magnificent mountains of East Greenland, stark and shimmering against the blue sky. It was a wonderful experience, and despite a certain anxiety, I felt really elated. In fact I can honestly say that this spontaneous and unauthorised cruise through Greenland pack-ice was one of the most exhilarating and memorable episodes of my whole life.

On a previous occasion, while we were steaming westwards along one of our survey-lines, I spied a ship hull-down below the horizon, fine on our starboard bow (a most unusual occurrence in those waters, where ships were few and far between). It was on an opposite course, it had a buff-coloured mast and funnel, and as it came over the horizon, it displayed a white hull. 'Looks remarkably like a Survey Ship,' said the Officer of the Watch jokingly. 'It damn well is!' I replied, 'Signalman, call her up on the ten-inch!' We exchanged identities. It was H.M.S. *Vidal*. She was running a line of soundings eastwards on the adjacent survey. 'Well, blow me down!' Neither of us was aware that the other was working anywhere near. We passed about three miles away, and I exchanged pleasantries with Tony Cooper, her Australian Captain, and arranged to meet up together in one of the Scottish lochs a week or two later.

Of course, working as we were, virtually on the edge of the Icelandic

Hecla *approaching ice-edge, East Greenland, 1967.*

submerged 'shelf', I took an early opportunity to visit Reykjavik for a week-end in May, largely to brief Petur Sigurdsson, the Hydrographer, on our work off-shore and to offer our services in any way he considered useful, e.g. to survey the waters around the new volcanic island of Surtsey, and the shape and extent of its coastline. Between us, we reckoned that this would be a useful project to be pursued jointly later that summer, and we laid plans accordingly.

A recurrent problem when using the Loran-'C' chains was lane-slippage. This could be easily detected and rectified if we were actually surveying, but it sometimes occurred when the ship was otherwise occupied, in which case it could play havoc with our work if proper checks were not made. The nearest land to the survey area was Vestmannaeyjar (the Westman Islands), and these, together with Surtsey (which was now static), provided a perfect means of fixing the ship's position. So whenever undetected lane-slippage was suspected, and always before resuming work after a break, I used to take the ship up to a reasonable distance off the islands and fix her position by horizontal sextant angles, at the same time checking the readings on the Loran-'C' receivers. So we got to know the islands rather well, and I was keen to pay them a formal visit.

One week-end in June, when the ship was alongside in Reykjavik, Pete

Spelling and I flew down to Heimaey, the only town and port in the islands, in our helicopter to call on the Mayor and to discuss with the Harbour Master the feasibility of bringing the ship into the harbour. It was 23 years since I had last been there, and the place had grown enormously. The port approaches, however, were much as I remembered them, and to bring the ship into such a constricted entrance, involving tight turns very close under the beetling cliffs, was going to be a tricky business. *Hecla* would be one of the largest ships ever to enter the harbour.

So despite the navigational hazards, I took *Hecla* into Heimaey harbour for a week-end, and berthed her alongside the modern wharf, which normally accommodated dozens of the local trawlers and drifters. Our presence aroused a lot of interest, and we were well received by the Mayor. While being entertained in his home, I remember discussing with him the state of the local volcano, which dominated the town and harbour entrance (and which my mother and I, with little Hrebna Benediktsson, had climbed all those years ago). Was it dormant – or extinct? The Mayor said that it was dormant, and had last erupted some 400 years previously. Some people, he said, thought that it was due to erupt again before very long. (As is well known, it did just that several years later, with disastrous results. The whole population had to be evacuated to the mainland, much of the town was destroyed, and the harbour entrance was almost sealed off).

Once again our mid-seasonal break for assisted maintenance, and to grant leave, was spent at Liverpool, and this time our programme coincided with that of our sister-ship, *Hecate*, both ships berthing together for ten days. This gave me the opportunity to compare notes with John Winstanley ('Winston'), her C.O., as *Hecate* had been working on a similar survey to ours, though further south. (An occasion had arisen earlier while we were both out working on our respective surveys, when we were both ordered to proceed with all despatch to assist H.M.S. *Vidal* after she had collided with a merchant-ship in mid-Atlantic! Although severely damaged, she did not in fact require assistance and the order was rescinded soon afterwards. It had seemed odd that an Ocean Survey Ship should find herself in trouble, and still odder that the only vessels near enough to help should be two other Ocean Survey Ships – and all of them British!)

At the end of June I took *Hecla* up to the head of Hvalfjord for a quiet week-end at anchor. I had a very special feeling for that place, and found the surroundings inspiring. It never failed to remind me of those days during the summer of 1940 when we had 'sweated so much blood' over that survey, and this time it was almost as peaceful as it had been then. Apart from one or two whale-catchers, we had the place to ourselves.

Early in July, while up in the Westman Islands, I had set up a joint survey of Surtsey with the Icelanders, the arrangement being that we detached one of our Surveying Motor Boats to work under the auspices of their Deputy Hydrographer (Commander Gunnar Bergsteinsson) and supported by the Coastguard gun-boat *Thor*.

The Commander of the Icelandic Coastguard Service was Petur Sigurdsson, the Hydrographer, and his fleet of modern gun-boats was not infrequently assigned to hydrographic duties, so there was no problem there. At the end of July I was joined by my son Nicholas, who, having previously expressed his intention of joining the Navy, was now showing strong signs of changing his mind. At this point, while *Hecla* was in process of setting up the joint survey, I exchanged calls with the Captain of the *Thor*, and he asked me if my son would be interested in signing on as a temporary member of his crew. What an intriguing invitation! I said that it seemed a splendid idea and that I would follow it up. The more I thought about it, the more it appealed to me. (Really, what an extraordinary offer, and what a marvellous opportunity to savour one aspect of naval life, with no commitments!)

That summer our daughter Virginia was spending her long vacation in Iceland. She had worked for the Icelandic Hydrographer as a draughtsman, before going up to York University – and this year she was studying Icelandic history and Old Norse. At one point Mary flew up to Reykjavik with her fishing-rod – and this coincided with one of our week-end visits, making it quite a family occasion.

That settled, we went ahead with the *Thor* project, and sailed for Iceland on 3rd August. Admiral Ritchie, the Hydrographer, had expressed a wish to visit Iceland to confer with Petur Sigurdsson, and I was keen to show him something of our work, and also something of that extraordinary country. So he joined us before leaving Londonderry, and we sailed wearing his flag. It was not a very calm passage, but once on the survey-ground, things began to look up.

We sailed up to the head of Hvalfjord, and I pointed out to the Admiral most of the natural features and marks that we'd used during the 1940 survey. I had arranged to fly him off to Reykjavik by helicopter, to be met by Petur Sigurdsson, and he agreed to take Nick with him. So I bade the Admiral and Nick farewell, and off they flew. We then went round to finish off the Surtsey Survey and recover our boat-party, and on 12th August we left Iceland for the last time. By mid-August, our detached party on the Isle of Skye had completed their survey of the Sound of Raasay, so we went straight down there to recover them. Our next commitment was a visit to

Harwich to demonstrate hydrographic and oceanographic survey techniques to delegates attending the Commonwealth Surveyors' Conference at Cambridge, which involved a day at sea and the dispensation of hospitality to some 30 or 40 of them.

My mother had never seen *Hecla*, and realising that our visit to Harwich would provide a last opportunity for her to do so, I had written to suggest that she should get Roger, my brother, (an ex-Battle of Britain Spitfire pilot) to come and drive her down there from Lincolnshire. I knew that this would be my last sea-going command, and I was keen to show the ship off to them both. They motored down to an hotel in Dovercourt, and I dined with them that night. Next day we went to sea with the Commonwealth surveyors, anchoring for the night close off Harwich after disembarking them. That evening my mother and Roger came off to dine with me on board, after which I gave them a conducted tour of the ship. I think they were duly impressed, as *Hecla* was really looking immaculate.

Our main task for the autumn was a survey north-west of Ireland, for which we established our two Lambda stations on Bloody Foreland (Co. Donegal) and at Saligo Bay (Islay). It was during the course of this survey that we set up a detachment, with two boats, at Killala (Co. Mayo) for a survey of the Bay on behalf of the Irish Government. Having this party ashore there enabled me, with a fairly clear conscience, to take the ship in to various loughs and anchorages on the west and north coasts of the Republic, either to shelter from the autumnal storms or to sustain and support our two detachments in Ireland. Thus, from time to time we would visit Blacksod Bay, Lough Swilly and Sheep Haven, as well as Killala Bay. I loved these wild parts of the Irish coast.

However, it was at Saligo Bay, towards the end of August, that we really fell foul of the locals, or rather of the local landlord. We had erected a Lambda-station, but before use, we had to establish its National Grid co-ordinates, and this meant theodolite observations from three or four previously co-ordinated triangulation-points scattered about the island of Islay. Weather conditions were a crucial factor, and time was of the essence. Sunday dawned bright and clear, so I ordered the helicopter to transport the observers to the points concerned, by far the quickest way of getting the job done. Pete Spelling dumped the parties, one after the other, skimming low over the moors, and returned to the ship, repeating the process in reverse an hour or two later when the observers had finished. It had been a very satisfactory day's work, and I was well pleased with the results. However, I had not reckoned with the fact that the whole island was owned by a Tory peer, Lord Margadale, who was not only in residence, but had assembled a large house-party intent on a big grouse-shoot the following day, plus some deer-stalking later that week.

The Noble Lord was hopping mad. He rang up the Navy Department in Whitehall and demanded an explanation. The helicopter had scattered his grouse and stampeded his deer. His forthcoming shoot was ruined, he said. His protests were relayed to the Hydrographer, who relayed them back to me! He sent me a blistering signal next day, adding strictures of his own. Had I not cleared the operations in advance with the local landlord? If not, why not? It was a travesty of 'Forward Planning' (a concept on which Admiral Ritchie had always set great store), etc., etc., etc. All I could do was to signal abject apologies – which I did – and write in similar vein to Lord Margadale. But it didn't end there. The affair rumbled on for some time afterwards, and I began to think mountains were being made out of molehills. Judging by the fuss they were kicking up, anyone might think a foreign aircraft had intruded on our airspace with sinister intent. Considering that we had operated our helicopter over foreign territory – South Africa, Iceland, the Irish Republic – without a murmur of protest, it was ironic that a perfectly legitimate 'Defence' operation over our own national territory should stir up so much rancour, even if it had upset His Lordship's sporting activities. In a letter to Admiral Ritchie, I said as much.

We plugged away at the main survey in the Western Approaches throughout the autumn, sheltering from time to time from the steadily deteriorating weather, usually in Lough Swilly, with an occasional visit to Londonderry or Lisahally for fuel. It was mid-November before we could begin the recovery of our camps on Islay and the Bloody Foreland, by which time the detached survey party at Killala had also finished their work. As it would probably be the very last time that I would be able to inspect and address the whole of my ship's company before we paid off, I made a particular point of completing all field-work and taking the ship in to Lough Swilly to spend Remembrance Day there, at anchor. Having inspected all hands at Divisions on the upper deck, and having had 'Church' rigged on the Flight Deck, I paraded everyone for the Service of Remembrance, an impressive and dignified occasion, after which I made my Farewell address. It was a milestone in my life, and quite an emotional one too.

The shipping channel through Lough Foyle runs close to the Republican shore, and right in front of my friend Terence Baird's house at Greencastle. A big white flagstaff stood in the garden of the next-door house, owned by his friend Liam McCormick, an Irish architect and amateur sailor, who used to dip his flag in salute whenever we passed. During our last visit to Londonderry, I was told by Terence that Liam was wondering how he could lower his 40-ft. mast to the ground for re-painting, and re-erect it afterwards. Could the Navy advise him? This seemed to me a golden opportunity for our sailors to practise some good old-fashioned seamanship, and I asked if Liam would like us to do the job for him. Obviously we could not send a naval working party overland through the Republic, but who would know if we sent it by boat, along the coast? The proposal was agreed. The Boatswain's party, equipped with sheer-legs, blocks and heavy tackles, lowered the mast to the ground, re-painted it, and, when the paint was dry, re-erected it, to the great joy and satisfaction of its owner. The sailors, well rewarded with beer and sandwiches, had thoroughly enjoyed a rare and useful experience, and I felt we had done something positive for Anglo-Irish relations. The mast gleamed, and the Irish tri-colour dipped in gratitude as we took our final departure. *Hecla* and *Hecate* returned to Devonport together at the end of November, and on 30th both ships paid off for re-fit and re-commissioning. After two and a half years, my last sea-going command was at an end.

CHAPTER XXIV

On Hydrographer's Staff, Whitehall and Taunton, 1968-70 – Followed by Promotion, 1971

M Y NEW APPOINTMENT was to the post of Assistant Hydrographer in Whitehall for the second time, and I was resigned to taking up the reins more or less where I had laid them down almost three years previously. At least I knew pretty well what I was in for when I took the job over early in the New Year.

However, I was not back in my old office. With the absorption of the three Armed Service Departments into the Ministry of Defence, the Navy had moved out of the Admiralty building and the Hydrographer's offices were now located in the old War Office building. A.H.'s office was nothing to write home about, but almost adjacent was the Admiral's superbly spacious octagonal room – which could one day be mine!

My recollections of the year 1968 are distinctly hazy, and obviously little of earth-shaking consequence could have occurred during this period. It was in 1969, on the way home from a glorious holiday in Sweden, that I heard the sad news of my mother's death. Although her health had been failing for some time, the end had come suddenly and was a considerable shock to those nearest to her. On returning to my office, I was asked by Steve Ritchie whether my mother's death had affected my plan to continue serving, and to take over from him as Hydrographer when his five years were up at the end of 1970. Since my mother's death I had given much thought to this very point, and was able to assure him that my plans had not changed. In that case, he said, I had better do a stint with Chart Branch at Taunton next year, to get the hang of the compilation and production processes. I would need experience in those fields before becoming 'the Boss Man'.

Hitherto, the Hydrographic Department had been split three ways: Chart Branch in Cricklewood, Production Division in Taunton, and Headquarters in Whitehall. One of Steve's major achievements had been to secure approval for the amalgamation of Chart Branch with Production Division, and to push ahead with a brand new purpose-built extension to the Taunton establishment, to house the Chart Branch offices. This had now come to fruition, and we now had some 800 staff located down at Taunton.

The Hydrographer was allowed 'by establishment' four Captains, two of whom were at sea and two ashore. The two Captains ashore both bore the title of Assistant Hydrographer. One of them was in charge of the Chart Branch (as Superintendent of Charts), and was known as A.H.(1). The other, in charge of naval personnel, H.Q. staff and the Survey Fleet, was A.H.(2). It had been my lot to serve twice in the latter post, and not at all in the former. However, with the amalgamation at Taunton, a new command structure had been formulated. The establishment there had been divided into three: Naval Division, Professional Division and Administration and Supply Division, each under an Assistant Director (A.D.(N), A.D.(P) and A.D.(A), and these three formed the Taunton Management Team. My next job was to be A.D.(N), the Assistant Director (Naval).

I started my new job as A.D.(N) at Taunton fairly early in the New Year. I found myself reasonable 'digs' in a guest house quite near the Department, so was able to walk to the office each morning. The new office-block, which housed the Naval and Professional Divisions, was an impressive building. As expected, I found myself much more concerned with charts and surveys than I had been as A.H. in Whitehall. Living on my own in 'digs' during the working week, I used to motor up to one or other of our homes, either Highgate or Legbourne, for week-ends. Eventually, however, we received a satisfactory offer for 'Westwind', the London house, and I immediately started inquiring about accommodation for Mary and me in the Taunton area. I eventually found that the Camp Commandant's married quarters at Sherford Army Camp, just to the west of Taunton, was not needed by the Major-General in command, and could be made available to me. Accordingly, early in the summer, we were formally 'marched in' – to use the Army parlance – and for the first time in my naval career, we had an official 'quarter'.

Much to my astonishment, I had been appointed an Honorary A.D.C. to Her Majesty the Queen. In fact, though I had not realised it, this was a normal attribute accorded to Captains who had reached the top of the 'Captains' List' and were in their ninth year, and therefore (in the ordinary course) due to retire at the end of it. The fact that, in my case, I was likely to be promoted to Flag rank at the end of the year, was neither here nor there – apparently! Anyway, I had to equip myself with the golden epaulette and aiguillette – against the unlikely event of my actually being called upon to render direct service to H.M. As it happened, the 125th anniversary of the foundation of the Hydrographic Office (by Alexander Dalrymple, in 1795) occurred that autumn, and to mark the occasion, H.R.H. Prince Philip, Duke of Edinburgh, graciously consented to visit us at Taunton. It was to be the one and only occasion on which it was appropriate for me to wear my new regalia.

We had a heli-pad in the grounds of the Department, specially provided for our own helicopters and for V.I.P. visits. Prince Philip duly plonked himself down on it, and was greeted on the spot by Admiral Ritchie. With the other two members of the Management Team, I was then introduced to him on the front doorstep. He was wearing his uniform as an Admiral of the Fleet, and all our naval personnel (normally attired in plain clothes) were wearing uniform also. H.R.H. was conducted round the whole establishment by the Hydrographer, and introduced to the Heads of Sections as he came to them. He spent much time chatting to all and sundry, but seemed only slightly interested in what I had to tell him (concerning Chart-correction, Notices to Mariners and so on), doubtless reckoning, as a naval officer, that he knew all about it anyway! Well, that was my moment of glory as an A.D.C.

It was during the summer of 1970, while I was down at Taunton, that Steve Ritchie was able to tell me that Board Approval had been given for my promotion next January to the rank of Rear Admiral, and that I was to relieve him as Hydrographer of the Navy in February. So that was that! I felt both relieved and subdued. It was a tremendous thing to have had it confirmed – at last – but it was a very sobering thought. I was to reach the top of the tree, the crowning point of my career, but what a huge responsibility I had been landed with! On the other hand, who in the whole Hydrographic Service had more experience of its workings, both at sea and ashore, than I had? I comforted myself with the knowledge that at least I could do the job as well as anyone else who might be available. But Steve Ritchie, with his many innovations, had really made a name for himself, and would be a hard man to follow. Anyway, Mary and I reckoned it was an occasion to celebrate, and we did.

In November, as I believe it was, I found myself leading a small delegation from the Department to attend a UNESCO Cartographic Conference in Tehran. My main mission at the Conference was to try to persuade Thailand, Malaysia, Indonesia and the Philippines to set up a South China Sea Hydrographic Commission on the lines of our North Sea Hydrographic Commission, but I could do little more than sow the seeds of the idea.

I was determined to get home by the week-end, and booked a seat on the only London-bound flight on the Saturday. It was an Iran-Air flight via Istanbul. After I had checked in at the airport, the fuelling-stop was changed from Istanbul to Moscow! It was too late to withdraw, and I had to face the prospect of flouting the strict prohibition placed on all Ministry of Defence staff against crossing the Iron Curtain. The fact that my brief-case was bulging with confidential documents made the prospect even more disconcerting, but in the event, when we reached Moscow, a Russian military guard was placed on the plane, and we were not permitted to leave it, nor were we searched. After 'sweating blood' on the ground, I craved a drink of water, and as soon as we were airborne again, I asked the Iranian stewardess for a glass of water. She brought a brimful tumbler, which I gratefully quaffed, and promptly choked on. 'Water?' I spluttered at her. 'So sorry, sir,' she answered, 'I thought you said vodka!'

CHAPTER XXV

Hydrographer of the Navy, 1971–5

IN FEBRUARY, 1971 I took over from Steve Ritchie at a ceremony in Taunton attended by most of the staff of the Department and also by our wives. The ceremony was primarily to bid farewell to an outstanding Hydrographer of the Navy, and to provide an occasion for me to present him, on behalf of the staff and the Surveying Service, with a set of valuable books, dear to his heart. Inside each volume had been pasted a beautifully inscribed book-plate commemorating his service and the affection and esteem in which he had been held. The wording of this I had based on the inscription engraved on the famous silver 'Owen Bowl' presented by his officers to Captain W.F.W. Owen some 140 years earlier. In making the presentation, I delivered a eulogistic and rather emotional speech, which

The 20th Hydrographer of the Navy, Whitehall, 1971.

almost reduced Steve and his wife to tears, but in the circumstances I could hardly have done less.

So now I was Hydrographer of the Navy, the twentieth holder of that post – which dated back to 1795 – and head of the oldest branch of Admiralty. It was a proud position to be in, and I relished it, both for what it was, and for the challenges which it presented. I was determined to do my best, and, if possible, to 'make my mark' on the Hydrographic Service. I was determined, also, not to make changes for the sake of change, even though I was less than enthusiastic about some of the changes made by Steve (e.g. his drive for metrication). Such changes had gone too far to be reversed, and chaos and confusion would have resulted from any attempt to revert to the 'status quo ante'. So my first directive to the Department (taken from the Fleet Signal Book) was 'Maintain present course and speed'.

I was resolved not to become too desk-bound, which would have been all too easy, with one office in Whitehall and another in Taunton. I had been instrumental during Admiral Irving's time in getting Board Approval for the Hydrographer to fly his flag when at sea in one of H.M. Surveying Ships, and both Egg and Steve had made good use of that dispensation. I decided that I would make the effort to spend time in each one of my thirteen ships every year, if possible while they were actually at work on the survey-ground. I also announced my intention of visiting every one of our 'out-stations' in U.K., and every branch and section of the Department at Taunton. Having wrestled, in previous shore appointments (S.O.B., O.C.S.C., A.H. and A.D.(N)), with the minutiae of innumerable problems, I took steps to see that the Hydrographer did not get bogged down with detail. My aim was to have every problem fully argued out by my staff-officers before being presented to me for a decision, a policy which, I felt, would leave me free to deal with the broader issues, and to get around as I wanted to.

I told my immediate superior (the Vice-Chief of Naval Staff) that my personal work-pattern would differ from that of my predecessors in that I would spend the beginning and end of the working week in Whitehall, and the middle of the week at Taunton. This would enable me to travel back and forth to Legbourne by train at week-ends, stay in our rented London flat on Monday, Tuesday and Thursday nights, and put up at the County Hotel in Taunton on Wednesday nights. It would give me two full days at Taunton and three at Whitehall (which, I felt, was the right balance), and though it meant a lot of train-travel, the journeys were long enough to deal with a fair amount of paper-work en route.

My first 'excursion' as Hydrographer was an official visit to see the Royal

Bulldog *and* Beagle *visiting Dartmouth, 1971.*

Naval College at Dartmouth, flying my flag in H.M.S. *Beagle*, with her consort *Bulldog* in company. I was received with full honours by the Captain-in-Charge (my old friend, Gordon Tait), with Guard and Band, which I had to inspect on the Parade Ground. Mary had already arrived, and we were accommodated overnight in considerable luxury in the Captain's official residence. Meanwhile the cadets were shown over the ships, getting their first insight into the Surveying Service, and great play was made by the Dartmouth beagles, with the whole pack swarming over my immaculate flagship, *Beagle*, (to the consternation of her First Lieutenant!).

A month later, in April, I headed a small delegation from the Office to the annual R.N./U.S.N. liaison meeting on the 'Polaris' Ocean Survey Programme with our American 'opposite numbers' in the U.S. Naval Oceanographical Office in Suitland, Maryland. We flew over to Washington, where I was taken in hand by the Oceanographer of the Navy, and together we decided to leave the business meetings to our respective subordinates, turning up to the plenary sessions at the start and finish, and to put our signatures to the resulting agreements. This left me free to see more of Washington, and to visit friends. On my last day in Washington, the capital was invaded by thousands of unruly civic 'protesters' intent on bringing the city to a standstill by occupying the main bridges and road-intersections. At five o'clock in the morning I got a close-up view of the way the police and armed forces dealt with these disruptive elements. A full-scale battle took place under my window, which I had to close in a hurry to keep out the tear-gas. Another battle took place on the way to the airport, with hundreds of motorists returning the missiles aimed at them from the sidewalks, and giving as good as they got.

As far as I can remember, I had to fly up to New York to catch the plane down to the West Indies, where I had planned to visit *Hecla*, whose C.O. had been unfavourably reported on. We landed on the island of Barbados, where the ship's helicopter was waiting to whisk me out to *Hecla* on her survey-ground north of the island. I spent several days inspecting the ship and watching her at work, and also visited her detached boat-party in the delightful Grenadines. We had a good look at a large French cruise-liner that had recently wrecked herself by trying to squeeze herself through a narrow rock-strewn passage, and we spent a pleasant lunch-hour at anchor off Mustique (Princess Margaret's holiday island), entertaining its owner, Colin Tennant and his wife. I returned to U.K. considerably reassured regarding the Captain's competence.

Shortly after I had taken over as Hydrographer, I was confronted with my first challenge in Whitehall. There had been a collision in the Dover Strait and the main shipping channel was blocked by two wrecks. I was asked by the Department of Trade to mount an emergency survey of an alternative route, 40 miles long, between two sandbanks known as The Varne and The Ridge, and to prove a 2-mile wide channel clear to a depth of 12 fathoms. Fortunately the three vessels of the Inshore Survey Squadron were just emerging from their winter lie-up, so I ordered them straight into the fray, and because the task was urgent, I called on the Naval Staff to provide assistance with minesweepers and patrol vessels. Four minesweepers and two frigates were assigned to the job (the frigate to keep the route clear of shipping) and placed under the tactical command of the Senior Officer Inshore Survey Squadron. Within a month 'Operation Varnesweep' had been successfully completed, the Navy earning high praise and congratulations from the Department of Trade.

About this time an unpleasant incident took place in Ireland which brought us unwittingly to the public eye. *Hecate* had left a detached survey party to finish off the previous season's work in Baltimore, Co. Cork (part of the 'quid pro quo' agreed with the Irish Government in return for our use of Lambda sites on their territory). The 35 ft. Survey motor boat lay at her moorings in the harbour overnight, and provided a tempting target for the I.R.A. They placed a bomb on board and duly blew it up, much to the dismay of the survey party and the consternation of the Irish authorities.

The latter did all in their power to bring the offenders to book, and made full restitution, compensation and apology to our Government. A hilarious cartoon by 'Giles' appeared in the *Daily Express*, and the original drawing was sent to me with the compliments of the author. (It now stands framed in a place of honour at home!)

A week or so after returning from the West Indies, I decided to kill three birds with one stone by flying over to Norway. I landed at Stavanger and was met by the Norwegian Hydrographer, Mr. Sundby, who at that time was Chairman of the North Sea Hydrographic Commission. He showed me over the charting establishment and impressed me with the difficulties he faced in maintaining up-to-date coverage of Norway's long and deeply-indented coastline with a very small staff and a 'shoe-string' budget. He put me up for the night at his home, and insisted on motoring me next day all the way to Oslo. It was a most interesting drive, initially along the coast, and he took great pleasure in pointing out to me the scene of Captain Vian's epic exploit in H.M.S. *Cossack* in rescuing all the British prisoners-of-war from the German ship *Altmark* in the early spring of 1940. (I remember the excitement which the incident caused at the time).

Mr. Sundby dropped me off alongside H.M.S. *Hecate*, which was visiting Oslo at the time, and I hoisted my flag in her (the second 'bird to be killed with one stone'). Next morning we sailed down the beautiful Oslo Fjord in brilliant sunshine, and continued overnight to Copenhagen. Here I was to 'kill my third bird' by making a formal visit to the Danish Hydrographer, Captain Knud Kjeergard, R.D.N. I had met him before, and he received me most warmly. The usual entertainments and receptions took place, ashore and on board, and after a diverting guided tour of Copenhagen's somewhat notorious 'attractions', and a night in one of its hotels, I took my leave of my Danish colleague and found my own way home.

For nearly two months during the spring of 1971 there was a nation-wide postal strike. The Hydrographic Department is probably more dependent than most organisations on the free flow of information, inward and outward. Obviously it is of no use to the mariner if its products and publications remain on the premises, and to a great extent the accuracy and up-to-dateness of these products rests on the receipt of reliable information from many quarters. Whereas we were able to use all sorts of alternative methods of distributing our wares to our 'customers' world-wide, the enormous daily influx of mail virtually dried up. Relieved of the task of dealing with it, we were at last able to catch up with the chronic backlog of work throughout the Department – only to become submerged by the avalanche which fell upon us when the strike ended. *Vidal*, the oldest of our

Vidal *(wearing the author's flag), back from the Indian Ocean and entering Portsmouth (en route to Chatham) to pay off, 1971.*

four Ocean Survey Ships, required 50% more crew members to man her than the ships of the 'Hecla' class. As naval manpower was a critical factor, we therefore decided to replace her and order a fourth 'Hecla'. When she returned from the Indian Ocean in August, I made a special point of boarding her off Portland so that she could wear my flag on the final leg of her last voyage, up-Channel and round to her home port, Chatham, to pay off. *Vidal* had given us twenty years of excellent service, but in these days of financial stringency she was no longer an economical asset. How long would we have to wait for her replacement?

That summer I spent several days with the three vessels of the Inshore Survey Squadron, working off the Norfolk coast. In a sense it was a nostalgic visit, because it was there that I'd had my first experience of surveying (in *Franklin* in 1938), and I actually found myself observing the self-same sextant-angle that had been assigned to me then, to practise on. At least in that quarter, sounding techniques had not changed much over the past 33 years. I also managed to fly my flag in the other two Inshore Survey Craft, *Woodlark* and *Waterwitch*, and was able to squeeze in a 48-hour visit to *Fox* between sessions of the Commonwealth Survey Officers' Conference at Cambridge, where I had to make an opening speech. Later, in the autumn, I managed to get to sea in *Fawn* and spent some time in *Hydra* before sending her off to the Indian Ocean.

Which reminds me: *Hydra's* C.O. was Roger Morris, who had served with me in *Owen*, and of whom I had quite a high opinion. As a Lieutenant-Commander, he had been granted the acting rank of Commander by virtue of his appointment, but had just been 'passed over' for promotion to the substantive rank. This irked me, and I argued very strongly that he should be promoted 'out-of-zone' (an almost unheard-of occurrence). To my astonishment and delight, on 30th June his name appeared in the half-yearly promotion-lists (together with another officer whom I had recommended), so my arguments had paid off. Just as well, because 14 years later, Roger Morris became Hydrographer of the Navy, with the rank of Rear Admiral! (How much can turn on the whim of an individual. Had I let matters take their ordinary course, who, I sometimes wonder, would have become the 22nd Hydrographer?).

During the winter I was able to announce that a firm order had been placed with Robb Caledon at Leith for our new ship, and that approval had been obtained to name her *Herald*. She would be an up-dated version of the 'Hecla'-class, with improvements drawn from our experience during the past six years. But that winter was dominated – both in the dockyards and at Taunton – by the coalminers' strike and the resulting Energy Crisis. Not only did this badly affect the refits of our ships, but it caused a 50% cut in our chart production.

During the early part of 1972 I became heavily involved in arguments and discussions between the Navy and the Marine Division of the Department of Trade regarding the need for extra hydrographic effort to ensure the safety of the growing number of very deep-draught super-tankers. There was mounting evidence that these enormous vessels were navigating through relatively shallow water in the English Channel and southern North Sea, with very little under-keel clearance, and there were mounting fears that this trend would lead to wrecks, oil spillage and devastating coastal pollution. My instincts were to press for an increase in the resources of the Hydrographic Service to cope with the increased task, and I was already arguing for this on the basis of the new requirements posed by our expanding fleet of deep-diving submarines (including our 'Polaris' force). The arguments raged back and forth, but I was up against obstructionism from the Department of Trade on the one hand, and a measure of jealousy from the Naval Staff on the other. The D. of T. would not stomach the idea of financing the Navy's functions, and the Naval Staff would not countenance apportioning more of the shrinking Defence Vote to the Hydrographic Service at the expense of its own warship-building programme.

These arguments, with variations, were to continue 'ad nauseam' throughout my period of office, with contributions, elaborations and changes of stance not only from the three main participants, but from other interests inside and outside the Government. My own thesis, basically, was that a prime function of the Royal Navy was to support British maritime trade – in peace and war. The physical protection of merchant shipping from enemy attack was a clear instance of this function in war-time, and its protection from piracy and natural hazards was a well-established function of the Navy in peace-time. After all, it was the realisation by the Admiralty that more ships were lost during the Napoleonic Wars through lack of adequate charts than through enemy action that brought the Hydrographic Service into being in the first place. So I continued to plug 'the Navy's responsibility for the support of maritime trade' as my main line throughout these arguments, and poured gentle scorn on the Civil Service concept that the Department of Trade should pay the Navy for this work. So far as I was aware, I said, the Admiralty had never sent a bill to the Board of Trade at the end of the War for the costs it had incurred in escorting convoys, sweeping mines from the shipping lanes, and shooting down attacking bombers! The Navy had simply been voted the extra funds it needed in order to perform these tasks.

However, as was usual in peacetime, the climate of public opinion was strongly in favour of cutting the Defence Vote, so there was no hope of enlarging it to meet the requirements of hydrography. On the other hand, there was growing public interest in the 'environment', and corresponding pressure to spend public money on its protection. Hydrography being a key factor in the protection of our coastal environment from oil-pollution, it followed that a parliamentary Vote in support of hydrography would receive a much smoother passage than a supplementary Vote (for the same purpose) for 'Defence'. Thus, as the internecine wrangling continued throughout Whitehall, I became more and more convinced that the solution to our problem lay in the setting up of a separate Hydrographic Vote, distinct from the Defence Vote, but administered, more or less, by the Navy Minister. As the arguments proceeded over the years, I found myself plugging that line as hard as I could.

Anyway, the upshot of the particular discussions that had taken place over the winter was that I pointed out to the Chamber of Shipping certain 'critical' areas in the English Channel that ought to be surveyed periodically in order to monitor gradual changes in depth and configuration affecting deep-draught navigation, while at the same time telling them that the depths were perfectly adequate for normal shipping (including warships), so I would be deploying the Surveying Fleet on tasks which, in 'Defence' terms, I judged to be of higher priority. This put the ball squarely in the Chamber of Shipping's court, with the result that they and a Consortium of the major British Oil Companies agreed to fund the surveys, to be carried out by commercial firms. We were to draw up the specifications for the work, assess the quality of the bids under a competitive tendering procedure, and deal with the results of the surveys. A contract was let to the most promising bidder, and the season began with a commercial survey firm, privately funded, taking over part of the Navy's historic task. It was an 'ad hoc' arrangement, forced on us in the absence of inter-Departmental agreement, and would not last.

In February I went over to the Hague to attend the 7th Conference of the North Sea Hydrographic Commission. At the end of it, the Norwegian Hydrographer, Mr. Sundby, handed over the chairmanship to the Dutch Hydrographer, Commodore Van Weelde, a man whom my predecessor had described as 'more British than the British themselves'.

All proceedings of the N.S.H.C. were conducted in English, a stumbling block for the adherence of France, whose possible membership was discussed. Belgium too was a problem (for other reasons), but since both countries had coasts bordering on the North Sea, they ought, logically, to be invited to join the Commission. Britain undoubtedly was the leading member, and this was reflected in the outcome of the meeting. Apart from the usual crop of 'Resolutions' (many of which I had to draft), there was a decision that a new 5-mile wide route for deep-draught shipping from the North Hinder to the Outer Silver Pit should be jointly surveyed and sonar-swept during the coming season, the U.K. being allocated 50 miles of it. More of an honour to us was a request by the Commission that we should investigate the feasibility and implications of expanding our Hydrographic School at Devonport to undertake the training of the hydrographic officers of all the N.S.H.C. countries.

A major event, in April, was the 10th quinquennial Conference of the International Hydrographic Organisation at Monaco. We spent a very busy fortnight in Monte Carlo. Several incidents stand out. My Chief Civil Hydrographic Officer, Mr. Pascoe, had been haranguing the assembled delegates on the importance of developing countries recognising the potential economic benefits of their off-shore waters, and the need to set up adequate hydrographic organisations to delineate and survey them. He spoke as one of The Group of Experts who had been summoned by the United

Nations Organisation in New York to draw up a Report on the state of
world hydrography, and he plugged the U.N. line which emerged from that
Report. I was to follow him with an exposition of our readiness to assist
these developing countries, by training their personnel and, if necessary,
helping to survey their waters for them (all grist to the B.A. chart mill). I
opened with the words: 'Mr. Pascoe has spoken for the United Nations. I
speak for the United Kingdom'. That went down rather well.

Halfway through the Conference, two of our Coastal Survey Vessels, *Fawn*
and *Fox*, entered the harbour, exciting much interest and comparing
favourably with the Surveying Ships of the U.S.A., France and West
Germany (which were already there). Where ours scored over the others,
however, was not only by taking the delegates (and their wives) to sea for
demonstrations (while wearing my flag), but by entertaining on board the
reigning Prince and Princess of Monaco. Though the standard of service and
quality of tableware left a good deal to be desired, Prince Rainier and
Princess Grace could not have been more charming and relaxed, and on
their departure, the Prince kindly presented me with a gold medal in a red
leather case. But the final triumph for Britain was the election, by an
overwhelming majority, of Rear Admiral G.S. Ritchie (my predecessor as
Hydrographer) to the post of President of the I.H.B. Directing Committee,
a position which he was to hold for the next ten years.

Woodlark *moving to transfer the author's flag to* Hecate, *English Channel, 1974.*

Once again I managed to spend periods at sea in almost all our ships, and among the more memorable of these were my formal visit, in *Hecate*, to the French Hydrographic Establishment at Brest, with *Woodlark* in company, where some useful business was conducted, and my visit to the Channel Islands in *Waterwitch*, in August, my first and only visit to those most outlying of the British Isles.

1972 was the centenary of *Challenger's* famous round-the-world voyage, which laid the foundations of oceanography, and I had been asked to give the opening address to the Second International Congress on the History of Oceanography, to be held in the Usher Hall in Edinburgh. I had spent a lot of time, and done a good deal of research, in preparing my speech. In it I laid great stress on the decisive role played by the Royal Navy, a role too often forgotten, ignored or taken for granted by present-day oceanographers, and I told the assembled scientists that their debt to our predecessors in the Navy's Hydrographic Service was well-nigh incalculable.

Several foreign oceanographical ships had gathered at Leith to mark this occasion, and *Hecate* was there as host-ship. It seemed a good opportunity for me to nip down to Robb Caledon's yard to inspect progress on the building of *Herald*, and what I saw was distinctly encouraging: construction was ahead of schedule, and there seemed good reason to expect the launching to take place next spring.

Towards the end of the season I spent several days in *Hecla* on her survey grounds in the Western Approaches. She was in process of re-surveying an area covering the Stanton Banks, which I had previously covered in a relatively small-scale exploratory survey in *Owen* twelve years earlier. This time, however, the work included a thorough sonar survey. This paid handsome dividends, because we located a significant rocky outcrop rising from an otherwise flat sandy sea-bed 80 fathoms deep, a feature of which the widely-spaced lines of the earlier survey had revealed no indication whatever.

Life continued fairly smoothly in the Hydrographic Service and in 1973 our ships were deployed in the Atlantic, the Caribbean and the Pacific, as well as in home waters, while the Department at Taunton was slowly developing, modernising and expanding, with all-round production gradually increasing. One of our headaches was recent Canadian Government legislation requiring all shipping in Canadian waters to use Canadian charts, a severe blow to both the world-wide Admiralty Chart concept and to the vast numbers of international shipping which relied on it. Needless to say, I had taken up the cudgels with the Canadians to persuade them to think again. To off-set this worry, it was decided that

H.R.H. the Prince of Wales (who was then serving as a Lieutenant in the Navy) should be appointed to one of my ships. I was quick to respond by selecting H.M.S. *Fox*, which was surveying in the West Indies. Her C.O., Commander John Myres (the Senior Officer of *Fox* and *Fawn*) was an excellent man, and I was confident that the Prince could not be in better hands.

In March I took Mary and my two sons, Nicholas and Adrian, to Buckingham Palace to witness my investiture by H.M. the Queen of the C.B. The Queen asked me about my job as Hydrographer, and said she thought it must be very interesting. 'Yes, it is, Ma'am,' I replied (quite truthfully). We all went on afterwards to a rather expensive West End restaurant.

At the end of April I led a small delegation from Taunton on our biennial visit to our 'opposite numbers' in America. Then, early in May, we flew up to Ottawa, where I had arranged to meet the Dominion Hydrographer and his staff. I had proposals to put to him which would mitigate the adverse effects of the recent Canadian Charting legislation, which bore heavily on the British Admiralty Chart system in particular, and on world-wide international shipping in general. I found the Canadians eager to achieve an acceptable compromise, which they would put to their Government, but in the event, their 'environmental lobby' was to prove too strong for them.

It was in June that the centenary of the famous *Challenger* expedition again impinged on me. The ship's figurehead, which had been adorning the grounds of Admiralty House at Northwood, was to be presented to the Institute of Oceanographical Sciences at Wormley as a centenary gift from the Admiralty, and I had been asked to make the presentation. I thought it would be appropriate to refer, in my speech, to the actual happenings in H.M.S. *Challenger* exactly one hundred years earlier, and was fortunate enough to find the ship's deck-log for that date. It had been a Sunday, and the ship had been working in the western Atlantic, keeping local time, three hours earlier than G.M.T. I was speaking at noon, B.S.T., so was able to describe (with a little imaginative colouring) the scene on board *Challenger* as she turned into the wind to occupy one of her many oceanographical 'stations' just after 0800 on that Sunday morning, and the attitude of the ship's officers to the effect that this would have on the state of the upper deck at the traditional Sunday morning Captain's Rounds! The assembled scientists and I.O.S. staff seemed to relish this thoroughly naval view-point, and afterwards asked for a copy of my speech. The figurehead had been mounted in a prominent position over the main entrance to the building, and I concluded my presentation by expressing the hope that it would 'stare down the centuries of the future as it had stared through the past, in silent witness to the continued expansion of British oceanography'!

Meetings of the North Sea Hydrographic Commission took place every eighteen months, and the next one fell due in September, with the Swedish Hydrographer, Commodore Hallbjorner, as host. He had arranged to hold it in an hotel on the shores of the Gulf of Bothnia, at a little sea-port called Harnosand. We achieved a lot during our business sessions, and found the Swedish approach to their survey problems quite fascinating. They had two Survey Ships alongside, but bad weather prevented them taking us to sea for a demonstration.

We had become inured to delays in the ship-building world (as in other industries) due to endless disputes, strikes and 'go-slows', so it was no surprise that the launch of our new ship had been deferred. However, in October she was at last ready for the Big Day. I had taken pains, in the office, to guide the Third Sea Lord's thinking in the right direction, so that the wife of the Hydrographer of the Navy was to be the ship's 'Sponsor' and perform the launching ceremony. Mary was delighted. She had always said that one of her great ambitions was to launch a ship, and this was her opportunity.

The author with his wife, Mary, and daughter Virginia, at the launch of Herald, *Leith 1974.*

We motored up to Edinburgh together, and on the journey Mary rehearsed her speech. We had been given a luxurious suite of rooms in the Caledonian Hotel by courtesy of Robb Caledon and Company, and the following morning their Chairman, Sir John Brown, appeared in our room with three beautiful brooches from which Mary was to choose one as a gift from the firm. She eventually chose the most unconventional of the three, a slab of gold 'filings' studded with diamonds and tourmalines. An official car took us down to the shipyard at Leith, where the white hull of the new ship towered above the gaily decorated rostrum and stands. It was drizzling, but the Royal Marine Band played cheerful airs as the 'top brass' and their ladies ascended the platform. Bouquets were presented, photographs taken, prayers were said and hymns sung. Mary voiced the immortal words, named the ship *Herald* and, with a mighty swing, smashed the suspended champagne bottle

Herald taking to the water after her launch, 1974.

against the port bow. She then pushed a lever and with slowly gathering sternway, our new ship gracefully took to the water amid the waves and cheers of the crowd, the blasts of dockyard hooters, and the strains of 'Rule Britannia' from the Band. It was a faultless performance and, as if to acknowledge it, *Herald* dropped a little curtsey to us as her bows left the slipway. Afterwards there was a reception followed by a big formal luncheon, at which Mary, the Lady Sponsor, made her speech. It was delightful, and very warmly applauded.

During October 1973 there was another round of active hostilities in the Arab-Israeli conflict, and this, coupled with the effects of the National Union of Mineworkers' strike and the consequent 3-day week, had reduced the country to the verge of economic disaster, and had brought home to many of us the disastrous effects of our reliance on foreign sources of energy. It occurred to me that it was utterly ridiculous in face of the fact that we had untold stocks of potential energy in our own backyard, beneath the sea-bed of the U.K. continental shelf, and, furthermore, the Hydrographic Service was in a unique position to do something about it. By switching our priorities from the purely navigational requirements of hydrography, we could deploy the resources of the Surveying Fleet to the systematic exploration of the continental shelf, and thus furnish the Government with the vital information that it needed to exploit this wealth. Accordingly, as a private individual writing from my home address, I sent off a strongly-worded letter to *The Times*, ending with a statement that 'it can be as true of to-morrow as it was of yesterday, that "it is upon the Navy under the Providence of God that the safety, honour and welfare of this realm do chiefly attend". We ignore the sea at our peril, and I suggest, Sir, that the time has come to get our national priorities right.'

This letter, written at the end of December, had not been published when I returned to the office early in January, due, no doubt to postal delays over the Christmas/New Year break. Accordingly, I rang the Editor to ask if he had received it. He had, but as to whether or not it would be printed, he would not commit himself. He asked whether I held an official post, and I explained my position. I said that I was considering sending a similar letter in my official capacity, but that would be difficult.

Next day I sat down and drafted an even better letter and sent it across to the Vice Chief of the Naval Staff with a request for permission to send it to *The Times*. He commended the letter, but said that as it was controversial, I could not sign it myself. He suggested that I should get a 'front man' to do so. I therefore rang up Admiral Sir Edmund Irving, read out the letter to him, and asked if he would be prepared to sign it. He agreed, and *The Times* published it prominently on January 18th. (Before doing so, they rang me up at home to say that it bore a marked resemblance to the one I had sent them on 30th December, and was there any connection? I gave them a full explanation). That was the start of a whole train of events which were to bring the Hydrographic Service very much to the forefront of Government attention during the year. It was also the start of a whole string of letters to *The Times* (many of which I drafted myself) which were to appear in that newspaper during the remaining months of my stewardship as Hydrographer.

The letter caused quite a stir. The Navy Minister was quizzed by certain M.P.s for his view of it, being told that the Hydrographer of the Navy was understood to endorse every word of it! The Minister's reply was that the matter was 'being given active consideration'. That was the truth, because things really started buzzing in the Ministry of Defence. I opened direct negotiations with the Director of the Institute of Geological Sciences, and also with the newly-formed Department of Energy, to offer our assistance in their efforts to solve the Energy Crisis. A tripartite Working Party, composed of representatives of the three organisations, was set up to work out a detailed plan of action, to identify the benefits and to assess the penalties. By mid-March a Plan had been produced, and I immediately submitted it to the Admiralty Board for approval.

Meanwhile, there had been a change of Government, and the Labour Party was now in power. There was an inevitable delay in obtaining ministerial decisions, but fortunately, the new Navy Minister (Mr. Frank Judd, M.P.), already known for his 'hydrographic sympathies', embraced the Plan with enthusiasm and asked that it be given 'maximum publicity'. With Board Approval now in the bag, I lost no time in swinging into action, and signalled all our ships to explain the change of direction and its effect on our programmes. *Hecate, Hecla* and, in due course, *Herald* would all be switched directly to the new task. The C.S.V.s and I.S.C.s would all be indirectly affected, but *Hydra*, in the Pacific, could continue undisturbed. She was working in the Solomon Islands.

Following the Minister's directive that maximum publicity should be given to our Plan, a high-level Press Release was issued, though in fact very little press coverage resulted. Another letter to *The Times* seemed to be indicated, and this time I hoped for a 'fair wind' from V.C.N.S. So I drafted a fairly reasonable and straightforward letter, to be signed by myself (in my official capacity) with the aim of informing the public as to what the Navy intended to do to help solve the Energy Crisis. I started by referring to the 'remarkable' letter published on January 18th from Admiral Irving, and went on to explain that it had coincided with plans then being formulated to do just what the Admiral had advocated, and that those plans had now come to fruition! I then described the measures to be taken, mentioning the three ships involved and the detailed co-operation of the other two organisations, and concluded with the words: 'This major effort is an important illustration of the Navy's traditional role in support of seaborne trade and the national economy'. As my letter was hardly controversial – and, moreover, put the Navy in rather a good light – I was fairly confident that the Board would approve it. In fact it did so – except for one word.

Instead of 'illustration' in the final paragraph, they substituted 'extension'. And with that alteration, my letter was duly published on May 6th.

By the time summer arrived, therefore, I was really feeling rather pleased with life. After all, a personal brainwave six months earlier had now been translated into massive action, with hundreds of participants involved, and when the vital information started flowing in from the ships, to be analysed by the I.G.S. and drawn up by our cartographers for the Department of Energy, I felt some cause for self-congratulation.

In my Annual Report, which came out in the spring 1974 and received wide distribution, I made a particular point of drawing attention to the crucial dilemma which faced us: how was our expanding task to be funded from a shrinking Defence Budget? I enlarged at some length on this theme, and the point was taken up by the Press, by M.P.s and by the Chamber of Shipping. The shipping community was so concerned that it forced the Department of Trade to take action. It called a joint meeting with the Ministry of Defence to air the whole matter. It emerged from this meeting that there was a need for wider consultations with other interests: the Department of Energy, the Offshore Operators, the National Ports Council, the Fishery Departments, the Scientists and the Foreign and Commonwealth Office. Accordingly, an inter-Departmental Committee was set up under M.O.D. chairmanship on which all such interests were represented. Its task was to report to the Cabinet by the end of the year on the extent to which the Hydrographic Service was required to meet commitments other than those of Defence, and the resources (in ships, manpower and money) needed to meet them, and how these could be provided. The Committee was to be known as 'The Hydrographic Study Group'.

This was a real break-through. Successive Hydrographers had been complaining ineffectually for more than a century that their work was inadequately funded, but had never brought the problem to a head. Now, for the first time in history, we had achieved a proper Government review of our whole expanding task, making sound recommendations for its future funding. At last the Government would have to listen — and act. I was well pleased with this development, and though the Hydrographic Study Group was to be chaired by a senior Civil Servant, it would be myself and my staff who would be making the running.

CHAPTER XXVI

The Final Year, 1975

IN MID-DECEMBER OF 1974 the Hydrographic Study Group (on which we had set great store) ran into 'heavy weather'. Not only was it going to be extremely difficult to extract increased public funds for an expansion of the Hydrographic Service, but the Marine Division of the Department of Trade (which was responsible for shipping), fearful of any claim on its own budget for hydrographic work, was doing its utmost to minimise the importance of surveys on our overseas trade-routes, contending that these were of relatively low priority and could wait. I strongly disagreed, and this led to a series of bitter clashes with the Head of that Division, whom I referred to as the Devil's Advocate, which hardly helped matters! More serious, however, was the fact that our Chairman (a fellow Civil Servant) seemed disposed to agree with him, thus undermining the case for expansion.

I discussed this development with the Vice Chief of Naval Staff (my immediate superior), and he advised me to 'canvass our case by a process of indirect "lobbying".' In response to this advice, I decided to re-enter *The Times* correspondence column with another letter to be signed by Admiral Irving. I sent him a draft which flowed naturally from the earlier letters (from the two of us) and which high-lighted the fact that the hydrographic effort had been switched from navigational to energy surveys in accordance with national priorities, an obvious expansion of our task, and called on Government to state how this expansion was to be funded. Christmas was upon us, and I reckoned that this letter would be published early in the New Year.

When I returned to the office in Whitehall on January 2nd, I learnt that Admiral Irving's wife Margaret, whom I had known for many years, had died. Nevertheless, 'Egg' had signed the letter I had sent him, and it was duly published in *The Times* on January 6th. This letter immediately sparked off a suggestion by the Nautical Institute (representing the international maritime profession) that they should follow up with a supporting letter, of which they sent me a draft. I thought their draft quite unsuitable for *The Times*, and tactfully suggested that we should get together and discuss it. Meanwhile, I had produced an alternative draft of my own! We spent a full three hours in my office, during which I had to exercise the utmost tact, before agreeing a final draft which, though based about 80% on mine and only 20% on theirs, they pronounced themselves delighted with. The letter was signed by Sir George Barnard, President of the Nautical Institute, and appeared in *The Times* on 17th January.

There followed two more letters to *The Times* that month (at my instigation), one from the Director of the Royal Institute of Navigation, and one from the Conservative M.P. for Taunton, Mr. Edward du Cann, which was a verbatim copy of the draft I had sent him. (Another excellent letter from Commander M.B.F. Ranken was regrettably not published). Mr. du Cann rang me up and told me that he had secured an Adjournment Debate in the House of Commons for 28th January, and intended to raise the question of funding the Hydrographic Service as the subject for the debate. He asked me for an early 'brief' on the situation – which I sent him – and then asked me to visit him in the House to discuss the matter further. I agreed to do so.

On the day in question (27th January) I began to wonder about the 'ethics' of briefing a member of Her Majesty's loyal Opposition on an official matter within the jurisdiction of Her Majesty's Government, and before going over to see Mr. du Cann, I decided it would be 'politic' to inform my own Minister, the Under Secretary of State for the Royal Navy, Mr. Frank Judd, M.P. I had difficulty in getting through to him on the 'phone, but finally, less than an hour before my visit, I made contact with his Private Secretary. The P.S. (a conceited young man whom I did not care for) doubted whether I ought to go through with the meeting 'as it would embarrass the Government'. I replied that I had agreed to see Mr. du Cann, and it was unthinkable that I should cancel the appointment at such short notice. He took my point, but said I could not discuss policy matters with du Cann. I replied that I would convey this 'injunction' to the M.P. when I met him.

I had about half an hour with Mr. du Cann in the House of Commons, and started by explaining the difficult position I was then in. He was most understanding, and apologised for the embarrassment he had caused me, even offering to write me a formal letter to that effect. Seeing that I had virtually brought the situation upon myself, I naturally declined this offer, and du Cann then said that 'for the record' he merely wished to up-date himself on facts and figures, and discuss one 'constituency matter'! We then talked freely ('off the record') about the whole Hydrographic dilemma, the 'separate Vote' concept, and the points he should bring out in the Debate. He showed me his draft speech, much of which he had taken verbatim from my own 'briefs'. I endorsed this, but asked him so far as possible to use his own words rather than mine, which, I said, would be widely recognised within the Ministry of Defence. Finally, I told him that virtually everything he needed as background for his speech had already been published – both in my last two Annual Reports, and in *The Times* correspondence.

As soon as I got back to the office, I composed a suitably abbreviated and circumspect report on what had transpired 'on the record' between du Cann and myself, and sent it across to the Minister's Private Secretary. Next morning (the day of the Debate), the P.S. rang me in great anger to say that 'action was being considered in higher quarters' as to how my 'contravention of a Ministerial Directive should be dealt with' – a Directive, furthermore, 'which had the backing of the Vice Chief of Naval Staff'!' Meanwhile I was to forward forthwith (by 12 noon) a full account of my conversation with Mr. du Cann, including details of the 'constituency matter' which he had raised with me!

In fact, of course, the 'constituency matter' had never been discussed, but I got my secretary to contact Mr. du Cann's and obtain the details, which I then incorporated in a report, together with a passable comment on it by me. Otherwise, apart from asserting that the Private Secretary's 'directive' had never been more than his personal advice, so far as I was concerned, my report, couched in coolly objective terms, consisted of little more than a somewhat amplified version of my earlier one. I sent a copy to V.C.N.S. and my Secretary delivered the original to the Minister's office two minutes before the noon deadline. I heard no more that day, and the Debate took place in the Commons that evening.

On my journey down to Taunton next morning, I read a brief report of the Debate in *The Times*.

As soon as I arrived, I was asked to ring V.C.N.S.'s office to fix an early meeting with him, and it was eventually arranged that I should do so at 8.30 a.m. on the Friday (Jan. 31st). It was naturally with some trepidation that I contemplated the prospect of this meeting, and I felt that some kind of reprimand from my 'boss' was the least that I could expect. If he were to go further than that, I was resolved to 'stand on my rights' and demand a Court Martial.

In the event, V.C.N.S. could not have been nicer. He said the Naval Staff had been following *The Times* correspondence with considerable interest, and reckoned I had been doing pretty well for myself, even to the point of having 'engineered a debate in the House'. To this I started to protest my innocence, but V.C.N.S. cut me short, saying 'All right, Droggy, we all know what's going on!'

He then went on to say that by getting myself involved in politics, I was now in hot water; the Minister was 'hopping mad', and I had forfeited all the good will I had previously enjoyed with him. His sincere advice to me now was to 'cool it', and I agreed to do so.

Having got thus far, V.C.N.S. then said that he had now received a note from the Minister to the effect that one of the M.P.s who had tried to speak in the Debate but had not done so, a Mr. Nelson, Conservative M.P. for Chichester, had informed him afterwards that he had that day received a letter from the Hydrographer. This I denied outright and categorically, labelling it as a pure fabrication. V.C.N.S. took note of my denial and said he would report it to the Minister.

Finally V.C.N.S. said he thought I ought to know – as a measure of the Minister's anger – that he had attempted to have me removed from office, but had been informed that that would not be possible!

I said that in my view the whole episode had been caused by a lack of communication between me and the Minister. Having made at least two previous attempts to communicate with him direct, and been thwarted, I only had the personal doubts of his Private Secretary to go on. If I had known that the Minister himself was against my seeing Mr. du Cann, I would almost certainly have called off the visit. I felt I owed the Minister an apology, and asked if I might see him for that reason. V.C.N.S. undertook to convey my request – together with my denial of the accusation concerning Mr. Nelson – to the Minister, and said that I would be informed of the outcome in due course.

Apart from being slightly shaken by the Minister's attempt to have me removed from office, I remained completely mystified about the M.P. for Chichester, of whom I had never heard. It was not until five weeks later that the explanation emerged. On 5th March, the Minister finally agreed to see me. By that time passions had cooled, and he regarded the whole episode as 'water under the bridge', though he felt it was not a good thing that the Navy should appear to be 'lobbying the Opposition', when it already enjoyed so much support from Ministers! However, he accepted my apology, but went on to allude 'en passant' to the case of Mr. Brotherton – without saying more. It was then immediately apparent to me that his accusation relating to Mr. Nelson had been based on a mis-identification of the member concerned. I had, in fact, written to Mr. Brotherton, my own M.P. (the member for Louth) a few days before the Debate – in strict confidence. Had the Minister correctly identified him, I could not, of course, have made my immediate and categorical denial. When Mr. Judd made his accusation – immediately after the Debate – he had not had the opportunity of reading the Hansard report on it (nor had I) – otherwise it would have been perfectly obvious that the member who had twice attempted to intervene in the debate (and to whom Mr. Judd had refused to give way) was Mr. Brotherton – and not Mr. Nelson. I had my lucky stars to thank for that error!

Anyway, the Debate (undoubtedly sparked off by *The Times* correspondence) had clearly given our case a very fair hearing. The upshot of my meeting with the Minister was that I had now made my peace with him. He undertook to see me again when the Hydrographic Study Group had completed its deliberations, and to listen to my views on its conclusions and recommendations.

This affair was a major preoccupation to me at the time. In a sense, it also illustrates the stresses and strains of 'Whitehall warfare', which are a constant aspect of daily life in the 'Corridors of Power'. I could not help but be affected by the unprecedented publicity which the Hydrographic Service was now attracting, and being so much in the national (and international) 'limelight', I was more than ever conscious of my considerable responsibilities. Not that these weighed all that heavily upon me. I had gradually grown up with them, after all, but they seemed to have increased with the enhanced publicity.

In June 1975 the Hydrographic Study Group made its Report, and the Cabinet gave it a 'first reading'. It had been printed – in glossy format, with maps and diagrams – at Taunton, for wide publication, but the Government had not yet sanctioned its general release. At the final full session of the Study Group, when we were formulating the Report's Conclusions and Recommendations, I had a public tussle with the Chairman, Mr. Jaffray (Assistant Under Secretary, Naval Staff). Civil Servants are notoriously reluctant to make firm and clear-cut recommendations, which could put their masters 'on the spot', and I knew that Jaffray would do all he could to water down anything of that sort in the final draft.

The Study Group made fourteen recommendations, the most important of which, from my point of view, was that the Survey Fleet should be expanded from its current strength of 13 ships (4 O.S.S., 4 C.S.V., 5 I.S.C.) to 20 ships (4 O.S.S., 8 C.S.V. and 8 I.S.C.). This was exactly what I had been arguing for, and I was delighted. But I could see that the Chairman was less than happy, and that a battle was brewing. I told my two Captains that we would have to get tough if we were to carry that recommendation as it stood. The Chairman directed that it should be re-worded thus: 'Consideration should be given to expanding the Survey Fleet...' I immediately objected. 'No,' I said, 'There's a world of difference between a recommendation to expand and a recommendation to consider expansion.

Why should we be mealy-mouthed about what we mean?' Silence on all sides. 'It will do no good, you know, to be too direct, and it will make no difference to the outcome,' replied the Chairman. 'That is the way the recommendation should be worded,' I said. 'I shall not endorse the Report, and other members of the Group may join me in rendering a dissenting report – if necessary a Minority Report – though we may find we're not in a minority.'

That put the cat among the pigeons, and the Chairman was non-plussed. This Report was very much his 'baby' – he had personally vetted every draft – and the last thing he wanted was anything less than unanimity. A dissenting report by the Hydrographer (of all people) would make a complete nonsense of the whole exercise. The Group comprised about 25 people, representing the whole maritime spectrum and six Departments of State. They were deadlocked. Several tentative compromises were offered, but we stood firm. Someone then suggested that the words 'if possible' should be inserted after 'The Survey Fleet should be expanded...' I considered this carefully. Obviously expansion would not be easy, but equally obviously it was certainly possible. Therefore the words 'if possible' made virtually no difference. I said I would accept the amendment, and the Chairman, visibly relieved, though still rather worried, settled for what he could get!

A further source of satisfaction for me was the recommendation that the concept of a separate Parliamentary Vote for Hydrography should be studied as soon as practicable – something I had argued for persistently. I had long felt that a separate Vote, distinct from the Defence Vote (though administered by the Navy Department), was the only logical way in which the funding of our work could be exposed and protected from pressure on Defence expenditure. Furthermore, it would have the additional advantage of providing explicit public recognition of one of the Navy's roles in support of the civil community – essentially a 'non-Defence' role. After all (as I pointed out in my final message before retiring), it had been said – by no less a personage than the First Sea Lord – that the work of the Hydrographic Service represented the greatest single contribution which the Royal Navy makes to the civil community in peacetime – and that the public should be made constantly aware of it.

Following the precedent set by my predecessors, I had planned a world tour to visit foreign and Commonwealth Hydrographers – and I was determined to take Mary with me. But in April the economic recession had begun to bite, and I was told to curtail the programme. Reluctantly, therefore, I cancelled my visits to the Far East and Pacific – although those countries were en route to scheduled meetings in America to which I was already committed.

So, with my Chief Civil Hydrographic Officer (Mr Newson) and our wives, we flew out in May to the Middle East – visiting in turn, the newly independent Gulf states, Bahrain and Qatar, before going on to Iran. My main mission in the Emirates was to explain that they were now responsible for surveying their own waters – though we were prepared to continue this work, if they wished, at their expense (which they could well afford). They saw the point, and agreed to consider the implications. (For us, it would mean funding some of our ships – which, otherwise, would probably have to be paid off).

In Iran the situation was somewhat different. At a recent C.E.N.T.O. conference that country had complained that the British Admiralty charts of their waters were obsolete and required up-dating. We had replied that this would be done on receipt from them of the relevant survey data (which, of course, was non-existent). My job, in a nutshell, was to get the Imperial Iranian Navy to agree to our re-surveying the whole of their coastal and off-shore waters, over a four-year period, at their expense – with on-the-job training for their officers as an additional 'quid pro quo'.

We had a whole series of interesting and constructive meetings with the Chief of the Imperial Navy and his staff, and with the Head of their National Geographic Office, explaining in detail the facilities we would require (e.g. to erect radio-location stations and sounding marks on their territory) – and the upshot was complete acceptance on their part of the whole plan – with the consequent financial aspects to be pursued on an inter-Governmental basis. I was more than satisfied with this agreement, which assured employment for up to four of our ships for several years ahead, and I reported this by signal to the M.O.D. and to our Ambassador. (I think it was the following year that the operation was in full swing – with our ships out there and actually working in their waters – when the Iranian Revolution occurred and the Shah was ousted, sadly aborting the entire project).

From Teheran we flew to India, where we had a wide range of subjects to discuss with their Government Hydrographer, including a new Charting Agreement. He, a Commodore in the Indian Navy, was based at Dehra Dun, in the foothills of the Himalayas – at least 1,000 miles from the sea. It was a most interesting meeting, lasting several days, during which we were royally entertained both by the Commodore and his Staff and also by a Gurkha Regiment based nearby. It was a memorable visit – and a very useful one. A great pity that we could not continue to Ceylon and beyond – and I now turned my thoughts across the Atlantic.

Some little time afterwards, on my return from a visit to America, I found that Henry Stanhope, the Defence Correspondent of *The Times*, had been trying to see me. So I rang him up and invited him round to my office in Whitehall. I had previously sent a copy of my Annual Report for 1974 to the Editor-in-Chief of *The Times*, so Stanhope was already fairly well briefed. He had heard about the H.S.G. Report, and asked for a copy of it. As, however, it had not then been released for general publication, I could only show it to him and expound on its main features, including its 14 recommendations. About a fortnight later, in mid-July, a splendid double-page article appeared in *The Times*, headlined 'Why we must find more money for the Navy's Survey Ships'. He set out the whole situation very fairly and clearly.

By mid-summer my time as Hydrographer of the Navy was beginning to run out. Since the end of the War, five years had become the norm for successive holders of the post, and that would have taken me up to February. However, I had already earmarked the officer (Chester Read) who should take over from my successor, David Haslam. If I and my immediate successor did a full term of five years each, it would have been too late for Chester Read to take over, since he would already have passed the point of retirement as Captain. Haslam and I had therefore agreed that we should each do four and a half years, so as to make it possible for Read to take over just as he reached the point of retirement. I decided that I would retire on 13th September, the 41st anniversary of the date on which I had joined the Navy, way back in 1934. I was 59, and already the oldest officer still serving.

In July the Cabinet Committee concerned with the Report of the Hydrographic Study Group agreed to its general release to all interested parties, and in August, as President of the Royal Geographical Society, Lord Shackleton opened the Commonwealth Survey Officers' Conference at Cambridge by waving it in the air and commending it to the assembled delegates as a historic document of great importance. The Report sparked off further articles in the national press, and several more letters to *The Times*, some of which were quite 'spontaneous'!

With all our ships working hard during that summer, I made a particular point of visiting all those within reach, and giving a farewell address to their ships' companies, in which I was able to outline recent developments 'in high places' and stress the greatly improved prospects for the Surveying Service arising from them. The last of these visits, in August, was to our new ship *Herald*, then working off the Outer Hebrides. After a big welcome from her Captain, I received lavish hospitality and spent my last night on board. Next day, before being landed by boat, I made my final farewell address to the ship's company on the Flight Deck, and as we drew away from the gangway, to the last shrill notes of the piping party, I watched, with a twinge of pride and sadness, my flag being slowly lowered from *Herald's* masthead.

Word now reached me that the Government had decided to postpone action on the financial recommendations of the H.S.G. Report until the autumn, and I felt it more than likely that unless pressure on them was maintained, they would continue to drag their feet. I therefore resolved that immediately prior to retiring, I would deliver a 'parting shot' in public, by sending a strongly worded and authoritative letter to *The Times* in my official capacity as Hydrographer of the Navy – off my own bat and without permission from my superiors, and damn the consequences! Letters and articles alluding to the Report continued to appear in the national Press, so it would not be difficult for me to hang my letter, when the time came, upon one of these. Meanwhile, in odd moments, I happily roughed out one or two possible drafts.

Mary came down with me for my last week, and she and my daughter Virginia helped at the farewell party I gave for the Whitehall staff and their wives in my large octagonal office. They also came down for the much larger party I threw at the Castle Hotel in Taunton for the Naval and Professional staff down there. And on my last evening, the Naval Officers fixed a splendid Guest Night dinner for Mary and me in the Officers' Mess at Sherford Camp.

That farewell Guest Night dinner was a really superb occasion. We wore Mess Undress and, with our wives in long evening dress, numbered about thirty. Captain John Winstanley (in charge of the Naval Division at Taunton) was Mess President, and Mary and I, as the Guests of Honour, sat on his left and right. As far as I can remember, David Haslam (Hydrographer-designate) sat on Mary's left. There were a number of speeches, of course, all heart-warming and rather eulogistic, to which I had to reply. I made a particular point, I remember, of praising the Surveying Service and saying what an interesting, exciting and satisfying career it offered, how greatly I had enjoyed my time in it, and that if I had my time over again, I would do exactly what I had done. In fact, looking back, I had absolutely no regrets whatsoever. But retirement, and the prospect of becoming my own master for the first time in my life, also had its points, I felt, and I was looking forward to it. I think I included all the right 'noises' too, commending my successor in flowery terms and thanking our hosts profusely. Warm applause was then followed by a formal presentation: for Mary a framed colour-photograph of a 19th-century View-sketch of a scene in the Hebrides, including Mull (which, in the original, she had admired in the Department's archives), and for me, an original of one of our earliest charts (of Algoa Bay, near Port Elizabeth) beautifully mounted in a gilt frame. Thursday, 11th September was my last day in the Taunton office, and I spent part of it putting the finishing touches to the 'magnum opus' (my parting letter to *The Times*), which I discussed with David Haslam. Since he might well have to live with the consequences, I felt it important that it should have his full backing. After dictating the letter to my secretary in Whitehall, Freda Filtness, and after David had assured me that he had now 'got the weight', I prepared to take my final departure. My heart rather sank as we approached the staircase leading down to the hall, as most of the staff had crowded on to it and around its foot, quite blocking our exit. A 'ceremony' of some kind was obviously imminent. Sure enough (despite my earlier protestations), David started making a speech. The upshot of this was that I was formally presented with a magnificent glass-topped coffee-table on which was inlaid a genuine copper printing plate of one of our charts. Not only was it a chart-plate of appropriate size, but the Department had actually selected a chart based mainly on my survey off Lamu in 1961/62 and partly on David's continuation of it in 1962/63 in H.M.S. *Owen*. In addition to the copper-plate coffee-table, they also gave me a teak-framed copy of the chart itself (Mataoni, Manda and Pate Bays and Approaches) to hang on my wall!

My last day as Hydrographer of the Navy was Friday, 12th September, and I spent it in Whitehall, finishing off the week's work and tying up the inevitable loose ends before my departure. Among these was my letter to *The Times*, which Freda had typed for my signature. I covered it with a personal letter to the Editor-in-Chief, asking that publication be withheld until the following Wednesday – 'for personal reasons' – and then told Freda to send it off. She was clearly uneasy about it, and I could understand why. I was breaking the Regulations by writing to the Press without prior clearance and authorisation, but I told her that in this instance, what the Hydrographer of the Navy had to say was, in my view 'in the Public Interest', and that this fact overrode all other considerations. My reason for withholding publication was that I was due to take formal leave of the Naval Secretary, the Navy Minister and the First Sea Lord, on the Monday and Tuesday, and Mary and I were also to have lunch with the First Sea Lord afterwards. It would have been most embarrassing had the letter been published while I was doing so!

I retired officially on Saturday, 13th September, but I was not yet out of the woods. We stayed in London for the week-end and gave up the lease on the flat, and on the Monday I started a round of farewell calls in Whitehall. My superiors, including the Minister, Frank Judd, were all very affable, and the Naval Secretary told me that Flag Officers were always subject to recall in emergencies (though this was unlikely). Admirals were simply transferred, when unemployed, from the Active to the Retired List, but retained their ranks. It was therefore incorrect to allow myself to be addressed as Rear Admiral (Retd.). The First Sea Lord (Admiral Sir Edward Ashmore) had a long discussion with me about the future of the Hydrographic Service, and agreed with me when I suggested that the Government had got its priorities wrong (a point which would emerge in my, as yet unpublished, letter to *The Times*). He gave a small lunch party for Mary and me (and one or two others) afterwards in his official quarters, which was very pleasant, and on the Tuesday afternoon we drove up to Legbourne, our country home.

Next day, Wednesday 17th September, my letter duly appeared – very prominently – in *The Times*, occupying two columns and headed 'Making Hydrography a National Priority' (not a heading I would have chosen myself). A sub-heading said: 'From the Hydrographer of the Navy', and at the bottom it carried my name, my Whitehall address, and the date, 12th September. It was a damned good letter (though I say it myself!) and I was prepared to stand by every word of it. Doubtless it would not be long before I was called to account.

Sure enough, when I got in that evening, after seeing about some new fencing, Mary told me that the Secretary to the First Sea Lord had rung, wanting to speak to me. She replied that I was out – she wasn't sure where – but that I had gone off to see about some fencing – and 'Lincolnshire is a very big county'. The Secretary left a message asking me to ring him when I got back. When I got hold of him, rather late in the day, he asked me to get down there as soon as possible, because the Secretary of State for Defence, Mr. Roy Mason, M.P., was seeing the First Sea Lord at noon next day (about my letter)! I told him that the earliest I could get there – assuming that my train was on time – would be shortly after 11.00 a.m. next morning.

I took the early train from Market Rasen on the Thursday, and had plenty of time to reflect on the situation during my journey south. I had no regrets. I had said what needed to be said – with all the authority and publicity that was possible – and I would pay the price. I had taken a carefully calculated risk. Short of a Court Martial (which was unlikely in view of the publicity, which would embarrass the Government and play straight into our hands), there was not much that the Admiralty Board could do, other than deliver some sort of a reprimand. Only through a Court Martial could they touch my pension, and since I now held no office, they could not remove me from that! An 'Expression of their Lordships' Displeasure' seemed the most likely penalty, and my action was well worth that. There comes a time in some people's lives, I felt, when a stand on principle has to be taken – at some personal sacrifice. I knew that, had I dodged the issue, I would have been unable to live with myself afterwards.

I arrived on time and was ushered in – after a ten-minute wait – to V.C.N.S.'s office. With a wry smile, he sat me down and said: 'Well, Droggy, it was a bloody good letter, but wouldn't it have been better if you'd written it from "Rose Cottage" or wherever it is you live?' 'No. Sir,' I replied, 'it would not have carried the same weight.' 'Maybe not,' he answered, 'but the fact is your letter has caused an almighty stink. The Minister is baying for your blood and wants to know what the Navy is going to do about it. The First Sea Lord sees him in half an hour's time, and will have to tell him. Clearly, we've got to do something.' 'I understand that,' I replied, 'and, presumably the Navy has to be seen to be taking some action.' 'Exactly,' said the V.C.N.S., 'the question is, what action? We don't want to make too much of a meal of it, and cause a real fuss, so what would you think of an 'Expression of their Lordships' Displeasure'?' 'That, Sir, is precisely what I had expected, and I think it would be entirely appropriate,' I replied. 'O.K.,' said 'V', 'But I just hope Roy will wear it.' So that was that, and I caught the next train back to Lincolnshire.

Two days later, on Saturday 20th September, I received a formal letter from a Civil Servant in the Ministry of Defence, which read:

'Sir, I am directed to refer to your interview with the Vice Chief of the Naval Staff on 18th September, 1975, concerning the publication in *The Times* newspaper dated 17th September 1975, without prior official approval, of your personal views about the role of the Hydrographic Service and the resources which you considered should be afforded to it. I am directed to inform you that, as a consequence of your unauthorised action, you have incurred the Severe Displeasure of the Admiralty Board of the Defence Council. I am, Sir, your obedient Servant...

'Fair enough,' I thought, 'No harm done, and honour satisfied on all sides!' My luck had held.

Two months later I received this letter from the Secretary of State:-

THE MINISTRY OF DEFENCE,
Main Building,
Whitehall, London, S.W.1

17 November 1975

Dear Admiral.

I have it in command from Her Majesty The Queen to convey to you on leaving the Active List of the Royal Navy her thanks for your long and valuable services.

May I take this opportunity of wishing you all good fortune in the future.

Yours Sincerely.

Ray Mason.

Secretary of State for Defence